T0113327

# THE
# QUOTABLE
# SPURGEON

## Charles Spurgeon

Harold Shaw Publishers
Wheaton, Illinois

*Much of the material in this book originally appeared in* Feathers for Arrows *by C.H. Spurgeon (Clapham, 1870).*

ISBN-13: 978-0-87788-710-2

Cover photo © 1990. Used with permission from Curry Library, William Jewel College.

**Library of Congress Cataloging-in-Publication Data**

Spurgeon, C. H. (Charles Haddon), 1834-1892.
    The quotable Spurgeon / Charles Spurgeon.
      p.    cm.
    "Much of the material in this book originally
appeared in Feathers for arrows . . ." —T.p. verso.
    ISBN 9780877887102
    1. Christian life—Baptist authors. I. Spurgeon, C. H.
(Charles Haddon), 1834-1894. Feathers for arrows. II. Title.
BV4501.2.S7142 1990
248.4'861—dc20                89-28076
                                 CIP

146502721

# Contents

# Introduction

"The impact of the ministry of Charles Haddon Spurgeon was unparalleled in the nineteenth century," declared historian Robert L. Duncan. The great German theologian and pastor Helmut Thielicke stated, "Sell all the books you have . . . and buy Spurgeon." As a preacher of the gospel, C.H. Spurgeon had few, if any, peers. His place in the history of the Christian pulpit is forever set. The nineteenth-century "Last of the Puritans"—as he was called by Prime Minister Gladstone—still touches the lives of multitudes of people today. The usefulness of Spurgeon's preaching and writing style possesses a dynamic relevance up to the contemporary moment even though he has been dead for almost a century. Several things feed into this reality.

## The Puritan Heritage of Spurgeon

The life of Spurgeon is a constant testimony to the Puritan legacy and its influence in his service to Christ. Due to rather stringent economic conditions, at eighteen months of age Charles was sent north to live with his grandparents in Stanbourne, Essex, northeast of London. The grandfather, James, was a staunch congregational Puritan pastor. At the age of six, little Charles one day happened into an old musty room in the manse at Stanbourne. The room exuded the odor of old leather-bound theological volumes. Most six-year-olds would have executed a hasty exit. But not Charles; he thought he had discovered a gold mine. Being already well able to read, he delved into the new-found treasure and picked up a copy of Bunyan's *Pilgrim's Progress*. It fascinated him—actually, he read it over one hundred times during his life. The Bunyan classic became something of the Puritan pattern for his own spiritual pilgrimage. That was the atmosphere in which Charles's early spiritual experience took place. Therefore, it is understandable why at the age of fifteen Charles was deeply under the conviction of sin and desperately seeking salvation. His conversion story, which he loved to share in his preaching, was typical of the Puritan approach. His search for Christ culminated one Sunday, January 1850, in a little primitive Methodist church in Colchester. An illiterate preacher looked at him and said, "Young man, look to Jesus." Spurgeon said, "I looked and I lived." It was a very dramatic experience and set him on the Puritan quest for biblical knowledge and ultimately to biblical preaching.

Four years later, at the age of nineteen, after a two-year pastorate in Waterbeach near Cambridge, Charles Spurgeon was called as a minister of the historic and prestigious New Park Baptist Church in Southwark, South London. John Rippon, Benjamin Keach, and theologian John Gill had been his illustrious predecessors at this significant church. So the "boy preacher" began his London ministry of nearly four decades. His first sermon at the New Park Street Church was heard by a mere eighty people. In six months, two thousand were being crammed into the old church building, while up to one thousand a Sunday were being turned away unable to get in. Soon the Metropolitan Tabernacle was constructed and Spurgeon preached to six thousand worshipers every Lord's day. It became the largest evangelical congregation in the world at its time. Although Spurgeon died in Mentone, France at the relatively young age of fifty-seven, the world has rarely seen a more productive, theologically-oriented pulpit ministry. Not only that, he started over twenty different social and evangelistic ministries through his great church. Two hundred new congregations emerged out of the ministry. The Pastor's College, which continues to this day, has trained thousands of men and women for ministry. The Stokwell Orphanage also carries on. Above all, the personal appeal of Spurgeon's writings and pulpit style blesses multitudes to the present hour. Permeating it all was his Puritan legacy. If Spurgeon was not "The Last of the Puritans," he certainly was one of the best.

## The Preaching Style of Spurgeon

Not only was Spurgeon deeply involved and immersed in Puritan theology and the necessity of a conversion experience, but his preaching effectiveness is almost unparalleled in the history of Christianity. His style was extemporaneous. He prepared his Sunday morning sermon on Saturday night and his Sunday evening sermon on Sunday afternoon. Yet, as one reads the sermons today, the eloquence, use of words, and the fervency that pulsates in every paragraph is quite phenomenal.

Perhaps the secret of Spurgeon's power in the pulpit was his deep, profound commitment to evangelistic preaching. He said, "The revealed word awakened me; but it was the preached word that saved me; I now think I am bound never to preach a sermon without preaching to sinners. I think that a minister who can preach a sermon without addressing sinners does not know how to preach." He went so far as to say in the *Sportsman* near the end of his days in September 1890, "The ordinary sermon should *always* be evangelistic."

Spurgeon was also tremendously sensitive to the absolute necessity of the work of the Holy Spirit in his pulpit style and ministry. He constantly affirmed, in the traditional Puritan fashion, the absolute necessity of God's sovereign act in effecting personal redemption. Therefore, he was a constant seeker for the mighty moving of the Holy Spirit to come upon the preaching of the Word so as to bring people to Christ. Spurgeon saw that outpouring of power. Revival came to the New Park Street almost simultaneously with his arrival in London. Actually, Spurgeon was something of a harbinger of the Prayer Revival of 1858, which reached all of Britain by 1860 after its inception in America.

No biographer, except Eric Eyick Haydan, has seen the full extent of the revival principle in the pulpit ministry of Charles Spurgeon. Often his success is explained merely on the grounds that he was a great preacher and social worker. But great preaching and ministry alone simply cannot explain the Spurgeon phenomenon. Spurgeon recognized it and said, "The times of refreshing from the presence of the Lord have at last dawned upon our land. There are signs of aroused activity in increased earnestness. A spirit of prayer is visiting our churches, and in its path is dropping fatness." The awakening surrounding Spurgeon's ministry was so profoundly deepened that for three years there were over one thousand people every Sunday turned away from the ten-thousand-seat-capacity Surrey Gardens Music Hall, where he preached to a packed building before the construction of the Metropolitan Tabernacle building.

Many things could be said about Spurgeon's preaching style, but perhaps central to it all was the fact that he was absolutely committed to the full authority of the Scriptures. The admonition to "preach the word" was taken with dead seriousness by the London preacher. He would take his text and elucidate it from every perspective. He certainly fulfilled the mandate of the Bible itself to be a proclaimer of the Word. This is so central to the preaching ministry of Spurgeon, and that is what gives it its lasting effect. It is true, he had a marvelous flow of words and an eloquence that parallels even that of Shakespeare. Further, he had a deep, rich resonant voice that vibrated with the warmth of his own heart. Yet it was his preaching of the Word of God and his delineating of Scriptures to people that give Spurgeon his tremendous lasting effect. He can be read to this day with much profit.

## Charles Spurgeon's Spirituality in His Preaching

Once again, Spurgeon reflects his Puritan orientation as one examines his spirituality. The London preacher's concept of the objective source of life in the Spirit was the Holy Scriptures. His spirituality demanded disciplined Bible study. He said, "There is a style of majesty about God's word. It's the living and incorruptible seed. It moves, it stirs itself, it lives, it communes with living man as the living word. You do not need to bring life to the scriptures. You should draw life from the scriptures." This moved Spurgeon not only into disciplined Bible study but into a life of earnest prayer and the seeking of the will of God in all matters. Maybe this is the final lasting quality of this great man of God and preacher of the Word.

## Conclusion

Much could be said concerning the life and ministry of Charles Haddon Spurgeon of London, England. Unquestionably he was a preaching giant of the nineteenth century. Yet his legacy so continues on that he is read with great profit to the present moment. Actually, there are more of his books in print today, a hundred years after his death, than any living or dead English writing author. This is hard to believe in the light of the myriad of books that are being produced. Yet it speaks of his Puritan legacy and theology, his deep commitment to the preaching of the word, to his unique style, and above all to his godly spirituality. Therefore he is a man to emulate. He is a man of more than a century.

Lewis A. Drummond

# The Sovereign Trinity

# The Mystery of the Trinity

When the kindness and love of God our Savior appeared, he saved us, not because of righteous things we had done, but because of his mercy. He saved us through the washing of rebirth and renewal by the Holy Spirit, whom he poured out on us generously through Jesus Christ our Savior, so that, having been justified by his grace, we might become heirs having the hope of eternal life. *Titus 3:4-7*

---

"It was reported of Alanus, that he promised his audience to discourse the next Sunday more clearly of the Trinity, and to make plain that mystery. While he was studying the point by the seaside, he spied a boy very busy with a little spoon trudging often between the sea and a small hole he had dug in the ground. Alanus asked him what he was doing.

"The boy answered, 'I intend to bring all the sea into this pit.'

"Alanus replied, 'Why do you attempt such impossibilities, and waste your time?'

"The boy answered, 'So do you, Alanus. I will as likely bring all the sea into this hole as you bring all the knowledge of the Trinity into your head. They are equally possible. We have begun together, we shall finish together. But of the two endeavors, mine is more hopeful.' "—*Thomas Adams*

# In the Palace of His Infinite Goodness

O LORD, our LORD, how majestic is your name in all the earth! You have set your glory above the heavens. From the lips of children and infants you have ordained praise because of your enemies, to silence the foe and the avenger. When I consider your heavens, the work of your fingers, the moon and the stars, which you have set in place, what is man that you are mindful of him, the son of man that you care for him? *Psalm 8:1-4*

---

I remember being taken one day to see a gorgeous palace at Venice, where every piece of furniture was made with most exquisite taste and of the richest material, where statues and pictures of enormous price abounded on all hands, and the floor of each room was paved with mosaics of marvelous art and extraordinary value. As I was shown from room to room and allowed to roam amid the treasures by its courteous owner, I felt a considerable timidity. I was afraid to sit anywhere, nor did I hardly dare to put my foot down, or rest my hand to lean. Everything seemed to be too good for ordinary mortals like myself. But when one is introduced into the gorgeous palace of infinite goodness, costlier and fairer far, one gazes wonderingly with reverential awe at the matchless vision. "How excellent is your lovingkindness, Oh God! I am not worthy of the least of your benefits. Oh, the depths of the love and goodness of the Lord."

# Humble Before God

The LORD said to Job: "Will the one who contends with the Almighty correct him? Let him who accuses God answer him! . . . Would you discredit my justice? Would you condemn me to justify yourself? . . ."

Then Job replied to the LORD: "I know that you can do all things; no plan of yours can be thwarted. You asked, 'Who is this that obscures my counsel without knowledge?' Surely I spoke of things I did not understand, things too wonderful for me to know. You said, 'Listen now, and I will speak; I will question you, and you shall answer me.' My ears had heard of you but now my eyes have seen you. Therefore I despise myself and repent in dust and ashes."

*Job 40:1-2, 8; 42:1-6*

---

The petty sovereign of an insignificant tribe in North America every morning stalks out of his hovel, bids the sun good morning, and points out to him with his finger the course he is to take for the day. Is this arrogance more contemptible than ours when we would dictate to God the course of his providence, and summon him to our bar for his dealings with us? How ridiculous does man appear when he attempts to argue with his God!

# God, the Condescending Father

The LORD is enthroned as King forever. The LORD gives strength to his people; the LORD blesses his people with peace. *Psalm 29:10-11*

As a father has compassion on his children, so the LORD has compassion on those who fear him. *Psalm 103:13*

---

A king sits with his council deliberating on high affairs of state involving the destiny of nations, when suddenly he hears the sorrowful cry of his little child who has fallen down or been frightened by a bee. He rises and runs to his relief, assuages his sorrows and relieves his fears. Is there anything unkingly here? Isn't this very natural? Does it not even elevate the monarch in your esteem? Why then do we think it dishonorable to the King of kings, our heavenly Father, to consider the small matters of his children? It is infinitely condescending, but is it not also superlatively natural that being a Father he should act as such?

# Only One Sun

Then I saw a new heaven and a new earth, for the first heaven and the first earth had passed away, and there was no longer any sea. I saw the Holy City, the new Jerusalem, coming down out of heaven from God . . . The city does not need the sun or the moon to shine on it, for the glory of God gives it light, and the Lamb is its lamp. *Revelation 21:1-2, 23*

"To him who sits on the throne and to the Lamb be praise and honor and glory and power, for ever and ever!" *Revelation 5:13*

---

"There was a cripple who spent his life in a room where he could not see the sun. He heard of its existence, he believed in it, and he had seen enough of its light to give him high ideas of its glory.

"Wishing to see the sun, he was taken out at night into the streets of an illuminated city. At first he was delighted with the bright lights, dazzled. But then he reflected on the sky, and realized there was darkness spread amid the lights. So he asked, 'Is this the sun?'

"Next he was taken out under a starry sky and was enraptured until, on reflection, he found that night covers the earth and was bewildered. Again he asked, 'Is *this* the sun?'

"Finally he was carried out on a bright day at noon, and no sooner did his eye open on the sky than all questions came to an end. There is only one sun! His eye was content; it had its highest object, and knew that there was nothing brighter.

"The same is true of the soul: it enjoys all lights, yet amid those of art and nature, the soul still inquires for something greater. But when the soul is led by the reconciling Christ into the presence of the Father, and he lifts upon it the light of his countenance, all thought of anything greater disappears. As there is only one sun, so there is only one God. The soul which once discerns and knows him, knows that there is none greater or brighter, and that the only possibility of ever beholding more glory is by drawing nearer."
—*Rev. W. Arthur*

# The Most Compassionate Father

*For as high as the heavens are above the earth, so great is his love for those who fear him; as far as the east is from the west, so far has he removed our transgressions from us. As a father has compassion on his children, so the LORD has compassion on those who fear him. Psalm 103:11-13*

---

When King Henry II was provoked to take up arms against his ungrateful and rebellious son, he besieged him in one of the French towns. The son, being near to death, desired to see his father and confess his wrongdoing, but the stern old sire refused to look the rebel in the face. The young man being sorely troubled in his conscience said to those about him, "I am dying, take me from my bed, and let me lie in sackcloth and ashes, in token of my sorrow for my ingratitude to my father."

Thus he died, and when the tidings came to the old man outside the walls that his boy had died in ashes, repentant for his rebellion, he threw himself upon the earth like another David, and said, "Would God I had died for him." The thought of his boy's broken heart touched the heart of the father.

If you, being evil, are overcome by your children's tears, how much more shall your father who is in heaven find in your bemoanings and confessions an argument for the display of his pardoning love through Christ Jesus our Lord? This is the eloquence God delights in, the broken heart and the contrite spirit.

# A God Who Knows

"There is no one holy like the LORD; there is no one besides you; there is no Rock like our God. Do not keep talking so proudly or let your mouth speak such arrogance, for the LORD is a God who knows, and by him deeds are weighed. *1 Samuel 2:2-3*

When I was woven together in the depths of the earth, your eyes saw my unformed body. All the days ordained for me were written in your book before one of them came to be. How precious to me are your thoughts, O God! How vast is the sum of them! Were I to count them, they would outnumber the grains of sand. *Psalm 139:15-18*

I am he who searches hearts and minds, and I will repay each of you according to your deeds. *Revelation 2:23*

---

A plate of sweet cakes was brought in and laid upon the table. Two children were playing on the hearthrug before the fire.

"Oh, I want one of these cakes!" cried the little boy, jumping up as soon as his mother went out, and going on tiptoe toward the table.

"No, no!" said his sister, pulling him back. "No, you must not touch."

"Mother won't know it. She did not count them," he cried, shaking her off, and stretching out his hand.

"If *she* didn't, perhaps *God* counted," the little girl answered.

The little boy's hand stopped.

Be sure that *God counts!*

# God, Our Sure Foundation

Every good and perfect gift is from above, coming down from the Father of the heavenly lights, who does not change like shifting shadows. *James 1:17*

"I am the Alpha and the Omega," says the Lord God, "who is, and who was, and who is to come, the Almighty." *Revelation 1:8*

"I the LORD do not change." *Malachi 3:6*

---

"There may be many Christians like young sailors, who think the shore and the whole land move when their ship sails and actually they themselves are moved. Just so not a few imagine that God moves, and sails, and changes places, because their giddy souls are under sail, and subject to alteration, to ebbing and flowing. But the foundation of the Lord abides sure."—*Samuel Rutherford*

# No Worries

How great is the love the Father has lavished on us, that we should be called children of God! *1 John 3:1*

"Look at the birds of the air; they do not sow or reap or store away in barns, and yet your heavenly Father feeds them. Are you not much more valuable than they? . . . See how the lilies of the field grow. They do not labor or spin. Yet I tell you that not even Solomon in all his splendor was dressed like one of these. If that is how God clothes the grass of the field, which is here today and tomorrow is thrown into the fire, will he not much more clothe you, O you of little faith? So do not worry." *Matthew 6:26, 28-31*

---

"One of my hearers had seven children who had come in rapid succession. He was hard-working and well spoken of. His children were all asleep when I went to visit him, and as I expressed the pleasure the sight of their peaceful little faces gave me, the father said, 'Yes, these are fine times for them; they don't need to take any thought for themselves.'

"On the following Sunday the man was in church. I spoke of the happy state of children, exempt from care as they were, and went on to say that believers were the children of God, that the Lord had commanded them to be careful for nothing, and promised that he would care for them. The man understood me, and it evidently pleased him to hear his expression repeated from the pulpit."—*Büchsel*

# Christ, the Head

For if the many died by the trespass of the one man, how much more did God's grace and the gift that came by the grace of the one man, Jesus Christ, overflow to the many! . . . For if, by the trespass of the one man, death reigned through that one man, how much more will those who receive God's abundant provision of grace and of the gift of righteousness reign in life through the one man, Jesus Christ. Consequently, just as the result of one trespass was condemnation for all men, so also the result of one act of righteousness was justification that brings life for all men. For just as through the disobedience of the one man the many were made sinners, so also through the obedience of the one man the many will be made righteous. *Romans 5:15, 17-19*

---

Everyone knows that it would be far better to lose our feet than our heads. Adam had feet to stand with, but we have lost them by his disobedience. Yet, glory be to God, we have found a Head, in whom we abide eternally secure, a Head which we shall never lose.

# Jesus, Our Example

Let us fix our eyes on Jesus, the author and perfecter of our faith, who for the joy set before him endured the cross, scorning its shame, and sat down at the right hand of the throne of God. Consider him who endured such opposition from sinful men, so that you will not grow weary and lose heart. *Hebrews 12:2-3*

For we do not have a high priest who is unable to sympathize with our weaknesses, but we have one who has been tempted in every way, just as we are—yet was without sin. Let us then approach the throne of grace with confidence, so that we may receive mercy and find grace to help us in our time of need. *Hebrews 4:15-16*

---

One thing which contributed to make Caesar's soldiers invincible was their seeing him always take his share in danger and never desire any exemption from labor and fatigue. We have a far higher incentive in the war for truth and goodness when we consider him who endured such contradiction of sinners against himself.

# The Only Hope

But as for me, I will always have hope; I will praise you more and more. My mouth will tell of your righteousness, of your salvation all day long, though I know not its measure. *Psalm 71:14-15*

Praise be to the God and Father of our Lord Jesus Christ! In his great mercy he has given us new birth into a living hope through the resurrection of Jesus Christ from the dead, and into an inheritance that can never perish, spoil or fade—kept in heaven for you. *1 Peter 1:3-4*

---

On a huge cross by the side of an Italian highway hung a hideous caricature of Jesus, the Beloved of our souls, who poured out his life for our redemption. Out of reverence to the living Christ we turned aside, disgusted from the revolting image, but not until we had seen the words *Spes Unica* in capitals over its head. Here was truth emblazoned on an idol. Yes, indeed, Jesus, our now exalted, but once crucified Lord is the sole and *only hope* of man. Assuredly, Oh Lord Jesus, you are *spes unica* to our souls.

> *Other refuge have we none,*
> *Hangs our helpless soul on thee.*

We found this diamond of truth in the mire of superstition: does it sparkle any the less?

# The Key to Covenant Blessings

Praise be to the God and Father of our Lord Jesus Christ, who has blessed us in the heavenly realms with every spiritual blessing in Christ. *Ephesians 1:3*

"He who loves me will be loved by my Father, and I too will love him and show myself to him." *John 14:21*

My purpose is that they . . . may have the full riches of complete understanding, in order that they may know the mystery of God, namely, Christ, in whom are hidden all the treasures of wisdom and knowledge. *Colossians 2:2-3*

---

There are many locks in my house and all with different keys, but I have one master-key which opens them all. The Lord has many treasures and secrets all shut up from carnal minds with locks which they cannot open. But he who walks in fellowship with Jesus possesses the master-key which will open to him all the blessings of the covenant and even the very heart of God. Through Jesus, the well beloved we have access to God, to heaven, and to every secret of the Lord.

# Christ, the Soul's Defense

Show the wonder of your great love, you who save by your right hand those who take refuge in you from their foes. Keep me as the apple of your eye; hide me in the shadow of your wings from the wicked who assail me, from my mortal enemies who surround me. *Psalm 17:7-9*

---

There is an ancient parable which says that the dove once made a pitiful complaint to her fellow birds that the hawk was a most cruel tyrant and was thirsting for her blood. One counseled her to fly low—but the hawk can stoop for its prey. Another advised her to soar aloft—but the hawk can mount as high as she. A third instructed her to hide herself in the woods—but that is the hawk's own territory. A fourth recommended that she stay in town—but there man hunted her, and she feared that her eyes would be put out by the cruel falconer to make sport for the hawk. At last one told her to rest herself in the clefts of the rock, there she would be safe; violence itself could not surprise her there.

The meaning is easy—do not fail to catch it and to act upon it. The dove is the poor defenseless soul; Satan is the cruel foe. Poverty cannot protect you, for sin can stoop to the poor man's level, devour him, and drag him to hell from a hovel. Riches are no security, for Satan can make these a snare as well; the bird of prey can follow to the heights to rend you in pieces. The busy world with all its cares cannot shelter you, for there the great enemy is most at home; he is the prince of this world and seizes those who find their joys therein as easily as a kite lays hold on a sparrow. Retirement cannot secure you either, for there are sins peculiar to quietude, and hell's dread vulture soars over lonely solitudes to find defenseless souls and rend them in pieces. There is but one defense. Jesus was wounded for sin; faith in him saves at once and forever.

# Our Only Rest

Cast all your anxiety on him because he cares for you. *1 Peter 5:7*

Therefore, since we have been justified through faith, we have peace with God through our Lord Jesus Christ, through whom we have gained access by faith into this grace in which we now stand. And we rejoice in the hope of the glory of God. *Romans 5:1-2*

---

"My heart can have no rest, unless it leans on Jesus Christ *wholly*, and then it feels his peace. But I am apt to leave my resting place, and when I ramble from it, my heart will quickly brew up mischief. Some evil temper now begins to boil, or some care would fain perplex me, or some idol wants to please me, or some deadness or some lightness creeps upon my spirit, and communion with my Savior is withdrawn. When these thorns stick in my flesh, I do not try, as before, to pick them out with my own needle, but carry all complaints to Jesus, casting every care on him. His office is to save, and mine to look for help."—*John Berridge*

# The Safety of the Christian

"My sheep listen to my voice; I know them, and they follow me. I give them eternal life, and they shall never perish; no one can snatch them out of my hand. My Father, who has given them to me, is greater than all; no one can snatch them out of my Father's hand. I and the Father are one." *John 10:27-30*

---

"A British subject may be safe although surrounded by enemies in a distant land—not that he has strength to contend alone against armed thousands, but because he is a subject of our queen. A despot on his throne, a horde of savages in their desert, have permitted a helpless traveler to pass unharmed, like a lamb among lions—although like lions looking on a lamb, they thirsted for his blood—because they knew his sovereign's watchfulness, and feared his sovereign's power. The feeble stranger has a charmed life in the midst of his enemies, because a royal arm unseen encompasses him as with a shield. The power thus wielded by an earthly throne may suggest and symbolize the perfect protection of Omnipotence. A British subject's confidence in his queen may rebuke the feeble faith of a Christian. 'Oh, you of little faith, why did you doubt?' Though there be fears within and fightings without, he who bought his people with his own blood cannot lose his inheritance, and will not permit any enemy to wrest from his hand the satisfaction of his soul. The man with a deceitful heart and a darkened mind, a feeble frame and a slippery way, a fainting heart and a daring foe—the man would stumble and fall. But the member of Christ's body cannot drop off; the portion of the Redeemer cannot be wrenched from his grasp. 'You are his.' Christ is the safety of a Christian."
—W. Arnot

# The Proof of Love

"My command is this: Love each other as I have loved you. Greater love has no one than this, that one lay down his life for his friends." *John 15:12-13*

"I have loved you with an everlasting love." *Jeremiah 31:3*

---

In the French revolution, a young man was condemned to the guillotine and shut up in one of the prisons. He was greatly loved by many, but there was someone who loved him more than all the others put together. That one was his own father, and the love he bore his son was proved in this way: when the lists were called, the father—whose name was exactly the same as the son's—answered to the name, and the father rode in the gloomy tumbrel out to the place of execution, and his head rolled beneath the axe instead of his son's, a victim to mighty love. See here an image of the love of Christ to sinners. For thus Jesus died for the ungodly.

# The Humility of Christ, the Vine

"I am the true vine, and my Father is the gardener. . . . I am the vine; you are the branches. If a man remains in me and I in him, he will bear much fruit; apart from me you can do nothing." *John 15:1, 5*

I am a rose of Sharon, a lily of the valleys. *Song of Songs 2:1*

---

"Of all trees, I observe, God has chosen the vine, a low plant that creeps upon the helpful wall; of all beasts, the soft and patient lamb; of all fowls, the mild and guileless dove. Christ is the rose of the field, and the lily of the valley. When God appeared to Moses, it was not in the lofty cedar, nor the sturdy oak, nor the spreading plane, but in a bush, a humble, slender, abject shrub—as if he would, by these choices, check the conceited arrogance of man."
*—Owen Feltham*

# The Gracious Wind of the Spirit

Now the Lord is the Spirit, and where the Spirit of the Lord is, there is freedom. And we, who with unveiled faces all reflect the Lord's glory, are being transformed into his likeness with ever-increasing glory, which comes from the Lord, who is the Spirit. *2 Corinthians 3:17-18*

He saved us through the washing of rebirth and renewal by the Holy Spirit, whom he poured out on us generously through Jesus Christ our Savior, so that, having been justified by his grace, we might become heirs having the hope of eternal life. *Titus 3:5-7*

---

My wind chime is not sounding, although a fine fresh wind is blowing in at the window. Why don't I hear its soft music strains? Because it was put away in the storage room because some of its strings were broken. There is a gracious revival in the church, and believers are greatly refreshed by the visitations of God's Spirit, but I am in a sadly worldly unbelieving condition. May it not be because I neglect private prayer, and have not been regular at corporate prayer, because my family concerns and business cares have kept my heart in the storage room, and my soul has lost her first love? Yes, these are the reasons. Lord, tune my heart, and I will again seek the places where the heavenly wind of your Spirit blows graciously and refreshingly. How can I bear to be silent when your daily mercies are all around me singing of your love?

# The Guide to the Truth

"But when he, the Spirit of truth, comes, he will guide you into all truth." *John 16:13*

---

"He will guide you into all truth." Truth may be compared to some cave or grotto, with wondrous stalactites reaching from the roof, and others reaching from the floor, a cavern glittering with spar and abounding in marvels. Before entering the cavern you enquire for a guide, who comes with his lighted torch. He conducts you down to a considerable depth, and you find yourself in the midst of the cave. He leads you through different chambers. Here he points you to a little stream rushing from amid the rocks and indicates its rise and progress. There he points to some peculiar rock and tells you its name, then takes you into a large natural hall, tells you how many persons once feasted in it, and so on. Truth is a grand series of caverns, it is our glory to have so great and wise a conductor as the Holy Spirit. Imagine that we are coming to the darkness of it. He is a light shining in the midst of us to guide us. And by the light he shows us wonderful things. He teaches us by suggestion, direction, and illumination.

# The Guarantee of Wonders to Come

*Now it is God who makes both us and you stand firm in Christ. He anointed us, set his seal of ownership on us, and put his Spirit in our hearts as a deposit, guaranteeing what is to come. 2 Corinthians 1:21-22*

---

In the early times when land was sold, the owner cut a section of turf and cast it into the cap of the purchaser as a token that it was his—or he tore off the branch of a tree and put it into the new owner's hand to show that he was entitled to all the products of the soil. And when the purchaser of a house received possession, the key of the door or a bundle of thatch from the roof signified that the building was yielded up to him. The God of all grace has given to his people all the perfections of heaven to be their heritage forever, and the down-payment of his Spirit is to them the blessed token that all things are theirs. The Spirit's work of comfort and sanctification is a part of heaven's covenant blessings—a turf from the soil of Canaan, a twig from the tree of life, the key to the mansions in the skies. Possessing the down-payment of the Spirit we have received possession of heaven.

# A Fragrance that Refreshes

But thanks be to God, who always leads us in triumphal procession in Christ and through us spreads everywhere the fragrance of the knowledge of him. For we are to God the aroma of Christ among those who are being saved and those who are perishing. *2 Corinthians 2:14-15*

And hope does not disappoint us, because God has poured out his love into our hearts by the Holy Spirit, whom he has given us. *Romans 5:5*

---

Frequently at the great Roman games the emperors, in order to gratify the citizens of Rome, would cause sweet perfumes to be rained down upon them through the awning which covered the amphitheater. Behold the vases, the huge vessels of perfume! There is nothing here to delight you so long as the jars are sealed, but let the vases be poured and let the drops of perfumed rain begin to descend, and everyone is refreshed and gratified thereby. Such is the love of God. There is a richness and a fullness in it, but it is not perceived till the Spirit of God pours it out like the rain of fragrance over the heads and hearts of all the living children of God. See, then, the need of having the love of God shed abroad in the heart by the Holy Ghost!

# The Heart of the Gospel

# The Heart of the Gospel

While we were still sinners, Christ died for us. *Romans 5:8*

"For the Son of Man came to seek and save what was lost." *Luke 19:10*

Christ Jesus came into the world to save sinners. *1 Timothy 1:15*

---

The late venerable and godly Dr. Archibald Alexander of Princeton had been a preacher of Christ for sixty years and a professor of divinity for forty. On his deathbed he was heard to say to a friend, "All my theology is reduced to this narrow compass—*Jesus Christ came into the world to save sinners.*"

# What Is the Road to Christ?

... from infancy you have known the holy Scriptures, which are able to make you wise for salvation through faith in Christ Jesus. All Scripture is God-breathed and is useful for teaching, rebuking, correcting and training in righteousness. *2 Timothy 3:15-16*

And beginning with Moses and all the Prophets, he explained to them what was said in all the Scriptures concerning himself. *Luke 24:27*

---

The best sermon is that which is most full of Christ. A Welsh minister, when preaching at the chapel of my dear brother Jonathan George, was saying that Christ was the sum and substance of the gospel, and he broke out into the following story.

A young man had been preaching in the presence of a venerable divine, and after he had finished, he foolishly went to the old minister and inquired, "What do you think of my sermon, sir?"

"A very poor sermon indeed," said the older man, "because there was no Christ in it. Don't you know, young man, that from every town, and every village, and every little hamlet in England, wherever it may be, there is a road to London?"

"Yes," said the young man.

"Ah!" said the old divine. "And so from every text in Scripture there is a road to the metropolis of the Scriptures, that is Christ. And, my dear brother, your business is, when you get to a text, to say, 'Now, what is the road to Christ?' and then preach a sermon, running along the road toward the great metropolis—Christ. I have never yet found a text that had not a plain and direct road to Christ in it. And if ever I should find one that has no such road, I will make a road; I would go over hedge and ditch but I would get at my Master. For a sermon is neither fit for the land nor yet for the garbage heap unless there is a savor of Christ in it."

# The Cross, the Center of the Gospel

For God was pleased to have all his fullness dwell in him, and through him to reconcile to himself all things, whether things on earth or things in heaven, by making peace through his blood, shed on the cross. *Colossians 1:19-20*

May I never boast except in the cross of our Lord Jesus Christ, through which the world has been crucified to me, and I to the world. *Galatians 6:14*

---

"Although the pulpit is intended to be a pedestal for the cross, even the cross itself is sometimes used as a mere pedestal for the preacher's fame. We may roll the thunders of eloquence, we may scatter the flowers of poetry, we may diffuse the light of science, we may enforce the precepts of morality, from the pulpit. But if we do not make Christ the great subject of our preaching, we have forgotten our errand and shall do no good. Satan trembles at nothing but the cross: at this he does tremble. And if we would destroy his power and extend that holy and benevolent kingdom, which is righteousness, peace, and joy in the Holy Ghost, it must be by means of the cross."—*J.A. James*

# Holding Forth the Cross of Christ

He humbled himself and became obedient to death—even death on a cross! Therefore God exalted him to the highest place and gave him the name that is above every name, that at the name of Jesus every knee should bow, in heaven and on earth and under the earth, and every tongue confess that Jesus Christ is Lord, to the glory of God the Father. *Philippians 2:8-11*

May I never boast except in the cross of our Lord Jesus Christ, through which the world has been crucified to me, and I to the world. *Galatians 6:14*

---

In a village in one of the Tyrolese valleys, we saw upon the pulpit an outstretched arm, carved in wood, the hand of which held a cross. We noted the emblem as full of instruction as to what all true ministry should be, and must be—a holding forth of the cross of Christ to the multitude as the only trust of sinners. Jesus Christ must be set forth evidently crucified among them. Lord, make this the aim and habit of all of us.

# Making It Clear

For Christ did not send me to baptize, but to preach the gospel—not with words of human wisdom, lest the cross of Christ be emptied of its power. *1 Corinthians 1:17*

He has reconciled you by Christ's physical body through death to present you holy in his sight, without blemish and free from accusation—if you continue in your faith, established and firm, not moved from the hope held out in the gospel. This is the gospel that you heard and that has been proclaimed to every creature under heaven. *Colossians 1:22-23*

---

When Dionysius, the tyrant, sent Lysander some rich Sicilian garments for his daughters, Lysander refused them, alleging that such fine clothes would make them look homely in comparison.

The truth of God is so comely in itself that the trappings of oratory are far more likely to lessen its glory than to increase it. Paul said that he preached the gospel "not with wisdom of words, lest the cross of Christ should be made of none effect."

# Music to the Spiritual Ear

" 'You will be ever hearing but never understanding; you will be ever seeing but never perceiving. For this people's heart has become calloused; they hardly hear with their ears, and they have closed their eyes. Otherwise they might see with their eyes, hear with their ears, understand with their hearts and turn, and I would heal them.' " *Matthew 13:14-15*

---

Alphonse Karr heard a gardener ask his master permission to sleep for the future in the stable, "for," said he, "there is no possibility of sleeping in the chamber behind the greenhouse, sir. The nightingales there do nothing but keep up a noise all night."

The sweetest sounds are an annoyance to those who have no musical ear. Doubtless the music of heaven would have no charms to carnal minds; certainly the joyful sound of the gospel is unappreciated so long as men's ears remain uncircumcised.

# Only Grace Will Do

And God raised us up with Christ and seated us with him in the heavenly realms in Christ Jesus, in order that in the coming ages he might show the incomparable riches of his grace, expressed in his kindness to us in Christ Jesus. For it is by grace you have been saved, through faith—and this not from yourselves, it is the gift of God—not of works, so that no one can boast. For we are God's workmanship, created in Christ Jesus to do good works, which God prepared in advance for us to do. *Ephesians 2:6-10*

---

"Take a toy away from a child and give him another, and he is satisfied. But if he is hungry, no toy will do.

As newborn babes, true believers desire the sincere milk of the Word, and the desire of grace in this way is grace."—*John Newton*

# Clothed with Christ

You are all sons of God through faith in Christ Jesus, for all of you who were baptized into Christ have been clothed with Christ. *Galatians 3:26-27*

Clothe yourselves with the Lord Jesus Christ. *Romans 13:14*

---

A great monarch was accustomed on certain set occasions to entertain all the beggars of the city. Around him were placed his courtiers, all clothed in rich apparel; the beggars sat at the same table in their rags of poverty. Now it came to pass, that on a certain day, one of the courtiers had spoiled his silken apparel, so that he dared not put it on, and he felt, "I cannot go to the king's feast today, for my robe is foul." He sat weeping until the thought struck him, "Tomorrow when the king holds his feast, some will come as courtiers happily decked in their beautiful array, but others will come and be made quite as welcome who will be dressed in rags. Well," said he, "so long as I may see the king's face and sit at the royal table, I will enter among the beggars." So without mourning because he had lost his silken habit, he put on the rags of a beggar, and he saw the king's face as well as if he had worn his scarlet and fine linen.

My soul has done this many times, when the evidences of my salvation have been dim. Your soul can do the same. If you cannot come to Jesus as a saint, come as a sinner; only do come with simple faith to him, and you shall receive joy and peace.

# Complete Surrender

May God himself, the God of peace, sanctify you through and through. May your whole spirit, soul and body be kept blameless at the coming of our Lord Jesus Christ. The one who calls you is faithful and he will do it. *1 Thessalonians 5:23-24*

---

When Henry VIII determined to make himself head of the English Church, he insisted that the convocation should accept his headship without limiting and modifying clauses. He refused to entertain any compromises, and vowed that "he would have no *tantums*," as he called them.

Sometimes a sinner parleys with his Savior, wishing he could have a little of the honor of his salvation, wanting to keep some favorite sin and amend the humbling terms of grace. But Jesus will be all in all, and the sinner must be nothing at all. The surrender must be complete; there must be no *tantums*, but the heart must submit to the sovereignty of the Redeemer without reserve.

# To See Ourselves Clearly

Do not merely listen to the word, and so deceive yourselves. Do what it says. Anyone who listens to the word but does not do what it says is like a man who looks at his face in a mirror and, after looking at himself, goes away and immediately forgets what he looks like. But the man who looks intently into the perfect law that gives freedom, and continues to do this, not forgetting what he has heard, but doing it—he will be blessed in what he does. *James 1:22-25*

---

How terribly trick mirrors distort the countenance! The man who looks into one of them sees his hair disheveled, his forehead smudged, his nose blotched, his eyes out of line, and a dozen other imaginary mischiefs. Trick mirrors are like those morbid, melancholy dispositions which pervert everything into gloom, and compel the most lovely characters to write bitter things against themselves! They may also be likened to depraved judgments, which lead men to impute deformity to perfection, and to censure even innocence itself. It would be better if all these good-for-nothing mirrors could be smashed to atoms, and the truth-reflecting glass of the word of God hung up in their places.

# The Three Whats

"I tell you the truth, whoever hears my word and believes him who sent me has eternal life and will not be condemned; he has crossed over from death to life." *John 5:24*

For all have sinned and fall short of the glory of God, and are justified freely by his grace through the redemption that came by Christ Jesus. God presented him as a sacrifice of atonement, through faith in his blood. *Romans 3:23-25*

In his great mercy he has given us new birth into a living hope through the resurrection of Jesus Christ from the dead, and into an inheritance that can never perish, spoil or fade—kept in heaven for you. *1 Peter 1:3-4*

---

Never forget the three whats. What from? Believers are redeemed from hell and destruction. What by? By the precious blood of Christ. What to? To an inheritance incorruptible, undefiled, and that will not fade away.

# One with Christ

He who unites himself with the Lord is one with him in spirit.
*1 Corinthians 6:17*

For you died, and your life is now hidden with Christ in God.
*Colossians 3:3*

---

There's a story of two friends who went into Vulcan's shop and begged a favor of him, which he granted. What was their request? That he would either beat them on his anvil or melt them in his furnace, both into one. But without make-believe, there is a far greater love in Christ, for he would be melted in the furnace of wrath, and beaten on the anvil of death, to be made one with us. And to declare the exceeding love, here were not both to be beaten on the anvil or melted in the furnace—but only he alone would be beaten, he alone would be melted that we might be spared.

# Invincible Proof

The Spirit himself testifies with our spirit that we are God's children. *Romans 8:16*

Be sure to fear the LORD and serve him faithfully with all your heart; consider what great things he has done for you. *1 Samuel 12:24*

---

An unbelieving lecturer gave people an opportunity to reply to him after his oration, and he was of course expecting that one or two rashly zealous young men would rise to advance the common arguments for Christianity, which he was quite prepared, by hook or by crook, to battle with or laugh down.

Instead, an old lady carrying a basket, wearing an ancient bonnet, and altogether dressed in an antique fashion that marked both her age and her poverty, came up on the platform. She began by saying, "I paid threepence to hear of something better than Jesus Christ, and I have not heard it. Now, let me tell you what religion has done for me. I have been a widow thirty years, and I was left with ten children. I trusted in the Lord Jesus Christ in the depth of poverty, and he appeared for me and comforted me, and helped me to bring up my children. None of you can tell what the troubles of a poor lone woman are, but the Lord has made his grace all-sufficient. You say that's all nonsense. Those who are young and foolish may believe you, but I know there is a reality in religion. Tell me something better than what God has done for me, or you have cheated me out of my threepence."

Such a mode of controversy was new to the lecturer, and therefore he gave up the contest, and merely said, "Really, the dear old woman was so happy in her delusion he should not like to undeceive her."

"No," she said, "that won't do. Truth is truth, and your laughing can't alter it. Jesus Christ has been all this to me, and I could not sit down in the hall and hear you talk against him without speaking up for him. I've tried and proved him, and that's more than you have."

The testing and proving of God, getting his love really shed abroad in the heart, is the great internal evidence of the gospel.

# Knowing with the Heart

Make every effort to add to your faith goodness; and to goodness, knowledge; and to knowledge, self-control; and to self-control, perseverance; and to perseverance, godliness; and to godliness, brotherly kindness; and to brotherly kindness, love. For if you possess these qualities in increasing measure, they will keep you from being ineffective and unproductive in your knowledge of our Lord Jesus Christ. *2 Peter 1:5-8*

---

I heard two people on the Wengern Alp talking by the hour of the names of ferns—not a word about their characteristics, uses, or habits, but a medley of crack-jaw titles and nothing more. They evidently felt that they were ventilating their botany and kept each other in countenance by alternate volleys of nonsense. Well, they were about as sensible as those doctrinalists who forever talk over the technicalities of religion but know nothing by experience of its spirit and power. Are we not all too apt to amuse ourselves after the same fashion? He who knows mere Linnean names, but has never seen a flower, is as reliable in botany as the theologian who can elaborate upon supralapsarianism but has never known the love of Christ in his heart.

# Our Sinful Nature

# Freedom from the Intolerable Bondage of Sin

At one time we too were foolish, disobedient, deceived and enslaved by all kinds of passions and pleasures. We lived in malice and envy, being hated and hating one another. But when the kindness and love of God our Savior appeared, he saved us, not because of righteous things we had done, but because of his mercy. *Titus 3:3-5*

For everything in the world—the cravings of sinful man, the lust of his eyes and the boasting of what he has and does—comes not from the Father but from the world. The world and its desires pass away, but the man who does the will of God lives forever. *1 John 2:16-17*

---

Our lusts are cords that bind us. Fiery trials are sent to burn and consume them. Who fears the flame which will bring him liberty from intolerable bonds?

# A Conscience Cold as Steel

The goal of this command is love, which comes from a pure heart and a good conscience and a sincere faith. . . . I give you this instruction in keeping with the prophecies once made about you, so that by following them you may fight the good fight, holding on to faith and a good conscience. Some have rejected these and so have shipwrecked their faith. *1 Timothy 1:5, 18-19*

---

It is a very terrible thing to let conscience begin to grow hard, for it soon chills into northern iron and steel. It is like the freezing of a pond. The first film of ice is scarcely perceptible; keep the water stirring and you will prevent the frost from hardening it. But once let it film over and remain quiet, the glaze thickens over the surface and it thickens still, and at last it is so firm that a wagon might be drawn over the solid ice. So with conscience, it films over gradually, until at last it becomes hard and unfeeling and is not crushed even with ponderous loads of iniquity.

# The Dark Gets Darker

In the beginning was the Word, and the Word was with God, and the Word was God. He was with God in the beginning. Through him all things were made; without him nothing was made that has been made. In him was life, and that life was the light of men. The light shines in the darkness, but the darkness has not understood it. *John 1:1-5*

For he has rescued us from the dominion of darkness and brought us into the kingdom of the Son he loves, in whom we have redemption, the forgiveness of sins. *Colossians 1:13-14*

---

When you have been sitting in a well-lighted room and are suddenly called into the outer darkness, how black it seems. And thus when a man has dwelt in communion with God, sin becomes exceedingly sinful, and the darkness in which the world lies appears like tenfold night.

# A Fish Out of Water

"The farmer sows the word. Some people are like seed along the path, where the word is sown. As soon as they hear it, Satan comes and takes away the word that was sown in them. Others, like seed sown on rocky places, hear the word and at once receive it with joy. But since they have no root, they last only a short time. When trouble or persecution comes because of the word, they quickly fall away. Still others, like seed sown among thorns, hear the word; but the worries of this life, the deceitfulness of wealth and the desires for other things come in and choke the word, making it unfruitful."
*Mark 4:14-19*

---

Fish sometimes leap out of the water with great energy, but it would be foolish to conclude that they have left the liquid element forever. In a moment they are swimming again as if they had never forsaken the stream. It was probably a fly that tempted them up, or a sudden urge; the water is still their home, sweet home.

When we see long-accustomed sinners making a sudden leap at religion, we may not make too sure that they are converts. Perhaps some gain lures them, or sudden excitement stirs them. If so, they will soon be back again at their old sins. Let us hope for the best, but let us not celebrate too soon.

# Looking for Trouble

He who is pregnant with evil and conceives trouble gives birth to disillusionment. He who digs a hole and scoops it out falls into the pit he has made. The trouble he causes recoils on him; his violence comes down on his own head. *Psalm 7:14-16*

---

Some people are never content with their lot, no matter what happens. Clouds and darkness are over their heads whether it rains or shines. To them every incident is an accident, and every accident a calamity. Even when they have their own way, they like it no better than your way, and, indeed, consider their most voluntary acts as matters of compulsion. We saw a striking illustration the other day of the infirmity we speak of in the conduct of a child about three years old. He was crying because his mother had shut the parlor door. "Poor thing," said a neighbor compassionately, "you have shut the child *out*."

"It's all the same to him," said the mother. "He would cry if I called him *in* and then shut the door. It is a peculiarity of that boy, that if he is left rather suddenly on either side of a door, he considers himself shut out and rebels accordingly."

There are older children who take the same view of things.

# Not Willing to See the Truth

They are darkened in their understanding and separated from the life of God because of the ignorance that is in them due to the hardening of their hearts. *Ephesians 4:18*

---

Nelson could not see the signal for suspending battle because he placed the glass to his blind eye, and man cannot see the truth as it is in Jesus because he has no mind to do so. Ungodly men are, as the country people say, "like the hogs in a harvest field," who will not come out for all your shouting. They cannot hear because they have no will to hear. Want of will causes paralysis of every faculty. In spiritual things man is utterly unable because resolvedly unwilling.

# Sin Cannot Be Hidden Long

"For there is nothing hidden that will not be disclosed, and nothing concealed that will not be known or brought out into the open." *Luke 8:17*

Be sure of this: The wicked will not go unpunished, but those who are righteous will go free. *Proverbs 11:21*

---

One danger of secret sin is that a person cannot commit it without its being eventually betrayed into a public sin. If a person commits one sin, it is like the melting of the lower glacier on the Alps, the others must follow in time. As certainly as you heap one stone on the landmark today, the next day you will cast another, until the heap, stone by stone, becomes an actual pyramid. See the coral insect at work, you cannot guess where it will create its pile. It will not build its rock as high as you please; it will not stay until an island is created. Sin cannot be held in with bit and bridle; it must be mortified.

# The Rebellious Nature

Indeed I would not have known what sin was except through the law. . . . But sin, seizing the opportunity afforded by the commandment, produced in me every kind of covetous desire. For apart from law, sin is dead. Once I was alive apart from law; but when the commandment came, sin sprang to life and I died. I found that the very commandment that was intended to bring life actually brought death. For sin, seizing the opportunity afforded by the commandment, deceived me, and through the commandment put me to death. So then, the law is holy, and the commandment is holy, righteous and good. *Romans 7:7, 8-12*

---

A contented citizen of Milan, who had never passed beyond its walls during the course of sixty years, being ordered by the governor not to stir beyond its gates, became immediately miserable and felt so powerful an inclination to do that which he had so long contentedly neglected, that on his application for a release from this restraint being refused, he became quite melancholy and at last died from grief.

How well this illustrates the apostle's confession that he would not have known lust unless the law had said to him, "Thou shalt not covet!" "When the commandment came," he said, "sin sprang to life in me." Evil often sleeps in the soul until the holy command of God is discovered, and then the enmity of the carnal mind rouses itself to oppose in every way the will of God. "Without the law," says Paul, "sin was dead." How vain to hope for salvation from the law, when through the perversity of sin it provokes our evil hearts to rebellion, and works in us neither repentance nor love.

# Shut the Door Against Sin

A simple man believes anything, but a prudent man gives thought to his steps. A wise man fears the LORD and shuns evil, but a fool is hotheaded and reckless. *Proverbs 14:15-16*

Be on your guard; stand firm in the faith. *1 Corinthians 16:13*

---

When sin is let in as a beggar, it remains in as a tyrant. The Arabs have a fable of a miller who one day was startled by a camel's nose thrust in the window of the room where he was sleeping. "It is very cold outside," said the camel, "I only want to get my nose in."

The nose was let in, then the neck, and finally the whole body. Presently the miller began to be extremely inconvenienced at the ungainly companion he had obtained in a room certainly not big enough for both.

"If you are inconvenienced, you may leave," said the camel. "As for myself, I shall stay where I am."

There are many such camels knocking at the human heart. A single worldly custom becomes the nose of the camel, and it is not long before the entire body follows. The Christian then finds his heart occupied by a vice which a little while before peeped in so meekly.

# Numbing the Conscience

An evil man is snared by his own sin. *Proverbs 29:6*

A man is a slave to whatever has mastered him. *2 Peter 2:19*

To the pure, all things are pure, but to those who are corrupted and do not believe, nothing is pure. In fact, both their minds and consciences are corrupted. *Titus 1:15*

---

Dr. Preston tells us of a believer who on one occasion was found drunk, and when depressed on account of his folly, the devil said to him, by way of temptation, "Do it again, do it again. For the grief you feel about it now you will never feel any more if you commit the sin again." Dr. Preston says that the man yielded to the temptation, and from that time he never did feel the slightest regret at his drunkenness, and lived and died a confirmed sot, though formerly he had been a very respected Christian.

# Turn Your Back on Sin

Do not set foot on the path of the wicked or walk in the way of evil men. Avoid it, do not travel on it; turn from it and go your way. For they cannot sleep till they do evil; they are robbed of slumber till they make someone fall. They eat the bread of wickedness and drink the wine of violence. The path of the righteous is like the first gleam of dawn, shining ever brighter till the full light of day. But the way of the wicked is like deep darkness; they do not know what makes them stumble. *Proverbs 4:14-19*

---

"Sin is to be overcome, not so much by maintaining a direct opposition to it, as by cultivating opposite principles. If you wish to kill the weeds in your garden, plant it with good seed. When the ground is well occupied there is less need for the labor of the hoe. If a man wished to quench fire, he might fight it with his hands until he was burned to death; the only way is to apply an opposite element."—*Andrew Fuller*

# Sin That Overpowers

Do not withhold your mercy from me, O LORD; may your love and your truth always protect me. For troubles without number surround me; my sins have overtaken me, and I cannot see. They are more than the hairs of my head, and my heart fails within me. Be pleased, O LORD, to save me; O LORD, come quickly to help me. *Psalm 40:11-13*

---

In the gardens of Hampton Court you will see many trees entirely vanquished and well nigh strangled by huge coils of ivy that are wound about them like snakes. There is no untwisting the folds, they are too giant-like, and fast fixed, and every hour the tiny roots of the climber are sucking the life out of the unhappy tree. Yet there was a day when the ivy was a tiny aspirant, only asking a little aid in climbing. Had it been denied then, the tree would never have become its victim, but by degrees the humble weakling grew in strength and arrogance, and at last it assumed the mastery, and the tall tree became the prey of the creeping, insinuating destroyer. The moral is too obvious. Sorrowfully do we remember many noble characters who have been ruined little by little with insinuating habits. Drink has been the ivy in many cases. Watch out, lest some slow advancing sin overpower you. Those who are murdered by slow poisoning die just as surely as those who take arsenic.

# Hate Sin with All Your Heart

Let those who love the LORD hate evil, for he guards the lives of his faithful ones and delivers them from the hand of the wicked. Light is shed upon the righteous and joy on the upright in heart. *Psalm 97:10-11*

Hate what is evil; cling to what is good. *Romans 12:9*

---

An Armenian arguing with a Calvinist remarked, "If I believed your doctrine and were sure that I was a converted man, I would take my fill of sin."

"How much sin," replied the godly Calvinist, "do you think it would take to fill a true Christian to his own satisfaction?"

Here he hit the nail on the head. "How can we that are dead to sin live any longer therein?" A truly converted person hates sin with all his heart, and even if he could sin without suffering for it, it would be misery enough to him to sin at all.

# Excuses, Excuses!

All a man's ways seem right to him, but the LORD weighs the heart. To do what is right and just is more acceptable to the LORD than sacrifice. *Proverbs 21:2-3*

---

A traveler in Venezuela illustrates the readiness of people to lay their faults on the locality, or on anything rather than themselves, by the story of a hard drinker who came home one night in such a condition that he could not for some time find his hammock. When this feat was accomplished, he tried in vain to get off his big riding boots. After many fruitless efforts he lay down in his hammock, and made a speech to himself, "Well, I have traveled all the world over. I lived five years in Cuba, four in Jamaica, five in Brazil. I have traveled through Spain and Portugal, and been in Africa, but I never yet was in such an abominable country as this, where a man is obliged to go to bed with his boots on."

We are commonly told by evildoers in excuse for their sins that no one could do otherwise in the same position, that there is no living at their trade honestly, that their workplace must be open on a Sunday, that their health required a trip to the beach on the Sabbath because their work was so difficult, that nobody could be religious in their workplace, and so on, all to the same effect—and about as truthful as the soliloquy of the drunkard of Venezuela.

# Just One Sin

For whoever keeps the whole law and yet stumbles at just one point is guilty of breaking all of it. *James 2:10*

Turn to me and have mercy on me, as you always do to those who love your name. Direct my footsteps according to your word; let no sin rule over me. *Psalm 119:132-33*

---

There was but one crack in the lantern, and the wind found it and blew out the candle. How great a mischief one unguarded point of character may cause us! One spark blew up the ammunition and shook the whole country for miles around. One leak sank the vessel and drowned all on board. One wound may kill the body, one sin destroy the soul.

# The Foolish Rose

An oracle is within my heart concerning the sinfulness of the wicked: There is no fear of God before his eyes. For in his own eyes he flatters himself too much to detect or hate his sin. The words of his mouth are wicked and deceitful; he has ceased to be wise and to do good. Even on his bed he plots evil; he commits himself to a sinful course and does not reject what is wrong. *Psalm 36:1-4*

---

While I was walking in the garden one bright morning, a breeze came through and set all the flowers and leaves a fluttering. Now that is the way flowers talk, so I pricked up my ears and listened.

Presently an old elder tree said, "Flowers, shake off your caterpillars!"

"Why?" said a dozen all together—for they were like some children, who always say "Why?" when they are told to do anything.

The elder said, "If you don't, they'll eat you up alive."

So the flowers set themselves a shaking until the caterpillars were shaken off.

In one of the middle beds there was a beautiful rose, who shook off all but one, and she said to herself, "Oh, that's a beauty! I'll keep that one."

The elder overheard her, and called out, "One caterpillar is enough to spoil you."

"But," said the rose, "look at his brown and crimson fur, and his beautiful black eyes, and scores of little feet. I want to keep him. Surely one won't hurt me."

A few mornings after, I passed the rose again. There was not a whole leaf on her. Her beauty was gone; she was all but killed, and had only life enough to weep over her folly, while the tears stood like dew-drops on her tattered leaves. "Alas! I didn't think one caterpillar would ruin me."

# Working Hard to Please the Devil

Flee the evil desires of youth, and pursue righteousness, faith, love and peace, along with those who call on the Lord out of a pure heart. Don't have anything to do with foolish and stupid arguments, because you know they produce quarrels. And the Lord's servant must not quarrel; instead he must be kind to everyone, able to teach, not resentful. Those who oppose him he must gently instruct, in the hope that God will grant them repentance leading them to a knowledge of the truth, and that they will come to their senses and escape from the trap of the devil, who has taken them captive to do his will. *2 Timothy 2:22-26*

---

Henry Ward Beecher says, "There was a man in the town where I was born who used to steal all his firewood. He would get up on cold nights and go and take it from his neighbors' woodpiles. A computation was made, and it was ascertained that he spent more time and worked harder to get his fuel than he would have been obliged to if he had earned it in an honest way at ordinary wages. And this thief is a type of thousands of men who work a great deal harder to please the devil than they would have to work to please God."

# In Beautiful Disguise

The coming of the lawless one will be in accordance with the work of Satan displayed in all kinds of counterfeit miracles, signs and wonders, and in every sort of evil that deceives those who are perishing. They perish because they refused to love the truth and so be saved. For this reason God sends them a powerful delusion so that they will believe the lie and so that all will be condemned who have not believed the truth but have delighted in wickedness. *2 Thessalonians 2:9-12*

---

"It is notable that nearly all the poisonous fungi are scarlet or speckled and the wholesome ones brown or grey, as if to show us that things rising out of darkness and decay are always most deadly when they are well dressed."—*Ruskin*

# Shooting Down Sin

For though we live in the world, we do not wage war as the world does. The weapons we fight with are not the weapons of the world. On the contrary, they have divine power to demolish strongholds. We demolish arguments and every pretension that sets itself up against the knowledge of God, and we take captive every thought to make it obedient to Christ. And we will be ready to punish every act of disobedience, once your obedience is complete. *2 Corinthians 10:3-6*

---

What swarms of rabbits the traveler sees on the commons and fields near Leatherhead (in Surrey), and yet a few miles further on one scarcely sees a single specimen of that prolific race. The creature is indigenous to both places, but at Leatherhead he is tolerated and therefore multiplies, while at the other places the gamekeepers diligently shoot down all they see. Sins are natural to all people, but it makes all the difference whether they are fostered or kept under. The carnal mind makes itself a warren for evil, but a gracious spirit wages constant war with every transgression.

# Stay Away from Infectious Sinners

Blessed is the man who does not walk in the counsel of the wicked or stand in the way of sinners or sit in the seat of mockers. But his delight is in the law of the LORD, and on his law he meditates day and night. *Psalm 1:1-2*

Test everything. Hold on to the good. Avoid every kind of evil. May God himself, the God of peace, sanctify you through and through. May your whole spirit, soul and body be kept blameless at the coming of our Lord Jesus Christ. *1 Thessalonians 5:21-23*

---

When a man is known to suffer from a sadly contagious disease, none of his friends will come near the house. There is little need to warn them off, they are all too alarmed to come near. Why is it people are not as much afraid of the contagion of vice? How dare they run risks for themselves and their children by allowing evil companions to frequent their house? Sin is as infectious and far more deadly than the smallpox or fever. Flee, then, from every one who might lead you into it.

# A Thorough Search by the Spirit

*Search me, O God, and know my heart; test me and know my anxious thoughts. See if there is any offensive way in me, and lead me in the way everlasting. Psalm 139:23-24*

---

When a wound in a soldier's foot refused to heal, the surgeon examined it very minutely, and manipulated every part. Each bone was there and in its place; there was no apparent cause for the inflammation, but yet the wound refused to heal. The surgeon probed and probed again, until his lancet came into contact with a hard foreign substance. "Here it is," he said, "a bullet lodged here. This must come out, or the wound will never close." Thus may some concealed sin work long disquiet in a seeking soul. May the Lord search us and try us, and see if there be any evil way in us and lead us in the way everlasting.

# Small Beginnings

Do not give the devil a foothold. *Ephesians 4:27*

"If you do not do what is right, sin is crouching at your door; it desires to have you, but you must master it." *Genesis 4:7*

---

The carpenter's gimlet makes but a small hole, but it enables him to drive a great nail. May we not here see a representation of those minor departures from the truth that prepare minds for grievous errors, and of those thoughts of sin that open a way for the worst of crimes! Beware, then, of Satan's gimlet.

# "I Don't Hate God!"

Jesus replied, "If anyone loves me, he will obey my teaching. My Father will love him, and we will come to him and make our home with him. He who does not love me will not obey my teaching." *John 14:23-24*

If anyone says, "I love God," yet hates his brother, he is a liar. For anyone who does not love his brother, whom he has seen, cannot love God, whom he has not seen. *1 John 4:20*

---

"After all, I do not hate God. No, you will not make me believe that. I am a sinner, I know, and do many wicked things. But after all, I have a good heart—I don't hate God."

Such was the language of a prosperous worldly man. He was sincere, but sadly deceived. A few months afterward, that God who had given him so many good things, crossed his path in an unexpected manner. A fearful torrent swept down the valley and threatened destruction to this man's large flour mill. A crowd was watching, in momentary expectation of seeing the mill fall, while the owner, standing in the midst of them, was cursing God to his face and pouring out the most horrid oaths.

He no longer doubted or denied that he hated God. But nothing in that hour of trial came out of his mouth that was not previously in his heart. God's account of the unrenewed heart is true: it is "deceitful above all things," as well as "desperately wicked." He who is wise will believe God's account of the state of his heart by nature, rather than the deceitful heart's account of itself.

# The Dangers of Smoke

We do not want you to become lazy, but to imitate those who through faith and patience inherit what has been promised. *Hebrews 6:12*

"I know your deeds, that you are neither cold nor hot. I wish you were either one or the other! So, because you are lukewarm—neither hot nor cold—I am about to spit you out of my mouth." *Revelation 3:15-16*

---

Two members of my congregation perished by a fire in their own house. They were not consumed by the flames, but they were suffocated by the smoke. No blaze was ever visible, nor could any remarkable sign of fire be seen from the street, yet they died as readily as if they had been burned to ashes by raging flames.

In this way sin also is deadly. Comparatively few of our hearers are destroyed by outrageous and flaming vices, such as blasphemy, theft, drunkenness, or uncleanness, but crowds of them are perishing by that deadly smoke of indifference that casts its stifling clouds of carelessness around them, and sends them asleep into everlasting destruction. Oh, that they could be saved from the smoke as well as from the flame!

# God's Grace

# Grace That Is Greater than Sin

We know that the one who raised the Lord Jesus from the dead will also raise us with Jesus and present us with you in his presence. All this is for your benefit, so that the grace that is reaching more and more people may cause thanksgiving to overflow to the glory of God. Therefore we do not lose heart. Though outwardly we are wasting away, yet inwardly we are being renewed day by day. *2 Corinthians 4:14-16*

---

Payson, when dying, expressed himself with great earnestness respecting the grace of God as exercised in saving the lost and seemed particularly affected that it should be bestowed on one so ill-deserving as himself. "Oh, how sovereign! Oh, how sovereign! Grace is the only thing that can make us like God. I might be dragged through heaven, earth, and hell, and I should still be the same sinful, polluted wretch, unless God himself renews and cleanses me."

# The Sweet Perfume of Grace

This is love: not that we loved God, but that he loved us and sent his Son as an atoning sacrifice for our sins. Dear friends, since God so loved us, we also ought to love one another. No one has ever seen God; but if we love each other, God lives in us and his love is made complete in us. We know that we live in him and he in us, because he has given us of his Spirit. And we have seen and testify that the Father has sent his Son to be the Savior of the world. If anyone acknowledges that Jesus is the Son of God, God lives in him and he in God. And so we know and rely on the love God has for us. *1 John 4:10-16*

---

The dahlia would surely be an empress among flowers if it had a perfume equal to its beauty—even the rose might have to look to her sovereignty. Florists have tried all their arts to scent this lovely child of autumn but in vain: no fragrance can be developed or produced. God has denied the boon, and human skill cannot impart it. The reflecting mind will be reminded of those admirable characters that are occasionally met with, in which everything of good repute and comely aspect may be seen, but true religion, that sweet ethereal perfume of grace, is wanting. If they had but love for God, what lovely beings they would be, the best of the saints would not excel them, and yet that fragrant grace they do not seek, and after every effort we may make for their conversion, they remain content without the one thing which is needful for their perfection. Oh, that the Lord would impart to them the mystic sweetness of his grace by the Holy Spirit!

# Saving Grace

I know that nothing good lives in me, that is, in my sinful nature. For I have the desire to do what is good, but I cannot carry it out. For what I do is not the good I want to do; no, the evil I do not want to do—this I keep on doing. . . . Who will rescue me from this body of death? Thanks be to God—through Jesus Christ our Lord! *Romans 7:18-19, 24-25*

If you live according to the sinful nature, you will die; but if by the Spirit you put to death the misdeeds of the body, you will live, because those who are led by the Spirit of God are sons of God. For you did not receive a spirit that makes you a slave again to fear, but you received the Spirit of sonship. *Romans 8:13-15*

---

The surgeon of a regiment in India relates the following incident: "A soldier rushed into the tent to inform me that one of his comrades was drowning in a pond, and nobody could save him because of the dense woods which covered the surface. We found the poor fellow manfully attempting to extricate himself from the meshes of rope-like grass that encircled his body. But the more he labored to escape, the more firmly they became coiled around his limbs. At last the floating plants closed in and left no trace of the disaster. After some delay, a raft was made and we put off to the spot. A native dived, holding on by a stake, and brought the body to the surface. I shall never forget the expression on the dead man's face—the clenched teeth and fearful distortion of the countenance, while coils of long trailing weeds clung to his body and limbs, the muscles of which stood out stiff and rigid, while his hands grasped thick masses, showing how bravely he had struggled for life."

This heart-rending picture is a terribly accurate representation of a man with a conscience alarmed by remorse, struggling with sinful habits but finding them too strong for him. Divine grace can save the wretch from his unhappy condition, but if he be destitute of that, his remorseful agonies will only make him more hopelessly the slave of his passions.

# Water That Satisfies

"Whoever drinks the water I give him will never thirst. Indeed, the water I give him will become in him a spring of water welling up to eternal life." *John 4:14*

---

The sharp shrill cry of "Acqua! Acqua!" constantly pierces the ear of the wanderer in the towns of Italy. The man who thus invites your attention bears on his back a burden of water, and in his hand glasses to hold the cooling liquid. In the streets of London he would find little patronage, but where fountains are few and the days are hot as an oven, he earns a livelihood and supplies a public need. The water-dealer is a poor old man bent sideways by the weight of his daily burden. He is worn out in all but his voice, which is truly startling in its sharpness and distinctness. At our call he stops immediately, glad to drop his burden on the ground, and smiling in prospect of a customer. He washes out a glass for us, fills it with sparkling water, receives payment with manifest gratitude, and trudges away across the square, crying still, "Acqua! Acqua!"

That cry, shrill as it is, has sounded sweetly in the ears of many a thirsty soul, and will for ages yet to come, if throats and thirst survive so long. How forcibly it calls to mind the Savior's favorite imagery, in which he compares the grace which he bestows on all who diligently seek it to "living water." And how much that old man is like the faithful preacher of the Word, who, having filled his vessel at the well, wears himself out by continually bearing the burden of the Lord, and crying, "Water! Water!" amid crowds of sinners who must drink or die. Instead of the poor Italian water-bearer, we see before us the man of God, whose voice is heard in the chief places of concourse, proclaiming the divine invitation, "Ho, every one that thirsts, come to the waters!" until he grows grey in the service, and people say, "Surely those aged limbs have need of rest." Yet he does not court rest, but pursues his task of mercy, never laying down his charge till he lays down his body, and never ceasing to work until he ceases to live.

---

# The Relief of Forgiveness

Seek the LORD while he may be found; call on him while he is near. Let the wicked forsake his way and the evil man his thoughts. Let him turn to the LORD, and he will have mercy on him, and to our God, for he will freely pardon. *Isaiah 55:6-7*

---

In certain places on Alpine summits the way is peculiarly dangerous on account of the frequent falling of avalanches, and the traveler walks in dread of instant destruction. Samuel Rogers puts it this way:

> *Then my guide*
> *lowering his voice addressed me: "Through this gap*
> *On and say nothing; lest a word, a breath,*
> *Bring down the winter's snow, enough to whelm*
> *An army."*

Thus when alarmed by an awakened conscience people walk in fear from hour to hour, trembling lest a thought or word of sin should bring down on them the impending wrath of God. Happy is he who has traversed that awful gap of terror and now breathes freely because sin is pardoned and therefore every apprehension is removed.

# The Glorious Restraints of Grace

Praise be to the God and Father of our Lord Jesus Christ, who has blessed us in the heavenly realms with every spiritual blessing in Christ. For he chose us in him before the creation of the world to be holy and blameless in his sight. In love he predestined us to be adopted as his sons through Jesus Christ, in accordance with his pleasure and will—to the praise of his glorious grace, which he has freely given us in the One he loves. In him we have redemption through his blood, the forgiveness of sins, in accordance with the riches of God's grace that he lavished on us with all wisdom and understanding. And he made known to us the mystery of his will according to his good pleasure. *Ephesians 1:3-9*

---

When we see a container wrenched open, the hinges torn away, or the clasp destroyed, we mark at once the hand of the Spoiler, but when we observe another container deftly opened with a master key, and the sparkling contents revealed, we note the hand of the Owner. Conversion is not, as some suppose, a violent opening of the heart by grace, in which will, reason, and judgment are all ignored or crushed. This is too barbarous a method for him who comes not as a plunderer to his prey, but as a possessor to his treasure. In conversion, the Lord who made the human heart deals with it according to its nature and constitution. His key insinuates itself into the wards; the will is not enslaved but enfranchised; the reason is not blinded but enlightened, and the whole man is made to act with a glorious liberty which it never knew till it fell under the restraints of grace.

# Complete Forgiveness

Have mercy on me, O God, according to your unfailing love; according to your great compassion blot out my transgressions. Wash away all my iniquity and cleanse me from my sin. *Psalm 51:1-2*

For as high as the heavens are above the earth, so great is his love for those who fear him; as far as the east is from the west, so far has he removed our transgressions from us. As a father has compassion on his children, so the LORD has compassion on those who fear him; for he knows how we are formed, he remembers that we are dust. *Psalm 103:11-14*

---

I have spilled ink over a bill and blotted it till it can hardly be read, but this is quite another thing from having the debt blotted out, for that is not accomplished until payment is made. A man may blot his sins from his memory and quiet his mind with false hopes, but the peace that this brings him is widely different from that which comes from God's forgiveness of sin through the satisfaction which Jesus made in his atonement. Our blotting is one thing; God's blotting out is something far higher.

# Deep Experience of Grace

It is written: "I believed; therefore I have spoken." With that same spirit of faith we also believe and therefore speak, because we know that the one who raised the Lord Jesus from the dead will also raise us with Jesus and present us with you in his presence. All this is for your benefit, so that the grace that is reaching more and more people may cause thanksgiving to overflow to the glory of God. *2 Corinthians 4:13-15*

---

In my house there is an extraordinarily deep well that reminds me of something better than the boasted deep experience of certain censorious believers who teach that to feel sin inwardly is the main thing, but to be delivered from it of small consequence. When this well was begun, the owner of the place resolved to have water, cost what it might. The well-sinkers dug through mud, clay, and stone, but found no water. Here was the deep experience of the corruptionist, all earth and no living spring, the filth revealed but not removed, the leper discovered but not healed. Another hundred feet of hard digging deep in the dark, but no water—still deeper experience. Then a third hundred feet, and still dirt, but no crystal—the very finest grade of your deeply experimental believer who ridicules the joys of faith as being of the flesh and presumptuous. Still on, on, on went the workers, till one day leaving their tools to go to dinner, upon their return they found that the water was rising fast and their tools were drowned. Be this last my experience—to go so deep as to reach the springs of everlasting love and find all my poor doings and efforts have broken in on me, covering all the mire, and rock, and earth of my poor, naturally evil heart.

# Grace to Depend On

To him who is able to keep you from falling and to present you before his glorious presence without fault and with great joy—to the only God our Savior be glory, majesty, power and authority, through Jesus Christ our Lord, before all ages, now and forevermore! Amen. *Jude 24-25*

---

In the old days the government of England resolved to build a wooden bridge over the Thames at Westminster. After they had driven a hundred and forty piles into the river, there occurred one of the most severe frosts in the memory of man, which tore the piles away from their strong fastenings, and snapped many of them in two. The apparent evil in this case was a great good; it led the commissioners to reconsider their purpose, and a substantial bridge of stone was erected.

It is a good thing when the worldly reformations of unregenerate people are broken to pieces, if thus they are led to fly to the Lord Jesus, and in the strength of his Spirit are brought to build solidly for eternity. Lord, if my resolves and hopes are carried away by temptations and the force of my corruptions, grant that this blessed calamity may drive me to depend wholly on your grace, which cannot fail me.

# The Secret Life in Christ

For you died, and your life is now hidden with Christ in God. When Christ, who is your life, appears, then you also will appear with him in glory. *Colossians 3:3-4*

We do, however, speak a message of wisdom among the mature, but not the wisdom of this age or of the rulers of this age, who are coming to nothing. No, we speak of God's secret wisdom, a wisdom that has been hidden and that God destined for our glory before time began. *1 Corinthians 2:6-7*

---

If you stand near telegraph wires you may often hear the mystic wailing and sighing of the winds among them, like the strains of an Aeolian harp, but you won't know anything of the message which is flashing among them. The inner language of those wires may be joyous, swift as lightning, far-reaching and full of meaning, but a stranger doesn't meddle with them. They become an apt emblem of the believer's inner life. Others hear our notes of outward sorrow wrung from us by external circumstances, but they can't perceive the message of celestial peace, the divine communings of a better land, the swift heartthrobs of heaven-born desire. The carnal see but the outer person, but the life hidden with Christ in God, flesh and blood cannot discern.

# The Beauty of the Spirit-Filled Life

Now the Lord is the Spirit, and where the Spirit of the Lord is, there is freedom. And we, who with unveiled faces all reflect the Lord's glory, are being transformed into his likeness with ever-increasing glory, which comes from the Lord, who is the Spirit. *2 Corinthians 3:17-18*

But the fruit of the Spirit is love, joy, peace, patience, kindness, goodness, faithfulness, gentleness and self-control. *Galatians 5:22-23*

---

We visited two palaces in Venice and realized the contrast of life and death. The first was tenanted by a noble family who delighted to maintain it in good repair, to adorn it with fresh beauties, and to furnish it in the most sumptuous manner. Everything was fresh, fair, bright, and charming. From the paving of mosaics in the hall one looked up to ceilings glowing with the creations of the artist's pencil, and in every chamber paintings, statues, ormolu, tapestry, and all things else of the richest kind surrounded you. The other was a palace, too, with marble pillars and carved work, but the stones were loosening, and the columns shifting; grass grew in the halls, and the roofs let in the rain. Decay was there, and desolation, yet the palace was as noble in its architecture as the first.

Thus when God dwells in a person, all his powers and faculties are bright with a sacred light, and joy and peace and beauty adorn his entire person; but if the Holy Spirit depart, the heart being empty and void becomes a ruin, everywhere decaying, and too often haunted by the demons of vice and iniquity.

# Sorrow, Fear, Love, and Faith

Godly sorrow brings repentance that leads to salvation and leaves no regret. *2 Corinthians 7:10*

We must all appear before the judgment seat of Christ, that each one may receive what is due him for the things done while in the body, whether good or bad. Since, then, we know what it is to fear the Lord, we try to persuade men. *2 Corinthians 5:10-11*

"He who loves me will be loved by my Father, and I too will love him and show myself to him." *John 14:21*

This righteousness from God comes through faith in Jesus Christ to all who believe. *Romans 3:22*

---

A discussion arose between some members of a Bible class in reference to the first Christian exercise of the converted soul. One contended that it was penitence or *sorrow*; another that it was *fear*, another *love*, another *hope*, another *faith*, for how could one fear or repent without belief? An elder, overhearing the discussion, relieved the minds of the disputants with this remark, "Can you tell which spoke of the wheel moves first? You may be looking at one spoke, and think that it moves first, but they all start together. Thus, when the Spirit of God operates on the human heart, all the graces begin to affect the penitent soul, though the individual may be more conscious of one than another."

# Guarded by Omnipotent Love

He who dwells in the shelter of the Most High will rest in the shadow of the Almighty. I will say of the LORD, "He is my refuge and my fortress, my God, in whom I trust." . . . If you make the Most High your dwelling—even the LORD, who is my refuge—then no harm will befall you, no disaster will come near your tent. . . . "Because he loves me," says the LORD, "I will rescue him; I will protect him, for he acknowledges my name. He will call upon me, and I will answer him; I will be with him in trouble, I will deliver him and honor him." *Psalm 91:1-2, 9-10, 14-15*

---

The image in Lowell's poem of "The Changeling" fascinates me. It is so much what I am and ever wish to be.

> *I feel as weak as a violet*
> *Alone 'neath the awful sky.*

Unable to defend myself and apparently undefended, yet guarded by omnipotent love, I would love to pour out a perfume of praise to the Great Invisible who watches over me, and would feel that under the care of Providence I may claim the sweetness of the poet's next stanza.

> *As weak, yet as trustful also;*
> *For the whole year long I see*
> *All the wonders of faithful nature*
> *Still worked for the love of me.*
> *Winds wander and dews drip earthward,*
> *Rains fall, suns rise and set,*
> *Earth whirls, and all but to prosper*
> *A poor little violet.*

# The Salt of Grace

But where sin increased, grace increased all the more, so that, just as sin reigned in death, so also grace might reign through righteousness to bring eternal life through Jesus Christ our Lord. *Romans 5:20-21*

---

My gardeners set out to remove a large tree which grew near a wall. As it would weaken the wall to stub up the roots, it was agreed that the stump should remain in the ground. But I wanted to make sure the stump would not grow and disfigure the gravel walk. The gardener's prescription was to cover it with a layer of salt. I mused awhile, and thought that the readiest way to keep down my ever-sprouting corruptions in the future would be to sow them well with the salt of grace. Oh Lord, help me to do so.

# Until Grace Prevails

For when we were controlled by the sinful nature, the sinful passions aroused by the law were at work in our bodies, so that we bore fruit for death. But now, by dying to what once bound us, we have been released from the law so that we serve in the new way of the Spirit, and not in the old way of the written code. *Romans 7:5-6*

---

George Shadford wrote, "One day a friend took me to see a hermit in the woods. After some difficulty we found his hermitage, which was a little place like a hog-sty, built of several pieces of wood, covered with tree bark, and his bed consisted of dry leaves. There was a narrow beaten path about twenty or thirty yards in length by the side of it, where he frequently walked to meditate.

"If one offered him food, he would take it, but if money were offered him, he would be angry. If anything was spoken which he did not like, he broke into a violent passion. He had lived in this cell seven cold winters, and after all his prayers, and separating himself from mankind, corrupt nature was still quite alive within him."

It does not matter whether we live among mankind or retire into a hermitage if we still carry with us our own hell, our corrupt evil tempers. Without a new heart and a right spirit, no condition can deliver a man from the powerful hold of his sins. Neither publicity nor solitude avails anything until grace prevails with us. The devil can tempt in the wilderness as well as in the crowd. We don't need seclusion but heavenly-mindedness.

# Sweet and Dreadful Doctrines

For he chose us in him before the creation of the world to be holy and blameless in his sight. In love he predestined us to be adopted as his sons through Jesus Christ, in accordance with his pleasure and will—to the praise of his glorious grace, which he has freely given us in the One he loves. *Ephesians 1:4-6*

And we know that in all things God works for the good of those who love him, who have been called according to his purpose. For those God foreknew he also predestined to be conformed to the likeness of his Son, that he might be the firstborn among many brothers. And those he predestined, he also called; those he called, he also justified; those he justified, he also glorified. *Romans 8:28-30*

---

Our forefathers were very fond of clipping their plants and training their flowers into quaint and grotesque forms, so that we read of great guns wrought in rosemary and sweet briars. But anyone who would have trembled at cannons which only shot forth flowers and darted perfume would have been very foolish. Let the poor trembler who is sincerely seeking Jesus rest assured that the seemingly dreadful doctrines of election and predestination are not one whit more terrible, and are far more sweetly fragrant.

# Stubbornly Refusing God's Grace

Do you show contempt for the riches of his kindness, tolerance and patience, not realizing that God's kindness leads you towards repentance? But because of your stubbornness and your unrepentant heart, you are storing up wrath against yourself for the day of God's wrath, when his righteous judgment will be revealed. *Romans 2:4-5*

---

When the dove was weary she remembered the ark and flew into Noah's hand at once. There are weary souls who know the ark, but will not fly to it. When an Israelite had slain, inadvertently, his fellow, he knew the city of refuge, he feared the avenger of blood, and he fled along the road to the place of safety. But multitudes know the refuge, and every Sunday we set up the signposts along the road, but yet they don't come to find salvation. The destitute waifs and strays of the streets of London find out the night refuge and ask for shelter; they cluster around the workhouse doors like sparrows under the eaves of a building on a rainy day. They piteously crave for lodging and a crust of bread. Yet crowds of poor benighted spirits, when the house of mercy is lighted up, and the invitation is plainly written in bold letters, "Whosoever will, let him turn in here," will not come, but prove the truth of Watts's verse:

*Thousands make a wretched choice,*
*And rather starve than come.*

# From the Ground Up

Instead of the thornbush will grow the pine tree, and instead of briars the myrtle will grow. This will be for the LORD's renown, for an everlasting sign, which will not be destroyed. *Isaiah 55:13*

---

I passed by a plot of land which some landowner had been enclosing, as those rascals always will filch every morsel of green grass. But I noticed that the enclosers had only fenced it in, but had not dug it up, nor plowed it, nor planted it. And though they had cut down the gorse, it was coming up again. Of course it would, for it was still a meadow, and a bit of fence or rail could not alter it. The gorse would come peeping up, and before long the enclosure would be as wild as the heath outside.

But this is not God's way of working. When God encloses a heart that has laid open to sin, does he cut down the thorns and the briars and then plant fir trees? No—he changes the soil so that from the ground itself, from its own vitality, the fir tree and the myrtle spontaneously start up. This is a most wonderful result. If a man remains at heart the same godless man, you can mend his habits, make him go to church, clothe him, keep him away from alcohol, and teach him not to talk filthily, and then say, "He's now a respectable man." But if these outward respectabilities and rightnesses are only skin deep, you have done nothing. At least, what you have done is nothing to be proud of. But suppose this man can be so changed that just as freely as he was accustomed to curse he now delights to pray, and just as heartily as he hated religion he now finds pleasure in it, and just as earnestly as he sinned he now delights to be obedient to the Lord. This is a wonder, a miracle which man cannot accomplish, a marvel which only the grace of God can work and which gives God his highest glory.

# To Be Continued . . .

Because of the LORD's great love we are not consumed, for his compassions never fail. They are new every morning; great is your faithfulness. *Lamentations 3:22-23*

The LORD will fulfill his purpose for me; your love, O LORD, endures forever. *Psalm 138:8*

---

It is always unpleasant when reading an interesting article in a magazine to find yourself pulled up short with the ominous words, "To be continued." Yet they are words of good cheer if applied to other matters. What a comfort to remember that the Lord's mercy and lovingkindness is *to be continued!* Much as we have experienced in the long years of our pilgrimage, we have by no means outlived eternal love. Providential goodness is an endless chain, a stream which follows the pilgrim, a wheel perpetually revolving, a star forever shining and leading us to the place where he is who was once a babe in Bethlehem. All the volumes which record the doings of divine grace are but part of a series *to be continued.*

# Grace Is the Primary Resource

His divine power has given us everything we need for life and godliness through our knowledge of him who called us by his own glory and goodness. Through these he has given us his very great and precious promises, so that through them you may participate in the divine nature and escape the corruption in the world caused by evil desires. *2 Peter 1:3-4*

---

The outlay in opening a mine is usually so great that they say to prepare a mine one must spend another mine. To open up the hidden preciousness of the promises, we need a mine of experience, and to gain this last a person needs an inexhaustible mine of grace.

# Blessings That Just Keep Coming

Praise be to the God and Father of our Lord Jesus Christ, who has blessed us in the heavenly realms with every spiritual blessing in Christ. *Ephesians 1:3*

---

A benevolent person gave Mr. Rowland Hill a hundred pounds to dispense to a poor minister a bit at a time, thinking it was too much too send him all at once. Mr. Hill forwarded five pounds in a letter, with only these words within the envelope, "More to follow." In a few days' time, the good man received another letter; this second messenger contained another five pounds, with the same motto, "And more to follow." A day or two after came a third and a fourth, and still the same promise, "And more to follow." Till the whole sum had been received, the astonished minister was made familiar with the cheering words, "And more to follow."

Every blessing that comes from God is sent with the same message, "And more to follow." "I forgive you your sins, but there's more to follow." "I justify you in the righteousness of Christ, but there's more to follow." "I adopt you into my family, but there's more to follow." "I educated you for heaven, but there's more to follow." "I give you grace upon grace, but there's more to follow." "I have helped you even to old age, but there's still more to follow." "I will uphold you in the hour of death, and as you are passing into the world of spirits, my mercy shall still continue with you, and when you land in the world to come there shall still be *more to follow.*"

# Safe in a Perilous Place

"Because he loves me," says the LORD, "I will rescue him; I will protect him, for he acknowledges my name. He will call upon me, and I will answer him; I will be with him in trouble, I will deliver him and honor him. With long life will I satisfy him and show him my salvation." *Psalm 91:14-16*

O LORD, you are my God; I will exalt you and praise your name, for in perfect faithfulness you have done marvelous things. . . . You have been a refuge for the poor, a refuge for the needy in distress, a shelter from the storm and a shade from the heat. For the breath of the ruthless is like a storm driving against a wall and like the heat of the desert. *Isaiah 25:1, 4-5*

---

When the instructed Christian sees his surroundings, he finds himself to be like a defenseless dove flying to her nest while against her tens of thousands of arrows are leveled. The Christian life is like that dove's anxious flight, as it threads its way between the death-bearing shafts of the enemy and by constant miracle escapes unhurt. The enlightened Christian sees himself to be like a traveler, standing on the narrow summit of a lofty ridge. On the right hand and on the left are gulfs unfathomable, yawning for his destruction. If it were not that by divine grace his feet are like hinds' feet, so that he is able to stand up on his high places, he would long before this have fallen to his eternal destruction.

# Salvation in Christ

# Protected by the Blood of Jesus

This righteousness from God comes through faith in Jesus Christ to all who believe. There is no difference, for all have sinned and fall short of the glory of God, and are justified freely by his grace through the redemption that came by Christ Jesus. God presented him as a sacrifice of atonement, through faith in his blood. *Romans 3:22-25*

---

Recently we read in the papers an illustration of the way of salvation. A man had been condemned in a Spanish court to be shot, but because he was an American citizen and also of English birth, the consuls of the two countries interposed, and declared that the Spanish authorities had no power to put him to death. What did they do to secure his life, when their protest was not sufficient? They wrapped him up in their flags, they covered him with the Stars and Stripes and the Union Jack and defied the executioners. "Now fire a shot if you dare, for if you do, you defy the nations represented by those flags, and you will bring the powers of those two great empires on you." There stood the man, and before him the soldiers, and though a single shot might have ended his life, yet he was as invulnerable as though encased in triple steel.

Even so Jesus Christ has taken my poor guilty soul ever since I believed in him and has wrapped around me the blood-red flag of his atoning sacrifice, and before God can destroy me or any other soul that is wrapped in the atonement, he must insult his Son and dishonor the sacrifice, and that he will never do, blessed be his name.

# Dying While Salvation Waits at Hand

We do not use deception, nor do we distort the word of God. On the contrary, by setting forth the truth plainly we commend ourselves to every man's conscience in the sight of God. And even if our gospel is veiled, it is veiled to those who are perishing. The god of this age has blinded the minds of unbelievers, so that they cannot see the light of the gospel of the glory of Christ, who is the image of God. *2 Corinthians 4:2-4*

---

It is said that some years ago a vessel sailing on the northern coast of the South American continent was observed to make signals of distress. When hailed by another vessel, they reported themselves as "Dying for water!"

"Dip it up then," was the response. "You are in the mouth of the Amazon river."

There was fresh water all around them, and they had nothing to do but to dip it up, and yet they were dying of thirst because they thought themselves surrounded by sea water.

People are often ignorant of their mercies. How sad that they should perish for lack of knowledge! Jesus is near the seeker even when he is tossed on oceans of doubt. The sinner has only to stoop down and drink and live; yet he is ready to perish, as if salvation were hard to find.

# Replaced with a Whole New Nature

Therefore, if anyone is in Christ, he is a new creation; the old has gone, the new has come! *2 Corinthians 5:17*

We were therefore buried with him through baptism into death in order that, just as Christ was raised from the dead through the glory of the Father, we too may live a new life. *Romans 6:4*

---

A raw countryman brought his gun to the gunsmith for repairs. The gunsmith examined it and found it almost too far gone for repairing. He said, "Your gun is in a very worn out, ruinous, good-for-nothing condition, what sort of repairing do you want for it?"

"Well," said the countryman, "I don't see as I can do with anything short of a new stock, lock, and barrel. That ought to set it up again."

"Why," said the smith, "you might just as well have a new gun altogether."

"Ah!" was the reply. "I never thought of that, and it strikes that's just what I do want. A new lock, stock, and barrel. That's about equal to a new gun, and that's what I'll have."

Man's nature requires just this sort of repairing. The old nature cast aside as a complete wreck and good for nothing, and a new one imparted.

# No One Can Do It for You

If you confess with your mouth, "Jesus is Lord," and believe in your heart that God raised him from the dead, you will be saved. For it is with your heart that you believe and are justified, and it is with your mouth that you confess and are saved. As the Scripture says, "Everyone who trusts in him will never be put to shame." *Romans 10:9-11*

---

A little girl, whom we will call Ellen, was some time ago helping to nurse a sick gentleman whom she loved very dearly. One day he said to her, "Ellen, it is time for me to take my medicine, I think. Will you pour it out for me? You must measure just a tablespoonful, and then put it in that glass close by." Ellen quickly did so, and brought it to his bedside. But, instead of taking it in his own hand, he quietly said, "Now, dear, will you drink it for me?"

"Me drink it! What do you mean? I am sure I would, in a minute, if it would cure you all the same, but you know it won't do you any good unless you take it yourself."

"Won't it really? No, I suppose not. But Ellen, if you can't take my medicine for me, I can't take your salvation for you. You must go to Jesus, and believe in him for yourself."

In this way he tried to teach her that each human being must seek salvation for himself, and repent, and believe, and obey, for himself.

# The Weight of Godliness

But thanks be to God that, though you used to be slaves to sin, you wholeheartedly obeyed the form of teaching to which you were entrusted. You have been set free from sin and have become slaves to righteousness. . . . But now that you have been set free from sin and have become slaves to God, the benefit you reap leads to holiness, and the result is eternal life. *Romans 6:17-18, 22*

But godliness with contentment is great gain. *1 Timothy 6:6*

---

The Princess Elizabeth carried the crown for her sister in the procession at Mary's coronation, and she complained to Noailles of its great weight. "Be patient," was the adroit answer. "It will seem lighter when on your own head."

The outward forms of godliness are as burdensome to an unregenerate person as was the crown to the princess. But once he is born again and so made a possessor of divine grace, they will sit easily enough upon his head, as his glory and delight.

# Hearers Only

Do not merely listen to the word, and so deceive yourselves. Do what it says. Anyone who listens to the word but does not do what it says is like a man who looks at his face in a mirror and, after looking at himself, goes away and immediately forgets what he looks like. But the man who looks intently into the perfect law that gives freedom, and continues to do this, not forgetting what he has heard, but doing it—he will be blessed in what he does. *James 1:22-25*

---

What a mistake to imagine that by hearing first one preacher and then another we can derive benefit to our souls! More is wanted than such hearing. A raven may fly from cage to cage, but it is not thereby changed into a dove. Go from room to room of the royal feast, and the sight of the tables will never relieve your hunger. The main thing is to have and hold the truth personally and inwardly. If you don't see to this, you will die in your sins, even if ten thousand voices direct you to the way of salvation. It is a pity that the bulk of hearers are hearers only, and are no more likely to go to heaven than the seats they sit on in the assembly of the saints.

# Now Is the Time

As God's fellow workers we urge you not to receive God's grace in vain. For he says, "In the time of my favor I heard you, and in the day of salvation I helped you." I tell you, now is the time of God's favor, now is the day of salvation. *2 Corinthians 6:1-2*

---

It is not after the storm has arisen, or the telegraph has reported that his ship has struck, that the merchant runs to insure his goods. He takes care of the insurance while the sun is shining and the air calm; he makes sure the insurance is in effect before the ship has cleared from the dock, or at all events before the ship has left the river. You should do the same, you living, but dying people! Now is the accepted time, today. God is with us waiting; his terms are still, "Whosoever will." Today you may enter into life; tomorrow the door may be shut.

# A True Change of Nature

You, however, are controlled not by the sinful nature but by the Spirit, if the Spirit of God lives in you. And if anyone does not have the Spirit of Christ, he does not belong to Christ. But if Christ is in you, your body is dead because of sin, yet your spirit is alive because of righteousness. And if the Spirit of him who raised Jesus from the dead is living in you, he who raised Christ from the dead will also give life to your mortal bodies through his Spirit, who lives in you. Therefore, brothers, we have an obligation—but it is not to the sinful nature, to live according to it. For if you live according to the sinful nature, you will die; but if by the Spirit you put to death the misdeeds of the body, you will live, because those who are led by the Spirit of God are sons of God. *Romans 8:9-14*

---

A vicious horse is none the better tempered because the kicking straps prevent his dashing the carriage to atoms. So a man is really none the better because the restraints of custom and providence may prevent his following that course of life which he would prefer. Poor fallen human nature behind the bars of laws, and in the cage of fear of punishment, is nonetheless a sad creature. If its Master unlocked the door, we would soon see what it would be and do. A young leopard that had been domesticated and treated as a pet licked its master's hand while he slept, and it so happened that it drew blood from a recent wound. The first taste of blood transformed the gentle creature into a raging wild beast. Yet it wrought no real change; it only awakened the natural ferocity that had always been there. A change of nature is required for our salvation—mere restraints are of small value.

# A Welcome for the Weary

"Come to me, all you who are weary and burdened, and I will give you rest. Take my yoke upon you and learn from me, for I am gentle and humble in heart, and you will find rest for your souls. For my yoke is easy and my burden light." *Matthew 11:28-30*

---

We are told that in stormy weather it is not unusual for small birds to be blown out of sight of land on to the sea. They are often seen by voyagers out of their reckoning and far from the coast, hovering over the masts on weary wings as if they wanted to alight and rest themselves, but fearing to do so. A traveler tells us that on one occasion, a little lark, which followed the ship for a considerable distance, was at last compelled through sheer weariness to alight. He was so worn out as to be easily caught. The warmth of the hand was so agreeable to him that he sat down on it, burying his little cold feet in his feathers and looking about with his bright eye not in the least afraid, and as if feeling assured that he had been cast among good kind people whom he could trust.

It makes a touching picture of the soul who is aroused by the Spirit of God and blown out of its own reckoning by the winds of conviction, and the warm reception of the weary little bird received at the hands of the passengers conveys but a faint idea of that welcome which will greet the worn-out, sin-sick souls who will commit themselves into the hands of the only Savior.

# Life-Changing Grace

And we, who with unveiled faces all reflect the Lord's glory, are being transformed into his likeness with ever-increasing glory, which comes from the Lord, who is the Spirit. *2 Corinthians 3:18*

---

A short time ago the manufacturers of lighting gas were puzzled to know how to dispose of the coal-tar left in the retorts. A more useless, nauseous substance was hardly known to exist. Chemistry came to the rescue, and today not less than thirty-six marketable articles are produced from this black, vile, sticky slime—solvents, oils, salts, colors, flavors. You eat a bit of delicious candy, happily unconscious that the exquisite taste that you enjoy so keenly comes from coal-tar. You buy at the drug store a tiny bottle labeled "Otto of Roses," little dreaming that the delicious perfume is wafted, not from "the fields of Araby," but from the foul gas retort.

Christianity is a moral chemistry. It would be a good thing for nations if Christianity held a higher place among their social economies. Tar-saving is all well enough, but soul-saving is better. Grace transforms a villain into an honest man, a harlot into a holy woman, a thief into a saint. Where fetid exhalations of vice alone ascended, prayer and praise are to be found. Where moral miasmata had their lair, righteousness and temperance pitch their tent. Every sort of good thing is produced by godliness, and that too in hearts once reeking with all manner of foulness. This should hold back every persecuting hand, hush every railing tongue, and incite every sanctified spirit to continued and increasing energy.

# We Cannot Save Ourselves

All of us have become like one who is unclean, and all our righteous acts are like filthy rags; we all shrivel up like a leaf, and like the wind our sins sweep us away. *Isaiah 64:6*

But God demonstrates his own love for us in this: While we were still sinners, Christ died for us. *Romans 5:8*

---

The squirrel in his wire cage continually in motion but making no progress reminds me of my own self-righteous efforts toward salvation, but the little creature is never half so wearied by his exertions as I was by mine. The poor scavenger in Paris trying to earn a living by picking dirty rags out of the kennel succeeds far better than I did in my attempts to obtain comfort by my own works. Dickens's cab-horse, which was only able to stand because it was never taken out of the shafts, was strength and beauty itself compared with my starving hopes propped up with resolutions and regulations. Wretches condemned to the galleys in the days of the old French kings, whose only reward for incessant toils was the lash of the keeper, were in a more happy plight than I when under legal bondage. Slavery in mines where the sun never shines must be preferable to the miseries of a soul goaded by an awakened conscience to seek salvation by its own merits. Some of the martyrs were shut up in a dungeon, and I remember the spiritual counterpart of that prison-house. Iron chains are painful enough, but what pain there is when the iron enters the soul! Tell us not of the writhings of the wounded and dying on the battlefield. Some of us, when our hearts were riddled by the artillery of the law, would have counted wounds and death a happy exchange. Oh blessed Savior, how blissful was the hour when all this horrid midnight of the soul was changed into the dawning of pardoning love!

# The Path of Repentance

"But the tax collector . . . would not even look up to heaven, but beat his breast and said, 'God have mercy on me, a sinner.' I tell you that this man . . . went home justified before God. For everyone who exalts himself will be humbled, and he who humbles himself will be exalted." *Luke 18:13-14*

---

In one of the coal mines of the north, the top of the pit fell in while a considerable number of the miners were down below, and the shaft was completely blocked. Those who were in the mine gathered to a spot where the last remains of air could be breathed. There they sat and sang and prayed after the lights had gone out because the air was unable to support the flame. They were in total darkness, but a gleam of hope cheered them when one of them said he had heard that there was a connection between that pit and an old pit which had been worked years ago. He said it was a long passage through which a man might get by crawling all the way, lying flat upon the ground—he would go and see if it were passable. The passage was very long, but they crept through it, and at last they came out to light at the bottom of the other shaft, and their lives were saved.

If my present way of access to Christ as a saint is blocked up by doubts and fears, if I cannot go straight up the shaft and see the light of my Father's face, there is an old working, the old-fashioned way by which sinners have gone of old, by which poor thieves go, by which harlots go. I will creep along it, lowly and humbly. I will go flat upon the ground. I will humble myself till I see my Lord and cry, "Father, I am not worthy to be called thy son, make me as one of thy hired servants, so long as I may but dwell in thy house." In our very worst case of despondency we may still come to Jesus as sinners. "Jesus Christ came into the world to save sinners." Call this to mind, and you may have hope.

# The Loving Pardon

In love he predestined us to be adopted as his sons through Jesus Christ, in accordance with his pleasure and will—to the praise of his glorious grace, which he has freely given us in the One he loves. In him we have redemption through his blood, the forgiveness of sins, in accordance with the riches of God's grace that he lavished on us with all wisdom and understanding. *Ephesians 1:4-8*

---

"You may have heard of some people condemned to execution, who at the scaffold were so obdurate and stiff-necked that not a cry or a tear came from them. Yet, just as they were going to lay their necks upon the block, a pardon came, and they were at once discharged from guilt, imprisonment, and death, they that were unable to weep a tear before, no sooner saw the pardon sealed and themselves acquitted, than they dissolved into tears of joy, thankfulness and surprise. So it is with believers. The more they see Christ in the pardon of sin, and the love of God in Christ to receive and embrace them, the more they melt."—*Tobias Crisp*

# No Righteousness of Our Own

I consider everything a loss compared to the surpassing greatness of knowing Christ Jesus my Lord, for whose sake I have lost all things. I consider them rubbish, that I may gain Christ and be found in him, not having a righteousness of my own that comes from the law, but that which is through faith in Christ—the righteousness that comes from God and is by faith. I want to know Christ and the power of his resurrection and the fellowship of sharing in his sufferings, becoming like him in his death, and so, somehow, to attain to the resurrection from the dead. *Philippians 3:8-11*

---

A ship on her way to Australia met with a very terrible storm and sprang a leak. As evils seldom come alone, a little while after another tempest assailed her. There happened to be a gentleman of the most nervous temperament aboard, whose garrulous tongue and important air began to alarm all the passengers. When the storm came on, the captain, who knew what mischief might be done by a suspicious and talkative individual, managed to get near him, intending to quiet him. The gentleman, addressing the captain, said in a tone of alarm, "What an awful storm! I am afraid we shall go to the bottom, for I hear the leak is very bad."

"Well," said the captain, "as you seem to know it and perhaps the others do not, you had better not mention it to anyone, lest you should frighten the passengers or dispirit my men. Perhaps as it is a very bad case, you would lend us your valuable help, and then we may possibly get through it. Would you have the goodness to stand here and hold hard on this rope? Do not leave it, but pull as hard as ever you can till I tell you to let it go."

So our friend clenched his teeth, and put his feet firmly down, and kept on holding this rope with all his might, till he earnestly wished for a substitute. The storm abated, the ship was safe, and our friend was released from his rope-holding. He expected a deputation would bring him the thanks of all the passengers, but they were evidently unconscious of his merits, and even the captain did not seem very grateful.

---

So our hero, in a roundabout style, hinted that such valuable services as his, having saved the vessel, ought to be rewarded at least with some few words of acknowledgment. He was shocked to hear the captain say, "What? You think *you* saved the vessel? Why, I gave you that rope to hold to keep you busy, that you might not be in such a feverish state of alarm."

This becomes a picture of how much self-righteous men contribute to their own salvation apart from Christ. They think they can certainly save themselves, and there they stand holding the rope with their clenched teeth and their feet tightly fixed, while they are really doing no more than our friend, who was similarly fooled. If ever you get to heaven, you will find that everything you did toward your own salvation, apart from the Lord Jesus, was about as useful as holding the rope; that, in fact, the safety of the soul lies somewhere else and not in you; and that what is wanted with you is just to get out of the way and let Christ come in and magnify his grace.

# Shining Stars in a Depraved Generation

As you have always obeyed—not only in my presence, but now much more in my absence—continue to work out your salvation with fear and trembling, for it is God who works in you to will and to act according to his good purpose. Do everything without complaining or arguing, so that you may become blameless and pure, children of God without fault in a crooked and depraved generation, in which you shine like stars in the universe as you hold out the word of life. *Philippians 2:12-16*

---

King Edward appointed William Wickham to build a stately church, and William Wickham performed his duty and finished by writing in the windows, "This work made William Wickham." When chastised by the king for assuming the honor of that work for himself as author, when he was really only the overseer, he answered that he did not mean that he made the work, but that the work made him: before he had been poor, and now he was well established financially.

Lord, when we read in thy Word that we must work out our own salvation, thy meaning is not that our salvation should be the effect of our work, but our work the evidence of our salvation.

# Living Faith

# Faith Is Stronger than Reason

*Now faith is being sure of what we hope for and certain of what we do not see. Hebrews 11:1*

An old writer said that Faith and Reason may be compared to two travelers. Faith is like a man in full health, who can walk his twenty or thirty miles at a time without suffering. Reason is like a little child, who can only, with difficulty, accomplish three or four miles. "Well," says the old writer, "on a given day Reason says to Faith, 'O good Faith, let me walk with you.' Faith replies, 'O Reason, you could never walk with me!' However, to try their paces, they set out together, but they soon find it hard to stay together. When they come to a deep river, Reason says, 'I can never ford this,' but Faith wades through it singing. When they reach a lofty mountain, there is the same exclamation of despair; and in such cases, Faith, in order not to leave Reason behind, is obliged to carry him on his back. Oh, what luggage is Reason to Faith!"

# Learning from the Inside Out

And this is my prayer: that your love may abound more and more in knowledge and depth of insight, so that you may be able to discern what is best and may be pure and blameless until the day of Christ, filled with the fruit of righteousness that comes through Jesus Christ—to the glory and praise of God. *Philippians 1:9-11*

---

"Orthodoxy can be learned from others; living faith must be a matter of personal experience. The Lord sent out his disciples, saying, 'You shall testify of me, because you have been with me from the beginning.' He only is a witness who speaks of what he has seen with his own eyes, heard with his own ears, and handled with his own hands. Orthodoxy is merely another form of rationalism, if it be learned from without."—*Buchsel*

# The Lifesaving Rope

For it is by grace you have been saved, through faith—and this not from yourselves, it is the gift of God—not by works, so that no one can boast. For we are God's workmanship, created in Christ Jesus to do good works, which God prepared in advance for us to do. *Ephesians 2:8-10*

Show me your faith without deeds, and I will show you my faith by what I do. . . . A person is justified by what he does and not by faith alone. . . . As the body without the spirit is dead, so faith without deeds is dead. *James 2:18, 24, 26*

---

The stupendous Niagara Falls have been spoken of in every part of the world. But while they are marvelous to hear of and wonderful to see, they have been very destructive to human life, when by accident some have been carried down the cataract. Some years ago, two men were in a boat and found themselves being carried so swiftly down the current that they must both inevitably be borne down and dashed to pieces. At last, however, one man was saved by a rope that was floated out to him, which he grasped. Another rope was floated to the other man, but at the same instant the rope came into his hand, a log floated by him. The thoughtless and confused man, instead of seizing the rope, laid hold on the log. It was a fatal mistake. They were both in imminent peril, but the one was drawn to shore because he had a connection with the people on the land, while the other, clinging to the loose, floating log, was borne irresistibly along, and was never heard of afterward. *Faith* has a saving connection with Christ. Christ is on the shore, so to speak, holding the rope, and as we lay hold of it with the hand of our confidence, he pulls us to shore. But our good works having no connection with Christ are drifted along down to the gulf of despair. Grapple our virtues as tightly as we may, even with hooks of steel, they cannot avail us in the least degree. They are the disconnected log that has no hold on the heavenly shore.

---

# Taking Him at His Word

The Spirit himself testifies with our spirit that we are God's children. Now if we are children, then we are heirs—heirs of God and co-heirs with Christ, if indeed we share in his sufferings in order that we may also share in his glory. *Romans 8:16-17*

---

The emperor Napoleon I was reviewing some troops upon the Place du Carrousel in Paris. In giving an order, he thoughtlessly dropped the bridle upon his horse's neck, which instantly set off in a gallop. The emperor was obliged to cling to the saddle. At this moment a common soldier of the line sprang before the horse, seized the bridle, and handed it respectfully to the emperor.

"Much obliged to you, captain," said the chief, in one word making the soldier a captain.

The man asked, "Of what regiment, sire?"

Napoleon replied, "Of my guards!" and galloped off.

The soldier then laid down his gun and, instead of returning to his comrades, approached the group of star officers.

"This fellow," replied the soldier proudly, "is captain of the guard."

"You? My poor friend! You are mad to say so!" one general said.

"*He* said it," replied the soldier, pointing to the emperor, who was still in sight.

"I ask your pardon, sir," said the general respectfully. "I was not aware of it."

Here, then, was exhibited a manifold faith. Since first the soldier believed the emperor, upon his word, because he heard him (as the Samaritans said of the Savior), and afterward, on the soldier's word, the general believed the emperor.

You now see how a person may be sure that God gives peace. It is by believing his testimony, just as this soldier believed that of his emperor. That is to say, as he believed himself to be a captain *before* wearing his uniform, so on the word and promise of God one believes himself to be a child of Jesus, *before* being sanctified by his Spirit.

# Sharing the Father's Riches

Every good and perfect gift is from above, coming down from the Father of the heavenly lights, who does not change like shifting shadows. He chose to give us birth through the word of truth, that we might be a kind of firstfruits of all he created. *James 1:17-18*

If you, then, though you are evil, know how to give good gifts to your children, how much more will your Father in heaven give good gifts to those who ask him! *Matthew 7:11*

---

"I once heard a father tell that when he moved his family to a new residence where the accommodation was much more ample and the substance much more rich and varied than that to which they had previously been accustomed, his youngest son, still a very little boy, ran around every room and scanned every article in sight, calling out in childish wonder at every new sight, 'Is this ours, father? And is this ours?'

"The child did not say 'yours,' and I observed that the father while he told the story was not offended with the freedom. You could read in his glistening eye that the child's confidence in appropriating as his own all that his father had was an important element in his satisfaction.

"Such, I suppose, will be the surprise, joy, and appropriating confidence with which the child of our Father's family will count all his own, when he is removed from the comparatively mean condition of things present and enters the infinite of things to come. When the glories of heaven burst on his view, he does not stand at a distance like a stranger, saying, 'Oh God, these are yours.' He bounds forward to touch and taste every provision those blessed mansions contain, exclaiming, as he looks in the Father's face, 'Father, this and this are ours!' The dear child is glad of all the Father's riches, and the Father is gladder of his dear child."—*W. Arnot*

# The Death Grip

But Christ is faithful as a son over God's house. And we are his house, if we hold on to our courage and the hope of which we boast. . . . We have come to share in Christ if we hold firmly till the end the confidence we had at first. *Hebrews 3:6, 14*

---

A sea captain once related a thrilling incident from his own experience. "A few years ago," said he, "I was sailing by the island of Cuba when the cry ran through the ship, 'Man overboard!' It was impossible to put up the helm of the ship, but I instantly seized a rope and threw it over the ship's stern, crying out to the man to seize it as for his life. The sailor caught the rope just as the ship was passing. I immediately took another rope and, making a slip noose of it, attached it to the other and slid it down to the struggling sailor and directed him to pass it over his shoulders and under his arms, and he would be drawn on board. He was rescued, but he had grasped the rope with such firmness, with such a death-grip, that it took hours before his hold relaxed and his hand could be separated from it. With such eagerness, indeed, had he clutched the object that was to save him, that the strands of rope became embedded in the flesh of his hands!"

Has not God let down from heaven a rope to every sinner on the earth? Is not every strand a precious promise, and ought we not to lay hold of it as for our very lives?

# A Shelter in the Royal Courts

The Lord is not slow in keeping his promise, as some understand slowness. He is patient with you, not wanting anyone to perish, but everyone to come to repentance. . . . You ought to live holy and godly lives as you look forward to the day of God and speed its coming. That day will bring about the destruction of the heavens by fire, and the elements will melt in the heat. But in keeping with his promise we are looking forward to a new heaven and a new earth, the home of righteousness. *2 Peter 3:9, 11-13*

---

A swallow having built its nest upon the tent of Charles V, the emperor generously commanded that the tent should not be taken down when the camp moved, but should remain until the young birds were ready to fly. Was there such gentleness in the heart of a soldier toward a poor bird that was not of his making, and shall the Lord deal harshly with his creatures when they venture to put their trust in him? Be assured that he has a great love to those trembling souls that fly for shelter to his royal courts. He that builds his nest on a divine promise shall find that it abides and remains until he shall fly away to the land where promises are lost in fulfillments.

# Confident Good Works

Cast your bread upon the waters, for after many days you will find it again. . . . Whoever watches the wind will not plant; whoever looks at the clouds will not reap. As you do not know the path of the wind, or how the body is formed in a mother's womb, so you cannot understand the work of God, the Maker of all things. Sow your seed in the morning, and at evening let not your hands be idle, for you do not know which will succeed, whether this or that, or whether both will do equally well. *Ecclesiastes 11:1, 4-6*

---

The spider casts her film out to the wind, feeling sure that somewhere or other it will adhere and form the beginning of her web. She commits the slender filament to the breeze believing that there is a place provided for it to fix itself. In this fashion we should believingly cast forth our endeavors in this life, confident that God will find a place for us. He who bids us pray and work will aid our efforts and guide us in his providence in a right way. Do not sit still in despair, but keep casting out the floating thread of hopeful endeavor, and the wind of love will bear it to its resting place.

# The Wickedness of Unbelief

The god of this age has blinded the minds of unbelievers, so that they cannot see the light of the gospel of the glory of Christ, who is the image of God. For we do not preach ourselves, but Jesus Christ as Lord, and ourselves as your servants for Jesus' sake. For God, who said, "Let light shine out of darkness," made his light shine in our hearts to give us the light of the knowledge of the glory of God in the face of Christ. *2 Corinthians 4:4-6*

---

The late Dr. Heugh, of Glasgow, a short time before he breathed his last, said, "There is nothing I feel more than the criminality of not trusting Christ without doubt—without doubt. Oh, to think what Christ is, what he did, and whom he did it for, and then not to believe him, not to trust him! There is no wickedness like the wickedness of unbelief!"

# An Active, Passionate Faith

Faith by itself, if it is not accompanied by action, is dead. . . . Show me your faith without deeds, and I will show you my faith by what I do. *James 2:17-18*

Do you not know that in a race all the runners run, but only one gets the prize? Run in such a way as to get the prize. *1 Corinthians 9:24*

---

The upper galleries at Versailles are filled with portraits, many of them extremely valuable and ancient. These are the likenesses of the greatest people of all lands and ages, drawn by the ablest artists. Yet more visitors wander through the rooms with little or no interest. In fact, after noticing one or two of the more prominent pictures, they hasten through the suite of chambers and descend to the other floors. Notice the change when the sightseers come to fine paintings like those of Horace Vernet, where the men and women are not inactive portraits but are actively engaged. There the warrior who was passed by without notice upstairs is seen hewing his way to glory over heaps of slain, or the statesman is observed delivering weighty words before an assembly of princes and peers. Not the people but their *actions* engross attention. Portraits have no charm when scenes of stirring interest are set in rivalry with them. After all, then, let us be who or what we may, we must push ourselves or be mere nobodies, chips in the porridge, forgotten shells on the beach. If we would impress we must act. The dignity of standing still will never win the prize; we must run for it. Our influence over our times will arise mainly from our doing and suffering the will of God, not from our office or person. Life, life in earnest, life for God—this will tell on the age. But mere orderliness and propriety, inactive and passionless, will be utterly inoperative.

# A God Who Can Shake the World

But I trust in you, O LORD; I say, "You are my God." My times are in your hands. *Psalm 31:14-15*

For you have been my hope, O Sovereign LORD, my confidence since my youth. From birth I have relied on you; you brought me forth from my mother's womb. I will ever praise you. I have become like a portent to many, but you are my strong refuge. My mouth is filled with your praise, declaring your splendor all day long. *Psalm 71:5-8*

---

During an earthquake, the inhabitants of a small village were very much alarmed, but they were at the same time surprised at the calmness and apparent joy of an old lady whom they all knew. At length one of them, addressing the old lady, said, "Ma'am, are you not afraid?"

"No," said the woman, "I rejoice to know that *I have a God who can shake the world.*"

# Climbing the Mountain of Assurance

Let us draw near to God with a sincere heart in full assurance of faith. *Hebrews 10:22*

But those who hope in the LORD will renew their strength. They will soar on wings like eagles; they will run and not grow weary, they will walk and not faint. *Isaiah 40:31*

---

Believe me, the life of grace is no dead level; it is not a marsh country, a vast flat. There are mountains, and there are valleys. There are tribes of Christians who live in the lowlands, like the poor Swiss of Valais, who live between the lofty ranges of mountains in the midst of the miasma, where the air is stagnant and fever has its lair and the human frame grows languid and enfeebled. Such dwellers in the lowlands of unbelief are forever doubting, fearing, troubled about their interest in Christ, and tossed to and fro; but there are other believers, who, by God's grace, have climbed the mountain of full assurance and near communion. Their place is with the eagle in his eyrie, high aloft; they are like the strong mountaineer who has trodden the virgin snow, who has breathed the fresh, free air of the Alpine regions, and therefore his sinews are braced, and his limbs are vigorous. These are they who do great exploits, being mighty men, men of renown.

# The Pilgrim Path

# Homesick for Heaven's Glories

I consider that our present sufferings are not worth comparing with the glory that will be revealed in us. The creation waits in eager expectation for the sons of God to be revealed. For the creation was subjected to frustration, not by its own choice, but by the will of the one who subjected it, in hope that the creation itself will be liberated from its bondage to decay and brought into the glorious freedom of the children of God. We know that the whole creation has been groaning as in the pains of childbirth right up to the present time. Not only so, but we ourselves, who have the firstfruits of the Spirit, groan inwardly as we wait eagerly for our adoption as sons, the redemption of our bodies. For in this hope we were saved. *Romans 8:18-24*

---

Have you ever seen a caged bird with its breast or wing bleeding from blows received by dashing against the wire of its cage? The poor creature dreamed of the forest and of the craggy rock, and, filled with aspirations for most sublime flight, it stretched its wings and flew upward, only to bring itself into sharp contact with its prison. Even thus the new-born nature, stirred in its inmost depths with longings suitable to its celestial origin, aspires after the joys of heaven, stretching all its wings to war toward perfection. But we who are in this body do groan; we find the flesh to be a prison, and so the more we long the more we pine. And pining, we sigh and cry, and wound our hearts with insatiable desires and bleeding discontents. The pangs of strong desire for the presence of the Lord in glory—who among believers has not felt them? Who among us has not found our flight upward brought to a painful pause by the stern facts of flesh and blood, and earth and sin?

# A Hard and Narrow Way

"Enter through the narrow gate. For wide is the gate and broad is the road that leads to destruction, and many enter through it. But small is the gate and narrow the road that leads to life, and only a few find it." *Matthew 7:13-14*

But join with me in suffering for the gospel, by the power of God, who has saved us and called us to a holy life—not because of anything we have done but because of his own purpose and grace. This grace was given us in Christ Jesus before the beginning of time, but it has now been revealed through the appearing of our Savior, Christ Jesus, who has destroyed death and has brought life and immortality to light through the gospel. And of this gospel I was appointed a herald and an apostle and a teacher. That is why I am suffering as I am. Yet I am not ashamed, because I know whom I have believed, and am convinced that he is able to guard what I have entrusted to him for that day. *2 Timothy 1:8-12*

---

Chrysostom says, the way is good if it is the way to a feast, even though it goes through a dark and miry lane. If it goes to an execution it is not good, even though it goes through the fairest street of the city. *Non qua sed quo.* Not the way but the end is to be mainly considered.

# Level Ground

Teach me to do your will, for you are my God; may your good Spirit lead me on level ground. *Psalm 143:10*

Now to him who is able to do immeasurably more than all we ask or imagine, according to his power that is at work within us, to him be glory in the church and in Christ Jesus throughout all generations, for ever and ever! Amen. *Ephesians 3:20-21*

---

An old authority assures us that "the Jews fancy, concerning the cloud that conducted Israel through the wilderness, that it did not only show them the way, but also leveled it; that it did not only lead them in the way which they must go, but also fit the way for them to go upon it; that it cleared all the mountains and smoothed all the rocks; that it cleared all the bushes and removed all the pitfalls."

What is probably a mere legend as to the type is abundantly true of the providence of God, which it so accurately represents. Our gracious God not only leads us in the way of mercy, but he prepares our path before us, providing for all our wants even before they occur.

# Moving Ahead

We ought always to thank God for you, brothers, and rightly so, because your faith is growing more and more, and the love every one of you has for each other is increasing. Therefore, among God's churches we boast about your perseverance and faith in all the persecutions and trials you are enduring. *2 Thessalonians 1:3-4*

---

Sailors would be loath to sail without using their log to test their pace and show their progress. The wonder is that so many professing Christians navigate the sea of life, and are utterly careless whether they are making headway or drifting from their course. Should we not all cast overboard our log? There are various ways by which with readiness we may measure our progress: our prayers, our labors, our patience, our faith, our communion with God, our humility, may all serve as logs by which to measure our sailing pace.

# He Keeps His Promises

His divine power has given us everything we need for life and godliness through our knowledge of him who called us by his own glory and goodness. Through these he has given us his very great and precious promises, so that through them you may participate in the divine nature and escape the corruption in the world caused by evil desires. . . . But do not forget this one thing, dear friends: With the Lord a day is like a thousand years, and a thousand years are like a day. The Lord is not slow in keeping his promise, as some understand slowness. He is patient with you, not wanting anyone to perish, but everyone to come to repentance. *2 Peter 1:3-4; 3:8-9*

---

Good old Spurstow says that some of the promises are like the almond tree—they blossom hastily in the very earliest spring. But, he says, there are others which resemble the mulberry tree—they are very slow in putting forth their leaves. Then what is a man to do, if he has a mulberry tree promise which is late in blossoming? Why, he is to wait till it does! If the vision tarry, wait for it to come, and the appointed time shall surely bring it.

# The Invisible Temptation

"Why are you sleeping?" he asked them. "Get up and pray so that you will not fall into temptation." *Luke 22:46*

---

Many horses fall at the bottom of a hill because the driver thinks the danger past and the need to hold the reins with firm grip less pressing. So it is often with us when we are not specially tempted to overt sin, we are the more in danger through slothful ease. I think it was Ralph Erskine who said, "There is no devil so bad as no devil." The worst temptation that ever overtakes us is, in some respects, preferable to our becoming carnally secure and neglecting to watch and pray.

*More the treacherous calm I dread*
*Than tempests rolling overhead.*

# Beware of the Smooth and Easy Path

So, if you think you are standing firm, be careful that you don't fall!
*1 Corinthians 10:12*

---

After crossing the Grimsel, on the way down toward Handeck, the traveler traverses a road cut in red marble so smoothly polished that, even when it is divested of its usual thin coating of snow it is dangerous in the extreme. Even though steps are hewn and rough marks made across the granite, he would be foolhardy who should try to ride along the slippery way, which is called Helle Parte (Hell Place) for reasons which glisten on the surface. "Dismount," a sign orders, and none are slow to obey it. There are many such Hell Places on the road to the celestial city—smooth places of pleasure, ease, flattery, self-content, and the like. It will be the wisest course, if any pilgrim has been fond of riding the high horse, for him to dismount at once and walk humbly with his God. That enchanted ground of which Bunyan tells us that the air naturally tended to make one drowsy, is just the spot to which we refer. Men whose path lies through that deceitful country need to be watchful.

# Enthusiastic Soldiers of the Cross

Never be lacking in zeal, but keep your spiritual fervor, serving the Lord. *Romans 12:11*

If God is for us, who can be against us? *Romans 8:31*

---

When the Spartans marched into battle they advanced with cheerful songs, willing to fight. But when the Persians entered the conflict, you could hear, as the regiments came on, the crack of the whips by which the officers drove the cowards to the fray. You need not wonder that a few Spartans were more than a match for thousands of Persians, that in fact they were like lions in the midst of sheep. So let it be with the church. Never should she need to be forced to reluctant action, but full of irrepressible life, she should long for conflict against everything which is contrary to God. If we were enthusiastic soldiers of the cross we would be like lions in the midst of herds of enemies, and through God's help nothing would be able to stand against us.

# Understanding the Deep Things of God

The Spirit searches all things, even the deep things of God. For who among men knows the thoughts of a man except the man's spirit within him? In the same way no one knows the thoughts of God except the Spirit of God. We have not received the spirit of the world but the Spirit who is from God, that we may understand what God has freely given us. *1 Corinthians 2:10-12*

We have not stopped praying for you and asking God to fill you with the knowledge of his will through all spiritual wisdom and understanding. *Colossians 1:9*

---

When a traveler is newly arrived in the Alps, he is constantly deceived in his reckoning. One man declared that he could climb the Righi in half an hour, but after several panting hours the summit was still ahead of him. Yet when he made the boast, some of us who stood by were much of his mind—the ascent did seem easy. This partly accounts for the mistakes people make in estimating eternal things: they have been too much used to molehills to be at home with mountains. Only familiarity with the sublimities of revelation can educate us to a comprehension of their heights and depths.

# The Path of the Pilgrim

You have made known to me the path of life; you will fill me with joy in your presence, with eternal pleasures at your right hand. *Psalm 16:11*

The path of the upright is a highway. . . . A man of understanding keeps a straight course. . . . The path of life leads upward for the wise. *Proverbs 15:19, 21, 24*

---

I heard a gentleman assert that he could walk almost any number of miles when the scenery was good, but, he added, "When it is flat and uninteresting, how one tires!" What scenery enchants the Christian pilgrim? The towering mountains of predestination, the great sea of providence, the rocks of sure promise, the green fields of revelation, the river that makes glad the city of God—all these compose the scenery that surrounds the Christian, and at every step fresh sublimities meet his view.

# The World Is Not a Firm Foundation

For no one can lay any foundation other than the one already laid, which is Jesus Christ. If any man builds on this foundation using gold, silver, costly stones, wood, hay or straw, his work will be shown for what it is, because the Day will bring it to light. It will be revealed with fire, and the fire will test the quality of each man's work. If what he has built survives, he will receive his reward. If it is burned up, he will suffer loss. *1 Corinthians 3:11-15*

---

In Chili where the ground is subject to frequent earthquakes, the houses are built of lowly height and of unenduring structure. It is of little use to dig deep foundations, and pile up high walls where the very earth is unstable. It would be foolish to build as for ages when the whole edifice may be in ruins in a week. Here we see a lesson for our worldly schemes and possessions. This poor fleeting world is not worth building our hopes and joys on it as though they could last long. We must treat it as a treacherous soil, and build but lightly on it, and we shall be wise.

# Be Careful with Unbelieving Friends

A righteous man is cautious in friendship, but the way of the wicked leads them astray. *Proverbs 12:26*

---

When cast by providence among sinful people who respect us, we ought to be particularly watchful. The hatred of the ungodly when poured on Christians in the form of persecution is seldom harmful to their spiritual nature, but the friendship of the world is always to be suspected. When the servants of the high priest allowed Peter to warm his hands at the fire, had Peter been a wise man, he would have been afraid that evil would come of it. We are disarmed by kindness, but it is never safe to be disarmed in an enemy's country. "Who," says the old proverb, "could live in Rome and yet be at war with the pope?" Who can have much to do with sinners and not have something to do with their sins? The smiling daughters of Moab did more mischief to Israel than all Balak's frowning warriors. All Philistia could not have blinded Samson if Delilah's charms had not deluded him. Our worst foes will be found among our ungodly friends. Those who are false to God are not likely to be true to us. Walk carefully, believer, if your way lies by the sinner's door, and especially if that sinner has acted a friendly part to you.

# Look Out for Meaningless Distractions

Let your eyes look straight ahead, fix your gaze directly before you. Make level paths for your feet and take only ways that are firm. Do not swerve to the right or the left; keep your foot from evil. *Proverbs 4:25-27*

---

Aesop's fable says, "A pigeon oppressed by excessive thirst saw a goblet of water painted on a signboard. Not realizing that it was only a picture, she flew toward it with a loud whirr and unwittingly dashed against the signboard, and jarred herself terribly. Having broken her wings by the blow, she fell to the ground and was killed by one of the bystanders."

The mockeries of the world are many, and those who are deluded by them not only miss the joys they looked for, but in their eager pursuit of vanity bring ruin on their souls. We call the dove silly to be deceived by a picture, however cleverly painted, but what epithet shall we apply to those who are duped by the transparently false allurements of the world!

# The World Is a Bog

Do not love the world or anything in the world. If anyone loves the world, the love of the Father is not in him. For everything in the world—the cravings of sinful man, the lust of his eyes and the boasting of what he has and does—comes not from the Father but from the world. The world and its desires pass away, but the man who does the will of God lives forever. *1 John 2:15-17*

---

Queen Elizabeth once said to a courtier, "They pass best over the world those who trip over it quickly; for it is but a bog: if we stop, we sink."

# Laying Aside Our Loads

Therefore, since we are surrounded by such a great cloud of witnesses, let us throw off everything that hinders and the sin that so easily entangles, and let us run with perseverance the race marked out for us. Let us fix our eyes on Jesus, the author and perfecter of our faith, who for the joy set before him endured the cross, scorning its shame, and sat down at the right hand of the throne of God. *Hebrews 12:1-2*

---

Crossing the Col D'Obbia, the mule laden with our luggage sank in the snow, nor could it be recovered until its load was removed. Then, but not till then, it scrambled out of the hole it had made and pursued its journey. It reminded us of mariners casting out the lading into the sea to save the vessel, and we were led to meditate upon the dangers of Christians heavily laden with earthly possessions, and the wise way in which the gracious Father unloads them by their losses that they may be enabled to pursue their journey to heaven and no longer sink in the snow of carnal-mindedness.

# Nothing Is Impossible

"What is impossible with men is possible with God." *Luke 18:27*

" 'Not by might nor by power, but by my Spirit,' says the LORD Almighty." *Zechariah 4:6*

This is the victory that has overcome the world, even our faith. *1 John 5:4*

---

Look at that bare perpendicular mountainside—why, it is worse than perpendicular; it overhangs the lake. Yet the bold Tyrolese have developed a road right along the bald face of the rock by blasting out a gallery, or, as it looks from below, by chiseling out a groove. One would have readily written down that feat as impossible, and yet the road is made and we have traveled it from Riva into the Tyrol, the Lago Garda lying far below our feet. Henceforth that road shall be to us a cheering memory when our task is more than usually difficult. If anything ought to be done it shall be done. With God in front, we shall soon leave difficulties in the rear, transformed into memorials of victory.

# The Blindness of the Unbelieving

By setting forth the truth plainly we commend ourselves to every man's conscience in the sight of God. And even if our gospel is veiled, it is veiled to those who are perishing. The god of this age has blinded the minds of unbelievers, so that they cannot see the light of the gospel of the glory of Christ, who is the image of God. For we do not preach ourselves, but Jesus Christ as Lord, and ourselves as your servants for Jesus' sake. For God, who said, "Let light shine out of darkness," made his light shine in our hearts to give us the light of the knowledge of the glory of God in the face of Christ. *2 Corinthians 4:2-6*

---

"Do not fear the frown of the world. When a blind man comes against you in the street you are not angry at him. You understand, 'He is blind, or he would not have hurt me.' Say the same of the people of this world when they speak evil of Christians—they are blind."—*McCheyne*

# Peace Like a River

And the peace of God, which transcends all understanding, will guard your hearts and your minds in Christ Jesus. *Philippians 4:7*

---

The believer's peace is like a river for *continuance*. Look at it, rising as a little brook among the mosses of the lone green hill. By and by it leaps as a rugged cataract; then it flows along that fair valley where the red deer wanders and the child loves to play. With hum of pleasant music the brook turns the village mill. Listen to its changing tune as it ripples over its pebbly bed or leaps down the wheel, or sports in eddies where the trees bend down their branches to kiss the current. Soon the small stream has become a river, and bears upon its flood full many a craft. Then its bosom swells, bridges with noble arches span it, and, grown vaster still, it becomes an estuary, broad enough to be an arm of old Father Ocean, pouring its water-floods into the mighty main. The river endures the lapse of ages; it is no evanescent morning cloud or transient rain flood, but in all its stages it is permanent.

*Men may come, and men may go,*
*But I flow on forever.*

Forevermore, throughout all generations, the river speeds to its destined place. Such is the peace of the Christian. He always has reason for comfort. He has not a consolation like a swollen torrent that is dried up under the hot sun of adversity, but peace is his rightful possession at all times. You shall discover the noble river when it mirrors the stars or sends back the sheen of the moon. You may see its waves in the hour of tempest by the lightning's flash, as well as in the day of calm when the sun shines brightly on them. The river is always in its place. And in the same way, come night, come day, come sickness, come health, come what will, the peace of God that passes all understanding will keep the Christian's heart and mind through Jesus Christ.

---

# Seeing through the Fog

So do not throw away your confidence; it will be richly rewarded. You need to persevere so that when you have done the will of God, you will receive what he has promised. For in just a very little while, "He who is coming will come and will not delay. But my righteous one will live by faith. And if he shrinks back, I will not be pleased with him." But we are not of those who shrink back and are destroyed, but of those who believe and are saved. Now faith is being sure of what we hope for and certain of what we do not see. *Hebrews 10:35-39, 11:1*

---

I once was surrounded by a dense mist, and I felt transported into a world of mystery where everything was swollen to a size and appearance more vast, more terrible, than is usual on this sober planet. A little mountain lake, scarcely larger than a farmer's horse pond, expanded into a great lake whose distant shores were leagues beyond the reach of my poor eyes. And as I descended into a valley, the rocks on one side like the battlements of heaven, and the descent on the other hand, looked like the dreadful lips of a yawning abyss. And yet when one looked back again in the morning's clear light there was nothing very dangerous in that pathway or terrible in those rocks. The road was a safe though sharp descent, devoid of terrors to ordinary mountain climbers. In the distance through the fog the shepherd "stalks gigantic" and his sheep are full-grown lions.

We often fall into such blunders in our life-pilgrimage. A little trouble in the distance is, through our mistiness, magnified into a crushing adversity. We see a lion in the way, although it is written that no ravenous beast shall go up there. A puny foe is swollen into a Goliath, and the river of death widens into a shoreless sea.

Come, heavenly wind, and blow the mist away, and then the foe will be despised, and the bright shores on the other side of the river will stand out clear in the light of faith!

# Keeping Your Heart in Line

Keep me safe, O God, for in you I take refuge. I said to the LORD, "You are my LORD; apart from you I have no good thing." . . . LORD, you have assigned me my portion and my cup; you have made my lot secure. The boundary lines have fallen for me in pleasant places; surely I have a delightful inheritance. I will praise the LORD, who counsels me; even at night my heart instructs me. I have set the LORD always before me. Because he is at my right hand, I will not be shaken. Therefore my heart is glad and my tongue rejoices; my body also will rest secure. *Psalm 16:1-2, 5-9*

---

The compass on board an iron vessel is very subject to aberrations. Yet, for all that, its evident desire is to be true to the pole. True hearts in this world and in this fleshly body are all too apt to swerve, but they still show their inward and persistent tendency to point toward heaven and God. On board iron vessels it is a common thing to see a compass placed aloft, to be as much away from the cause of aberration as possible: a wise hint to us to elevate our affections and desires. The nearer to God, the less swayed by worldly influences.

# Looking for the Blessed Hope

You ought to live holy and godly lives as you look forward to the day of God and speed its coming. That day will bring about the destruction of the heavens by fire, and the elements will melt in the heat. But in keeping with his promise we are looking forward to a new heaven and a new earth, the home of righteousness. *2 Peter 3:11-13*

---

"I was told of a poor peasant in the mountains who, month after month, year after year, through a long period of declining life, opened his casement every morning, as soon as he awoke, and looked toward the east to see if Jesus Christ were coming. He had not calculated the date of Christ's coming, or he would not have needed to look at all. He was ready for Christ's coming, or he would not have been in such a hurry to seek him. He was willing for Christ's coming, or he would rather have looked another way. He loved, or Christ would not have been the first thought of the morning. His Master did not come, but eventually a messenger did, to fetch the ready one home. The same preparation sufficed for both; his longing soul was satisfied with either.

Often the child of God awakes in the morning, weary and encumbered with troubled thoughts, and his Father's secret presence comes to mind. He looks up (if not out) to feel (if not to see) the glories of that last morning when the trumpet shall sound and the dead shall arise indestructible—no weary limbs to bear the spirit down; no feverish dreams to haunt the vision; no dark forecasting of the day's events, no returning memory of the griefs of yesterday."—*Fry*

# Climbing Above

Since, then, you have been raised with Christ, set your hearts on things above, where Christ is seated at the right hand of God. Set your minds on things above, not on earthly things. *Colossians 3:1-2*

On your way to Italy, no sooner do you pass the brow of the St. Gothard pass than you are on the sunny side of the Alps. The snow lying there is nothing in comparison to the vast accumulation upon the Swiss side of the summit where the wind ceases to be sharp and cutting, and a very few minutes' ride brings you into a balmy air which makes you forget that you are so greatly elevated above the sea level. There is a very manifest difference between the southern side and the bleak northern aspect.

He who climbs above the cares of the world and turns his face to his God has found the sunny side of life. The world's side of the hill is chilly and freezing to a spiritual mind, but the Lord's presence gives a warmth of joy which turns winter into summer. Some pilgrims to heaven appear never to have passed the summit of religious difficulty. They are still toiling over the Devil's Bridge, or loitering at Andermatt, or plunging into the deep snowdrifts of their own personal unworthiness, ever learning, but never coming to a full knowledge of the truth. They have not attained to a comfortable perception of the glory, preciousness, and all-sufficiency of the Lord Jesus, and therefore they abide amid the winter of their doubts and fears. If they had but faith to surmount their spiritual impediments, how changed would everything become! It is fair traveling with a sunny land smiling before your eyes, especially when you retain a grateful remembrance of the bleak and wintry road which you have traversed. But it is sorry work to be always stopping on the Swiss side of the mountain.

# God's Holy Word

# Illuminated by the Light of the Word

The word of God is living and active. Sharper than any double-edged sword, it penetrates even to dividing soul and spirit, joints and marrow; it judges the thoughts and attitudes of the heart. Nothing in all creation is hidden from God's sight. Everything is uncovered and laid bare before the eyes of him to whom we must give account. *Hebrews 4:12-13*

---

When a lazy housemaid was scolded for the untidiness of the rooms, she exclaimed, "I'm sure the rooms would be clean enough if it were not for the nasty sun which is always showing the dirty corners." In the same way men revile the gospel because it reveals their own sin. Thus all agitations for reforms in Church and State are opposed, and all manner of mischief attributed to them as if they created the evils which they bring to light. The lover of the right courts anything which may manifest the wrong, but those who love evil never have a good word for those disturbing beams of truth which show up the filthy corners of their hearts and lives.

# Nutrition for a Hungry Reader

The law of the LORD is perfect, reviving the soul. The statutes of the LORD are trustworthy, making wise the simple. The precepts of the LORD are right, giving joy to the heart. The commands of the LORD are radiant, giving light to the eyes. The fear of the LORD is pure, enduring forever. The ordinances of the LORD are sure and altogether righteous. They are more precious than gold, than much pure gold; they are sweeter than honey, than honey from the comb. By them is your servant warned; in keeping them there is great reward. *Psalm 19:7-11*

---

An old man once said, "For a long period I puzzled myself about the difficulties of Scripture, until at last I came to the resolution that reading the Bible was like eating fish. When I find a difficulty I lay it aside and call it a bone. Why should I choke on the bone when there is so much nutritious meat for me? Some day, perhaps, I may find that even the bone may afford me nourishment."

# Butterflies or Bees?

*All Scripture is God-breathed and is useful for teaching, rebuking, correcting and training in righteousness, so that the man of God may be thoroughly equipped for every good work. 2 Timothy 3:16-17*

---

"To some the Bible is uninteresting and unprofitable because they read too fast. Among the insects which subsist on the sweet sap of flowers, there are two very different classes. One is remarkable for its imposing plumage; and as you watch its jaunty gyrations over the fields, and its dance from flower to flower, you cannot help admiring its graceful activity. But in the same field there is another worker, whose brown vest and businesslike straight-forward flight may not have arrested your eye. His fluttering neighbor darts down here and there, and sips elegantly wherever he can find a drop of ready nectar; but this dingy plodder makes a point of alighting everywhere, and wherever he alights he either finds honey or makes it. He explores all about till he discovers it, and then having ascertained the knack of it, joyful as one who has found great spoil, he sings his way down into its luscious recesses. His rival, of the painted velvet wing, has no patience for such dull and long-winded details. But the one died last October along with the flowers, while the other is warm in his hive tonight, amid the fragrant stores which he gathered beneath the bright beams of summer.

"To which do you belong—the butterflies or the bees? Do you search the Scriptures, or do you only skim them? Do you dwell on a passage till you bring out some meaning, or till you can carry away some memorable truth or immediate lesson? Or do you flit along on heedless wing, only on the lookout for novelty? Does the Word of God dwell in you richly, that in the vigils of a restless night, or in the bookless solitude of a sick room, or in the winter of old age or exclusion from ordinances, its treasured truths would perpetuate summer round you and give you meat to eat which the world knows not of?"—*James Hamilton, D.D.*

---

# The Ultimate Authority

We do not use deception, nor do we distort the word of God. On the contrary, by setting forth the truth plainly we commend ourselves to every man's conscience in the sight of God. *2 Corinthians 4:2*

---

"The mother of a family was married to an unbeliever who made fun of religion in the presence of his own children; yet she succeeded in bringing them all up in the fear of the LORD. I asked her one day how she preserved them from the influence of a father whose sentiments were so opposed to her own. This was her answer: 'Because to the authority of a *father* I do not oppose the authority of a *mother*, but that of God. From their earliest years my children have always seen the Bible on my table, and the holy book constituted their entire religious instruction. I was silent that I might allow it to speak. If they asked a question, evidenced a fault, or performed a good action, I opened the Bible, and the Bible answered, reproved, or encouraged them. The constant reading of the Scriptures has accomplished that which surprises you.' "—*Adolph Monod*

# "I Love the Bible"

Your word, O LORD, is eternal; it stands firm in the heavens. Your faithfulness continues through all generations; you established the earth, and it endures. Your laws endure to this day, for all things serve you. If your law had not been my delight, I would have perished in my affliction. I will never forget your precepts, for by them you have renewed my life. . . . Oh, how I love your law! I meditate on it all day long. *Psalm 119:89-93, 97*

---

When Mr. Hone, who wrote the "Every-day Book" and was of skeptical views, was traveling through Wales, he stopped at a cottage to ask for a drink of water, and a little girl answered him, "Oh, yes! Sir, I have no doubt mother will give you some milk. Come in." He went in and sat down. The little girl was reading her Bible.

Mr. Hone said, "Well, my little girl, are you doing your duty?"

"No, sir, I am not," she replied, "I am reading the Bible."

"Yes," said he, "and are you satisfying your duty in doing so?"

"Oh, no," she replied, "it is no duty to read the Bible; I love the Bible."

"And why do you love the Bible?" said he.

Her simple, childlike answer was, "I thought everybody loved the Bible." Her own love to the precious volume had made her innocently believe that everybody else was equally delighted to read God's Word. Mr. Hone was so touched with the sincerity of that expression that he read the Bible himself and, instead of being an opponent to the things of God, came to be a friend of divine truth.

# The Lifeboat

I am not ashamed of the gospel, because it is the power of God for the salvation of everyone who believes: first for the Jew, then for the Gentile. For in the gospel a righteousness from God is revealed, a righteousness that is by faith from first to last, just as it is written: "The righteous will live by faith." *Romans 1:16-17*

---

"The lifeboat may have a tasteful shape and beautiful decoration, but these are not the qualities for which I prize it: it was my salvation from the howling sea! So the interest which a regenerate soul takes in the Bible is founded on a personal application to the heart of the saving truth which it contains. If there is no taste for this truth, there can be no relish for the Scriptures."—*J.W. Alexander, D.D.*

# Zigzagging

I have chosen the way of truth; I have set my heart on your laws.... I run in the path of your commands, for you have set my heart free. Teach me, O LORD, to follow your decrees; then I will keep them to the end. Give me understanding, and I will keep your law and obey it with all my heart. Direct me in the path of your commands, for there I find delight. *Psalm 119:30, 32-35*

---

First to the right, then to the left, the road was ever ascending but always twisting, and thus, by easy marches, we were able to reach the summit of the pass. A straight line would have been shorter for the eagle's wing, but no human foot could have followed it. Nobody called us inconsistent for reaching our destination in this way; we kept to the road, and no one could complain.

If we honestly desire to gain the heights of divine truth, we shall find many zigzags in the road. Here we shall face divine sovereignty with all its lofty grandeur, and soon we shall turn in the opposite direction, toward the frowning peaks of human responsibility. What does it matter if we appear to be inconsistent, so long as we keep to the highway of Scripture, which is our only safe road to knowledge! Angels may, perhaps, be systematic divines. For men it should be enough to follow the word of God, let its teachings wind as they may.

# When Reason Is Lost in Wonder

As you do not know the path of the wind, or how the body is formed in a mother's womb, so you cannot understand the work of God, the Maker of all things. *Ecclesiastes 11:5*

My heart is not proud, O LORD, my eyes are not haughty; I do not concern myself with great matters or things too wonderful for me. But I have stilled and quieted my soul; like a weaned child with its mother, like a weaned child is my soul within me. *Psalm 131:1-2*

---

The great boulders which lie along the valley of Storo in the Tyrol are of a granite unknown in that region; they must have come from a great distance. Now it might be hard to explain the method by which they arrived in the valley, but it would be absurd to deny that they are there. Most unaccountable is the fact, but a very strong and stubborn fact it is, for there they lie, huge as houses and yet perfectly alien to the country. There are truths in Scripture which puzzle us; we cannot understand their relation to other portions of revelation. They are mysteries, apparently alien to the spirit of other passages. What then? Although we cannot account for them, that does not alter the fact that there they are, and it would be extreme folly to deny their existence because they puzzle us. Rather let us find room for adoring faith where reason is lost in wonder.

# Children of the King

For he has rescued us from the dominion of darkness and brought us into the kingdom of the Son he loves, in whom we have redemption, the forgiveness of sins. *Colossians 1:13-14*

The Spirit himself testifies with our spirit that we are God's children. Now if we are children, then we are heirs—heirs of God and co-heirs with Christ, if indeed we share in his sufferings in order that we may also share in his glory. *Romans 8:16-17*

---

One looks with interest on that ancient stone at Kingston-upon-Thames, on which so many Saxon kings were crowned, but far more reverent is the gaze we fix on those texts of Scripture whereby (through God's grace) many have been made kings unto our God. We rail them off in a special enclosure and place them where the highways meet, that others may look on them and find their coronations at the same spot.

# Preserving the Vitality of the Gospel

The word of God is living and active. *Hebrews 4:12*

That which was from the beginning, which we have heard, which we have seen with our eyes, which we have looked at and our hands have touched—this we proclaim concerning the Word of life. The life appeared; we have seen it and testify to it, and we proclaim to you the eternal life, which was with the Father and has appeared to us. *1 John 1:1-2*

---

Petrarch's works are said to have laid so long in the roof of St. Mark's, at Venice, that they became turned into stone, although by what process they do not say. To many men it seems as if the Word of God has become petrified, for they receive it as a hard, lifeless creed, a stone on which to sharpen the daggers of controversy, a stumbling block for young beginners, a millstone with which to break opponents' heads, after the manner experienced by Abimelech at Thebez. A man must have a stout digestion to feed on some men's theology—no sap, no sweetness, no life, but all stern accuracy and fleshless definition. Proclaimed without tenderness, and argued without affection, the gospel from such men rather resembles a missile from a catapult than bread from a Father's table. Teeth are needlessly broken over the grit of systematic theology, while souls are famishing. To turn stones into bread was a temptation of our Master, but how many of his servants yield readily to the far worse temptation to turn bread into stone! They should go away, off to a stone-yard to break granite, so as not to stand in the way of loving spirits who would feed the family of God with living bread. The inspired Word is to us spirit and life, and we cannot afford to have it hardened into a huge monolith or a spiritual Stonehenge—sublime, but cold; majestic, but lifeless. It would be better to have it as our own household book, a bosom companion, the poor man's counselor and friend.

---

# Apply Your Heart to Understanding

If you accept my words and store up my commands within you, turning your ear to wisdom and applying your heart to understanding, and if you call out for insight and cry aloud for understanding, and if you look for it as for silver and search for it as for hidden treasure, then you will understand the fear of the LORD and find the knowledge of God. For the LORD gives wisdom, and from his mouth come knowledge and understanding. *Proverbs 2:1-6*

---

"How is it, my dear," inquired a school teacher of a little girl, "that you do not understand this simple thing?"

"I don't know," she answered, with a perplexed look, "but I sometimes think I have so many things to learn that I do not have enough time to understand."

There may be much hearing, much reading, much attendance at public services, and very small result, and all because the word was not the subject of thought, and was never embraced by the understanding. What is not understood is like meat undigested, more likely to be injurious than nourishing.

# Truth Shall Reign Forever

For you have been born again, not of perishable seed, but of imperishable, through the living and enduring word of God. For, "All men are like grass, and all their glory is like the flowers of the field; the grass withers and the flowers fall, but the word of the LORD stands forever." *1 Peter 1:23-25*

---

How wonderfully has the Lord provided for the continuance of the vegetable world. He causes the plant to scatter broadcast a multitude of seeds, and bids the winds convey them far and wide. The fowls of the air are commissioned to bear berries and fruits to their proper soils, and even to bury them in the earth, while scores of four-footed creatures, engaged in storing up food for themselves, become planters of trees and propagators of plants. Seeds bear a charmed life about them; they will germinate after being buried for centuries. They have been known to flourish when turned up from the borings of wells from the depth of hundreds of feet, and when ponds and lakes have been dried, the undrowned vegetable life has surprised the beholders by blossoming with unknown flowers. Can we imagine that God has been thus careful of the life of the mere grass of the field, which is the very emblem of decay, and yet is negligent of his Word that lives and abides forever? It is not to be dreamed of. Truth, the incorruptible seed, is ever scattering itself. Every wind is laden with it, every breath spreads it. It lies dormant in a thousand memories, it preserves its life in the abodes of death. The Lord has but to give the word, and a band of eloquent men shall publish the gospel, apostles and evangelists will rise in abundance, like the warriors who sprang from the fabled dragon's teeth. Converts will spring up like flowerets at the approach of spring; nations will be born in a day, and truth, and God the Lord of truth, shall reign forever.

# Excavating the Treasures of Scripture

The law of the LORD is perfect, reviving the soul. The statutes of the LORD are trustworthy, making wise the simple. The precepts of the LORD are right, giving joy to the heart. The commands of the LORD are radiant, giving light to the eyes. The fear of the LORD is pure, enduring forever. The ordinances of the LORD are sure and altogether righteous. They are more precious than gold, than much pure gold; they are sweeter than honey, than honey from the comb. By them is your servant warned; in keeping them there is great reward. *Psalm 19:7-11*

---

There is gold in the rocks that fringe the Pass of the Splugen, gold even in the stones that mend the roads, but there is too little of it to be worth extracting. Alas, how like too many books and sermons! Not so the Scriptures; they are much fine gold, and their very dust is precious.

# An Appetite for God's Word

As the deer pants for streams of water, so my soul pants for you, O God. My soul thirsts for God, for the living God. When can I go and meet with God? *Psalm 42:1-2*

I meditate on all your works and consider what your hands have done. I spread out my hands to you; my soul thirsts for you like a parched land. . . . Let the morning bring me word of your unfailing love, for I have put my trust in you. *Psalm 143:5-6, 8*

---

Lord Bacon tells of a bishop who used to bathe regularly twice every day. On being asked why he washed so often, he replied, "Because I cannot conveniently do it three times." If those who love the Scriptures were asked why they read the Bible so often, they might honestly reply, "Because we cannot find time to read it more often." The appetite for the Word grows on that which it feeds on. We would say with Thomas à Kempis, "I would be always in a nook with a book."

# Glorious Liberty

It is for freedom that Christ has set us free. Stand firm, then, and do not let yourselves be burdened again by a yoke of slavery. *Galatians 5:1*

The LORD is my shepherd, I shall lack nothing. He makes me lie down in green pastures, he leads me beside quiet waters, he restores my soul. He guides me in paths of righteousness for his name's sake. . . . Surely goodness and love will follow me all the days of my life, and I will dwell in the house of the LORD forever. *Psalm 23:1-3, 6*

---

In his *Practical Illustrations of Character*, the late William Jay said, "What a difference must a Christian and a minister feel between the shackles of some systems of divinity and the advantage of Scriptural freedom, the glorious liberty of the sons of God. The one is the horse standing in the street in harness, feeding indeed, but on the contents of a bag tossed up and down. The other, the same animal in a large, fine meadow, where he lies down in green pastures, and feeds beside the still waters."

# Optical Illusion

Many live as enemies of the cross of Christ. Their destiny is destruction, their god is their stomach, and their glory is their shame. Their mind is on earthly things. But our citizenship is in heaven. And we eagerly await a Savior from there, the Lord Jesus Christ, who, by the power that enables him to bring everything under his control, will transform our lowly bodies so that they will be like his glorious body. *Philippians 3:18-21*

---

From far off one can hardly tell a mountain from a cloud. The clouds rise with peaks and summits, all apparently as solid, and certainly as glistening, as the snow-clad Alps, so that the clearest eye might readily be deceived. Yet the mountain is unsubstantial as the cloud, and the cloud is never permanent as the mountain. So do the things of time appear to be all-important, far-reaching and enduring, and eternal things are not always of equal weight to the soul with those nearer at hand. Yet, despite all our instinctive judgments may suggest to the contrary, nothing earthly can ever be lasting, nothing in time can be worth considering compared with eternity. The cloudy philosophies of men may assume the shape of eternal truth, but the wind shall scatter them, while the great mountains of the divine word shall stand fast forever and ever.

# Preoccupied from the Lord's Work

He saved us through the washing of rebirth and renewal by the Holy Spirit, whom he poured out on us generously through Jesus Christ our Savior, so that, having been justified by his grace, we might become heirs having the hope of eternal life. . . . Stress these things, so that those who have trusted in God may be careful to devote themselves to doing what is good. These things are excellent and profitable for everyone. But avoid foolish controversies and genealogies and arguments and quarrels about the law, because these are unprofitable and useless. *Titus 3:5-7, 8-9*

---

There was among learned men such a rage for Aristotle that his ethics were frequently read to the people instead of the gospel, and the teachers themselves were employed either in wresting the words of Scripture to support the most monstrous opinions, or in discussing the most trivial questions. Think of men gravely debating whether the angel Gabriel appeared to the Virgin Mary in the shape of a serpent, of a dove, of a man, or of a woman? Did he seem to be young or old? In what dress was he? Was his linen clean or foul? Did he appear in the morning, noon, or evening? What was the color of the Virgin's hair? Etc. Think of all this nonsense veiled in learned terms and obscure phrases! While human minds were engaging in weaving such cobwebs as these, no progress was made in real knowledge, and the gloom of the dark ages deepened into tenfold night.

We are much in danger of the same evil from another quarter. The reign of obscure nonsense and dogmatic trifling may yet return. An ultra-spiritual sect has arisen whose theological language is a jargon, whose interpretations are mystical, whose prophetical hypotheses are ridiculous, and whose arrogance is superlative. To leave the consideration of well-known and soul-saving truths to fight over unimportant subtleties is to turn our corn fields into poppy gardens. True spirituality shuns the obscure and the *dilettanti,* and delights in the plain and practical.

# Accepting the Whole Seed

"I am the living bread that came down from heaven. If a man eats of this bread, he will live forever. This bread is my flesh, which I will give for the life of the world." *John 6:51*

---

There are two ways of treating the seed. The botanist splits it up and discourses on its curious characteristics. The simple farmer eats and sows, sows and eats. Similarly there are two ways of treating the gospel. A critic dissects it, raises a mountain of debate about the structure of the whole, and relation of its parts, and when he is done with his argument, he is done. To him the letter is dead. He neither lives on it himself, nor spreads it for the good of his neighbors; he neither eats nor sows. The disciple of Jesus, hungering for righteousness, takes the seed whole; it is bread for today's hunger, and seed for tomorrow's supply.

# The Power of Prayer

# The Power of Prayer, and the Lack of Power without Prayer

Be clear-minded and self-controlled so that you can pray. *1 Peter 4:7*

Is any one of you in trouble? He should pray. Is anyone happy? Let him sing songs of praise. Is any one of you sick? He should call the elders of the church to pray over him and anoint him with oil in the name of the Lord. And the prayer offered in faith will make the sick person well; the Lord will raise him up. If he has sinned, he will be forgiven. Therefore confess your sins to each other and pray for each other so that you may be healed. The prayer of a righteous man is powerful and effective. Elijah was a man just like us. He prayed earnestly that it would not rain, and it did not rain on the land for three and a half years. Again he prayed, and the heavens gave rain, and the earth produced its crops. *James 5:13-18*

---

In Payson's diary is the following entry: "Sept. 23—Was quite dull and lifeless in prayer, and in consequence had no success in study."

# God Hears Prayer—You Can Believe It!

This is the assurance we have in approaching God: that if we ask anything according to his will, he hears us. And if we know that he hears us—whatever we ask—we know that we have what we asked of him. *1 John 5:14-15*

---

Is it not a sad thing that we should think it wonderful for God to hear prayer? A little boy in one of the schools in Edinburgh, who had attended a prayer meeting, had much better faith. He said to his teacher who had conducted the prayer meeting, "Teacher, I wish my sister could be made to read the Bible. She never reads it."

"Why should your sister read the Bible, Johnny?"

"Because if she should once read it, I am sure it would do her good, and she would be converted and be saved."

"Do you think so, Johnny?"

"Yes, I do, sir, and I wish the next time there's a prayer meeting you would ask the people to pray for my sister that she may begin to read the Bible."

"Well, it shall be done, John."

So the teacher mentioned that a little boy was very anxious that prayer should be offered that his sister might begin to read the Bible. John was observed to get up and go out. The teacher thought it very rude of the boy to disturb the people in a crowded room, and so the next day when the lad came, he said, "John, I thought it was very rude of you to get up in the prayer meeting and go out. You ought not to have done so."

"But sir," said the boy, "I did not mean to be rude. I thought I would just go home and see my sister reading her Bible for the first time."

In the same way we ought to believe and watch with expectation for answers to our prayer. Do not say, "Lord, turn my darkness into light," and then go out with your candle as though you expected to find it dark. After asking the Lord to appear for you, expect him to do so, for according to your faith he will answer.

# Praying and Working

The prayer of a righteous man is powerful and effective. *James 5:16*

If a man is lazy, the rafters sag; if his hands are idle, the house leaks. *Ecclesiastes 10:18*

We hear that some among you are idle. They are not busy; they are busybodies. Such people we command and urge in the Lord Jesus Christ to settle down and earn the bread they eat. And as for you, brothers, never tire of doing what is right. *2 Thessalonians 3:11-13*

---

A scholar at a boarding school near London was commended for repeating her lessons well. A school companion, who was always idly inclined, said to her one day, "How is it that you always say your lessons perfectly?"

She replied, "I always *pray* that I may say my lessons well."

"Do you?" replied the other. "Then I'll pray, too." But the next morning she could not repeat one word of her lesson. Very much confounded she ran to her friend. "I prayed," said she, "but I could not repeat a word of my lesson."

"Perhaps," rejoined the other, "you took no pains to learn it."

"Learn it! Learn it!" answered the first. "I did not learn it at all. I didn't know I needed to learn it, when I *prayed* that I might say it." She loved her idleness, poor girl. And her praying was but a mockery.

# Giving It Up to God

But godliness with contentment is great gain. *1 Timothy 6:6*

He fell to the ground in worship and said: "Naked I came from my mother's womb, and naked I will depart. The LORD gave and the LORD has taken away; may the name of the LORD be praised." In all this, Job did not sin by charging God with wrongdoing. *Job 1:20-22*

---

The habit of resignation is the root of peace. A godly child had a ring given him by his mother, and he greatly prized it. But he suddenly and unhappily lost his ring, and he cried bitterly. Recollecting himself, he stepped aside and prayed. His sister laughingly said to him, "What is the good of praying about a ring—will praying bring back your ring?"

"No, sister," said he, "perhaps not, but praying has done this for me: it has made me quite willing to do without the ring, if it is God's will. And is not that almost as good as having it?"

Thus faith quiets us by resignation, as a babe is hushed in his mother's bosom. Faith makes us quite willing to do without the mercy which once we prized; and when the heart is content to be without the outward blessing, it is as happy as it would be with it, for it is at rest.

# Power of a Refreshed Spirit

As the rain and the snow come down from heaven, and do not return to it without watering the earth and making it bud and flourish, so that it yields seed for the sower and bread for the eater, so is my word that goes out from my mouth: It will not return to me empty, but will accomplish what I desire and achieve the purpose for which I sent it. You will go out in joy and be led forth in peace; the mountains and hills will burst into song before you, and all the trees of the field will clap their hands. *Isaiah 55:10-12*

---

In driving piles, a machine is used by which a huge weight is lifted up and then made to fall upon the head of the pile. Of course the higher the weight is lifted the more powerful is the blow which it gives when it descends. Now, if we wish to impact our age and society with ponderous blows, we must see to it that we are uplifted as near to God as possible. All our power will depend upon the elevation of our spirits. Prayer, meditation, devotion, communion, are like a windlass to wind us up aloft. It is not lost time which we spend in such sacred exercises, for we are thus accumulating force, so that when we come down to our actual labor for God, we shall descend with an energy unknown to those to whom communion is unknown.

# Our Loving Guide and Father

The LORD will guide you always; he will satisfy your needs in a sun-scorched land and will strengthen your frame. You will be like a well-watered garden, like a spring whose waters never fail. *Isaiah 58:11*

If you, then, though you are evil, know how to give good gifts to your children, how much more will your Father in heaven give good gifts to those who ask him! *Matthew 7:11*

---

If the Lord has enriched you in material things, though you have not feared him, have you not every reason to expect that he will do as well for you in spiritual things, if you ask him to do so? If you call at a friend's house on horseback, he takes your horse into his stable and is remarkably attentive to it. The creature is well groomed, well housed, well fed. You are not at all afraid that *you* will be shut out for surely there is a warm place in the parlor for the rider, when a horse is so well accommodated in the stable. Now, your body, which we may liken to the horse, has enjoyed temporal prosperity in abundance, and surely the Lord will take care of your soul if you seek his face! Let your prayer be, "My God, my Father, be my guide. Since you have dealt so well with me in these external matters, give me true riches, give me to love your Son and trust in him, and be forevermore your child."

# God Hears the Intercession of Saints

And pray in the Spirit on all occasions with all kinds of prayers and requests. With this in mind, be alert and always keep on praying for all the saints. *Ephesians 6:18*

Build yourselves up in your most holy faith and pray in the Holy Spirit. Keep yourselves in God's love as you wait for the mercy of our Lord Jesus Christ to bring you to eternal life. *Jude 20-21*

---

We saw in Venice a picture of St. Mark and other holy champions delivering the fair city from the devil, who had resolved to raise a great storm in the Adriatic, flood the lagoons, and drown the inhabitants of the "bride of the sea." The whole story is merely a legend, but even so the picture is capable of mirroring the truth that the intercession of saints and God's peculiar regard for them have oftentimes delivered the church.

# Unity through Prayer

Be completely humble and gentle; be patient, bearing with one another in love. Make every effort to keep the unity of the Spirit through the bond of peace. There is one body and one Spirit—just as you were called to one hope when you were called—one Lord, one faith, one baptism; one God and Father of all, who is over all and through all and in all. *Ephesians 4:2-6*

Don't have anything to do with foolish and stupid arguments, because you know they produce quarrels. *2 Timothy 2:23*

---

Two neighbors, a cooper and a farmer, were spending the evening together. Both were professors of religion, but of different denominations. Their conversation was first on topics relating to practical religion, but after a time it diverged to the points of difference between the two denominations to which they belonged. It first became a discussion, and then a dispute. The cooper was the first to perceive its unprofitable and injurious tendency, and remarked, "We are springing apart from each other. Let us pray." They kneeled down and prayed together, after which they spent the remainder of the evening lovingly together, conversing on the things of the kingdom in which they both felt an equal interest. The suggestion of the cooper was an excellent one, and it were well if it were acted on more frequently by those who, like him, are members of the household of Christ.

# Restorative Power of Daily Prayer

Morning by morning, O LORD, you hear my voice; morning by morning I lay my requests before you and wait in expectation. *Psalm 5:3*

Satisfy us in the morning with your unfailing love, that we may sing for joy and be glad all our days. *Psalm 90:14*

O LORD, be gracious to us; we long for you. Be our strength every morning, our salvation in time of distress. *Isaiah 33:2*

---

On the first of May in the olden times, according to annual custom, many inhabitants of London went into the fields to bathe their faces with the early dew upon the grass under the idea that it would render them beautiful. Some writers call the custom superstitious. It may have been so, but this we know, that to bathe one's face every morning in the dew of heaven by prayer and communion, is the sure way to obtain true beauty of life and character.

# Pull the Rope Boldly

Therefore, since we have a great high priest who has gone through the heavens, Jesus the Son of God, let us hold firmly to the faith we profess. For we do not have a high priest who is unable to sympathize with our weaknesses, but we have one who has been tempted in every way, just as we are—yet was without sin. Let us then approach the throne of grace with confidence, so that we may receive mercy and find grace to help us in our time of need. *Hebrews 4:14-16*

---

Prayer pulls the rope below and the great bell rings above in the ears of God. Some scarcely stir the bell, for they pray so languidly. Others give but an occasional pluck at the rope. But he who wins with heaven is the man who grasps the rope boldly and pulls continuously, with all his might.

# Prayers Like Mountains

During the days of Jesus' life on earth, he offered up prayers and petitions with loud cries and tears to the one who could save him from death, and he was heard because of his reverent submission. *Hebrews 5:7*

I urge, then, first of all, that requests, prayers, intercession and thanksgiving be made for everyone. . . . This is good, and pleases God our Savior, who wants all men to be saved and to come to a knowledge of the truth. *1 Timothy 2:1, 3*

---

"Philip James Spener had a son of eminent talents, but he was perverse and extremely vicious. All means of love and persuasion were without success. The father could only *pray*, which he continued to do, that the Lord might yet be pleased to save his son at any time and in any way. The son fell sick, and while lying on his bed in great distress of mind, nearly past the power of speech or motion, he suddenly started up, clasped his hands, and exclaimed, 'My father's prayers, like mountains, surround me!' Soon after his anxiety ceased, a sweet peace spread over his face, his malady came to a crisis, and the son was saved in body and soul. He became another man. Spener lived to see his son a respectable man, in public office, and happily married. Such was the change of his life after his conversion."—*N.E. Puritan*

# He Meets the Needs of the Faithful

My God will meet all your needs according to his glorious riches in Christ Jesus. *Philippians 4:19*

"Ask and it will be given to you; seek and you will find; knock and the door will be opened to you. For everyone who asks receives; he who seeks finds; and to him who knocks, the door will be opened." *Matthew 7:7-8*

---

On a tradesman's table I noticed a book labeled WANT BOOK. What a practical suggestion for a man of prayer! He should put down all his needs on the tablets of his heart, and then present his "want book" to his God. If we knew all our needs, what a large book we would need! How comforting to know that Jesus has a supply book, which exactly meets our want book! Promises, providences, and divine visitations combine to meet the necessities of all the faithful.

# Active Service

# Always Ready for Service

Do your best to present yourself to God as one approved, a workman who does not need to be ashamed and who correctly handles the word of truth. . . . he will be an instrument for noble purposes, made holy, useful to the Master and prepared to do any good work. *2 Timothy 2:15, 21*

Therefore, prepare your minds for action; be self-controlled; set your hope fully on the grace to be given you when Jesus Christ is revealed. *1 Peter 1:13*

---

Brutus visiting Ligarius found him ill and said, "What! Are you sick, Ligarius?"

"No, Brutus," he said, "if you have a noble enterprise at hand, then I am well."

So should the believer say of Christ. What might excuse us from other labor shall never prevent our engaging in *his* service.

# An Honor to Be Used in His Service

Yet, O LORD, you are our Father. We are the clay, you are the potter; we are all the work of your hand. Do not be angry beyond measure, O LORD; do not remember our sins forever. Oh, look upon us, we pray, for we are all your people. *Isaiah 64:8-9*

---

I thought I looked and saw the Master standing, and at his feet lay an earthen vessel. It was not broken, not unfitted for service, yet there it lay, powerless and useless, until he took it up. He held it awhile, and I saw that he was filling it, and soon I beheld him walking in his garden, where he had "gone down to gather lilies." The earthen vessel was yet again in his hand, and with it he watered his beautiful plants and caused their fragrances to be shed forth more abundantly. Then I said to myself, "Sorrowing Christian, hush! Hush! Peace, be still! You are this earthen vessel, powerless, it is true, yet not broken, still fit for the Master's use. Sometimes you may be laid aside altogether from active service, and the question may arise, what is the Master doing with me now? Then may a voice speak to your inmost heart, 'He is filling the vessel, yes, only filling it to be ready for use.' Don't ask how he will use you. Be silent. Is it not all too great an honor for you to be used by him at all? Be content, whether thou art employed in watering the lilies or in washing the feet of the saints. It doesn't really matter. Surely it is enough for an earthen vessel to be in the Master's hands and employed in the Master's service."

# To Fight Foremost in the Ranks of the Prince

Fight the good fight of the faith. Take hold of the eternal life to which you were called when you made your good confession in the presence of many witnesses. In the sight of God, who gives life to everything, and of Christ Jesus, who while testifying before Pontius Pilate made the good confession, I charge you to keep this commandment without spot or blame until the appearing of our Lord Jesus Christ, which God will bring about in his own time—God, the blessed and only Ruler, the King of kings, and Lord of Lords, who alone is immortal and who lives in unapproachable light, whom no one has seen or can see. To him be honor and might forever. *1 Timothy 6:12-16*

---

When the Spartan king advanced against the enemy, he always had with him someone that had been crowned in the public games of Greece. And they tell us that a Lacedaemonian, when large sums were offered him on condition that he would not enter the Olympic lists, refused them. Having with much difficulty thrown his antagonists in wrestling, one put this question to him, "Spartan, what will you gain by this victory?"

He answered with a smile, "I shall have the honor to fight foremost in the ranks of my prince."

The honor that appertains to office in the church of God lies mainly in this: that the person who is set apart for such service has the privilege of being first in holiness of example, abundance of liberality, patience of longsuffering, zeal in effort, and self-sacrifice in service. Gracious King of kings, if you have made me a minister or deacon in your church, enable me to be first in every good word and work, shunning no sacrifice, and shrinking from no suffering.

# Serving Despite Difficulties

Blessed is the man who perseveres under trial, because when he has stood the test, he will receive the crown of life that God has promised to those who love him. *James 1:12*

For our light and momentary troubles are achieving for us an eternal glory that far outweighs them all. So we fix our eyes not on what is seen, but on what is unseen. For what is seen is temporary, but what is unseen is eternal. *2 Corinthians 4:17-18*

---

Consider the miller on the village hill. How does he grind his grist? Does he bargain that he will only grind in the west wind, because its gales are so full of health? No, he grinds in the east wind, which searches joints and marrow, makes the millstones revolve, and together with the north and south it is yoked to his service. Even so should it be with you who are true workers for God. All your ups and your downs, your successes and your defeats, should be turned to the glory of God.

# Worn Out in the Master's Service

If you suffer for doing good and you endure it, this is commendable before God. To this you were called, because Christ suffered for you, leaving you an example, that you should follow in his steps. *1 Peter 2:20-21*

The testing of your faith develops perseverance. Perseverance must finish its work so that you may be mature and complete, not lacking anything. *James 1:3-4*

---

The minstrel sang of the old hero:

*With his Yemen sword for aid;*
*Ornament it carried none,*
*But the notches on the blade.*

What nobler decoration of honor can any godly man seek after than his scars of service, his losses for the cross, his reproaches for Christ's sake, his being worn out in his Master's service!

# Looking to God for Reward

"Surely the righteous still are rewarded; surely there is a God who judges the earth." *Psalm 58:11*

Whatever you do, work at it with all your heart, as working for the Lord, not for men, since you know that you will receive an inheritance from the Lord as a reward. It is the Lord Christ you are serving. *Colossians 3:23-24*

---

When Calvin was banished from ungrateful Geneva, he said, "Surely if I had merely served man, this would have been a poor recompense. But it is my happiness that I have served him who never fails to reward his servants to the full extent of his promise."

# Each One Is Needed to Make the Message Known

All this is from God, who reconciled us to himself through Christ and gave us the ministry of reconciliation: that God was reconciling the world to himself in Christ, not counting men's sins against them. And he has committed to us the message of reconciliation. We are therefore Christ's ambassadors, as though God were making his appeal through us. *2 Corinthians 5:18-20*

---

A certain band of warlike knights had been exceedingly victorious in all their conflicts. They were men of valor and of indomitable courage and had subdued province after province for their king. But all of a sudden they said in the council chamber, "We have at our head a most valiant warrior. Would it not be better if, leaving a few such as he to go out to the fight, the mere men-at-arms, who make up the ordinary ranks, were to rest at home? We should be much more at our ease, our horses would not so often be covered with foam, nor our armor be bruised. Many would enjoy abundant leisure, and great things would be done by the valiant few."

Now, the foremost champions, with fear and trembling, undertook the task and went to the conflict, and they fought well, as the rolls of fame can testify. But still, from the very hour in which that scheme was planned and carried out, no city was taken, no province was conquered. Then the champion spoke out, saying, "How did you think that a few men could do the work of all the thousands? When you all went to the fight, and every man took his share, we dashed upon the foe like an avalanche and crushed him beneath our feet."

If we, as Christians, are to subdue the earth, every one of us must join in the fight. We must not exempt a single soldier of the cross, neither man nor woman, rich nor poor, but each must fight for the Lord Jesus according to his or her ability, that his kingdom may come, and that his will may be done in earth even as it is in heaven. We shall see great things when all agree to this and put it in practice.

# One at a Time

In your hearts set apart Christ as Lord. Always be prepared to give an answer to everyone who asks you to give the reason for the hope that you have. *1 Peter 3:15*

---

I once heard a story of a foolish man who declared he could fight the whole British army. When he was asked how he could draw so long a bow as that, he said, "This is what I would do. I know I am the best swordsman in the world, so I would go and challenge one British soldier and kill him, then take another, and kill him. In this way I only want time enough and I would kill the whole British army."

It was a ridiculous boast, but there is something in it that I could not bring out so well in any other way. If we want to conquer the world for the Lord Jesus Christ, rest assured we must do it in this foolish man's fashion. We must take people one by one, and these must be brought to Christ. Otherwise the great mass will remain untouched. Do not imagine for a moment that you are going to convert a nation at once. You are to convert the people of that nation, one by one, through the power of God's Holy Spirit. It is not for you to suit your machinery and arrange your plans for the moving of a mass as such. You must look to the salvation of the units.

# Like a Life-Giving Tree

The righteous will flourish like a palm tree, they will grow like a cedar of Lebanon; planted in the house of the LORD, they will flourish in the courts of our God. They will still bear fruit in old age, they will stay fresh and green, proclaiming, "The LORD is upright; he is my Rock, and there is no wickedness in him." *Psalm 92:12-15*

Therefore we do not lose heart. Though outwardly we are wasting away, yet inwardly we are being renewed day by day. For our light and momentary troubles are achieving for us an eternal glory that far outweighs them all. *2 Corinthians 4:16-17*

---

"On the barren flank of a rock grows a tree with dry leaves. Its large woody roots can scarcely penetrate into the stone. For several months of the year not a shingle shower moistens its foliage. Its branches appear dead and dried, but when the trunk is pierced there flows from it a sweet and nourishing milk. It is at the rising of the sun that this vegetable fountain is most abundant. The natives are then seen hastening from all quarters, furnished with large bowls to receive the milk, which grows yellow and thickens at its surface. Some empty their bowls under the tree itself; others carry the juice home to their children."—*Alexander von Humboldt*, on the cow-tree.

May not the earnest Christian ministering good on all sides be imaged in this marvelous tree? He may often consider himself a withered and dead tree, but there is within him a living sap, which wells up with blessing to all around. His surroundings are all against him, the soil in which he grows is hostile to grace, yet he not only lives on, but luxuriates. He derives nothing from earth, his fountain is from above, but he enriches the sons of earth with untold blessings, and though they often wound him they experimentally know his value. Many of the poor and needy look up as to a friend in need; he is full of the milk of human kindness. Where he cannot give in golden coin he distributes comfort in words of sympathy and words of cheer.

# Works That Endure

If any man builds on this foundation using gold, silver, costly stones, wood, hay or straw, his work will be shown for what it is, because the Day will bring it to light. It will be revealed with fire, and the fire will test the quality of each man's work. If what he has built survives, he will receive his reward. *1 Corinthians 3:12-14*

"When the Son of Man comes in his glory, and all the angels with him, he will sit on his throne in heavenly glory. . . . Then the King will say to those on his right, 'Come, you who are blessed by my Father; take your inheritance, the kingdom prepared for you since the creation of the world. For I was hungry and you gave me something to eat, I was thirsty and you gave me something to drink, I was a stranger and you invited me in, I needed clothes and you clothed me, I was sick and you looked after me, I was in prison and you came to visit me.' Then the righteous will answer him, 'Lord, when did we see you hungry and feed you, or thirsty and give you something to drink? When did we see you a stranger and invite you in, or needing clothes and clothe you? When did we see you sick or in prison and go to visit you?' The King will reply, 'I tell you the truth, whatever you did for one of the least of these brothers of mine, you did for me.'" *Matthew 25:31, 34-40*

---

Here is a good searching question for a man to ask himself as he reviews his past life: *Have I written in the snow?* Will my life-work endure the lapse of years and the fret of change? Has there been anything immortal in it, which will survive the speedy wreck of all sublunary things? The boys inscribe their names in capitals in the snow, and in the morning's thaw the writing disappears. Will it be so with my work, or will the characters that I have carved outlast the brazen tablets of history? Have I written in the snow?

# Indifference Is Impossible

Never be lacking in zeal, but keep your spiritual fervor, serving the Lord. *Romans 12:11*

Whatever your hand finds to do, do it with all of your might. *Ecclesiastes 9:10*

---

It appears that Themistocles, when a boy, was full of spirit and fire, quick of apprehension, naturally inclined to bold attempts, and likely to make a great statesman. His hours of leisure and vacation he spent not—like other boys—in idleness and play, but he was always inventing and composing declamations, the subjects of which were either impeachments or defenses of some of his schoolmates, so that his teacher would often say, "Boy, you will be nothing common or indifferent. You will either be a blessing or a curse to the community."

So remember, you who profess to be followers of the Lord Jesus, that to you indifference is impossible! You *must* bless the church and the world by your holiness, or you will curse them both by your hypocrisy and inconsistency. In the visible church it is most true that "no man liveth unto himself, and no man dieth unto himself."

# Light Labors of Love

Let us not become weary in doing good, for at the proper time we will reap a harvest if we do not give up. Therefore, as we have opportunity, let us do good to all people, especially to those who belong to the family of believers. *Galatians 6:9-10*

As for you, brothers, never tire of doing what is right. *2 Thessalonians 3:13*

---

It is of the utmost importance to keep up our interest in the holy work in which we are engaged, for the moment our interest flags the work will become wearisome. Humboldt says that the copper-colored native of central America, far more accustomed than the European traveler to the burning heat of the climate, yet complains more when upon a journey, because he is stimulated by no interest. The same Indian who would complain, when in botanizing, he was loaded with a box full of plants, would row his canoe fourteen or fifteen hours at a time against the current without a murmur, because he wished to return to his family. Labors of love are light. Routine is a hard master. Love much, and you can do much. Impossibilities disappear when zeal is fervent.

# The Impossibility of Two Masters

"No servant can serve two masters. Either he will hate the one and love the other, or he will be devoted to the one and despise the other. You cannot serve both God and Money." The Pharisees, who loved money, heard all this and were sneering at Jesus. He said to them, "You are the ones who justify yourselves in the eyes of men, but God knows your hearts. What is highly valued among men is detestable in God's sight." *Luke 16:13-15*

---

"You cannot serve two masters—you must serve one or another. If your work is first with you, and your fee second, work is your master, and the Lord of work, who is God. But if your fee is first with you, and your work second, fee is your master, and the Lord of fee, who is the devil. So there you have it in brief terms—work first, you are God's servants; fee first, you are the fiend's. And it makes a difference, now and ever, believe me, whether you serve him who has on his vesture and thigh written, 'King of kings,' and whose service is perfect freedom, or him on whose vesture and thigh the name is written, 'Slave of slaves,' and whose service is perfect slavery."—*John Ruskin*

# Striking a Balance

God is not unjust; he will not forget your work and the love you have shown him as you have helped his people and continue to help them. We want each of you to show this same diligence to the very end, in order to make your hope sure. We do not want you to become lazy, but to imitate those who through faith and patience inherit what has been promised. *Hebrews 6:10-12*

---

It is a wise thing to exhibit prudence and hopefulness in their proper degrees and seasons. Some are so exultant at success as to become rash, and thereby secure for themselves a disaster. Others are so depressed by a defeat as to be incapable of further action. When we are most unsuccessful in our Lord's work we should rally all our forces for new attempts, hoping that the tide will turn, and believing that the crown is certain for those who persevere. On the other hand when the Lord favors us with the largest degree of blessing, we must watch with holy anxiety lest by any negligence or sin we should grieve the Holy Spirit and so forfeit all hope of future triumph.

# A Question of Priorities

"Why do you worry about clothes? See how the lilies of the field grow. They do not labor or spin. Yet I tell you that not even Solomon in all his splendor was dressed like one of these. If that is how God clothes the grass of the field, which is here today and tomorrow is thrown into the fire, will he not much more clothe you, O you of little faith? So do not worry, saying 'What shall we eat?' or 'What shall we drink?' or 'What shall we wear?' For the pagans run after all these things, and your heavenly Father knows that you need them. But seek first his kingdom and his righteousness, and all these things will be given to you as well." *Matthew 6:28-33*

But be sure to fear the LORD and serve him faithfully with all your heart; consider what great things he has done for you. *1 Samuel 12:24*

---

A gentleman of Boston, an intimate friend of Professor Agassiz, once expressed his wonder that a man of such abilities as Agassiz possessed should remain contented with such a moderate income.

"I have enough," was Agassiz's reply. "I have not *time* to make money. Life is not sufficiently long to enable a man to get rich and do his duty to his fellow men at the same time."

Do we Christians have time to serve our God and yet to give our whole souls to gaining wealth? The question is left for conscience to answer.

# A Difficult but Satisfying Calling

"Come, let us return to the LORD. He has torn us to pieces but he will heal us; he has injured us but he will bind up our wounds. After two days he will revive us; on the third day he will restore us, that we may live in his presence. Let us acknowledge the LORD; let us press on to acknowledge him. As surely as the sun rises, he will appear; he will come to us like the winter rains, like the spring rains that water the earth." *Hosea 6:1-3*

---

Artificial piety, like flowers in wax, droops not in the hour of drought, but the fair lily of true grace hangs its head if the rain of heaven be denied. True faith, like fire, has its attendant smoke of unbelief, but presumption like a painted flame is all brightness. Like ships at sea, true Christian have their storms, but mere professors of the faith, like pictured galleys on the canvas, ride on an unruffled ocean. Life has its changes, but death abides the same. Life has muscle, sinew, brain, spirit, and these vary in physical condition; but the petrified limbs of death lie still until the worm has devoured the carcass. Life weeps as well as smiles, but the ghastly grin of death does not relax with anxiety or fear. As no weather can give ague to marble, as no variation of temperature can bring fever to iron, so to some men the events of life, the temptations of prosperity, or the trials of adversity bring little change. Yet it would be better to ebb and flow forever like the sea than to rot in endless stagnation of false peace. Better to be hunted by the hounds of hell, and so driven to the shelter of the cross, than to dwell at ease and be fattening for the devil's shambles.

# The Bond of Gentleness

Live a life worthy of the calling you have received. Be completely humble and gentle; be patient, bearing with one another in love. Make every effort to keep the unity of the Spirit through the bond of peace. *Ephesians 4:1-3*

---

It is said of that eminent saint and martyr Bishop Hooper, that on one occasion a man in deep distress was allowed to go into his prison to tell his tale of conscience, but Bishop Hooper looked so sternly upon him and addressed him so severely at first, that the poor soul ran away and could not get comfort until he had sought another minister of a gentler aspect. Hooper really was a gracious and loving soul, but the sternness of his manner kept the penitent off.

# Shepherding Believers, a Heavy Responsibility

To the elders among you, I appeal as a fellow elder, a witness of Christ's sufferings and one who also will share in the glory to be revealed: Be shepherds of God's flock that is under your care, serving as overseers—not because you must, but because you are willing, as God wants you to be; not greedy for money, but eager to serve; not lording it over those entrusted to you, but being examples to the flock. And when the Chief Shepherd appears, you will receive the crown of glory that will never fade away. *1 Peter 5:1-4*

---

John Brown of Haddington said to a young minister who complained of the smallness of his congregation, "It is as large a one as you will want to give account for in the day of judgment." The admonition is appropriate, not to ministers alone, but to all teachers.

# Useful in Christ's Kingdom

Land that drinks in the rain often falling on it and that produces a crop useful to those for whom it is farmed receives the blessing of God. But land that produces thorns and thistles is worthless and is in danger of being cursed. . . . God is not unjust; he will not forget your work and the love you have shown him as you have helped his people and continue to help them. *Hebrews 6:7-8, 10*

---

Many true saints are unable to render much service to the cause of God. See, then, the gardeners going down to the pond and dipping their watering pots to carry the refreshing liquid to the flowers. A child comes into the garden and wishes to help, and yonder is a little watering pot for him. Note well the little water pot, though it does not hold so much, yet carries the same water to the plants. And it does not make any difference to the flowers that receive that water, whether it came out of the big pot or the little pot, so long as it is the same water, and they get it. You who are as little children in God's church, you who do not know much, but try to tell others what little you know. If it be the same gospel truth, and be blessed by the same Spirit, it will not matter to the souls who are blessed by you whether they were converted or comforted under a person of one or ten talents.

# A Crystal Stream in a Thirsty Land

See, a king will reign in righteousness and rulers will rule with justice. Each man will be like a shelter from the wind and a refuge from the storm, like streams of water in the desert and the shadow of a great rock in a thirsty land. Then the eyes of those who see will no longer be closed, and the ears of those who hear will listen. The mind of the rash will know and understand, and the stammering tongue will be fluent and clear. *Isaiah 32:1-4*

A generous man will prosper; he who refreshes others will himself be refreshed. *Proverbs 11:25*

---

"On a hot summer day, some years ago, I was sailing with a friend in a tiny boat on a miniature lake, enclosed like a cup within a circle of steep, bare Scottish hills. On the shoulder of the brown sun-burned mountain, and in full sight was a well with a crystal stream trickling over its lip and making its way down toward the lake. Around the well's mouth and along the course of the rivulet, a belt of green stood out in strong contrast with the iron surface of the rocks all around. We soon agreed as to what should be made of it. There it was, a legend clearly printed by the finger of God on the side of these silent hills, teaching the passerby how needful a good man is, and how useful he may be in a desert world."—*W. Arnot*

# A Driving Force from Above

So I say, live by the Spirit, and you will not gratify the desires of the sinful nature. For the sinful nature desires what is contrary to the Spirit, and the Spirit what is contrary to the sinful nature. . . . But the fruit of the Spirit is love, joy, peace, patience, kindness, goodness, faithfulness, gentleness and self-control. Against such things there is no law. Those who belong to Christ Jesus have crucified the sinful nature with its passions and desires. Since we live by the Spirit, let us keep in step with the Spirit. *Galatians 5:16-17, 22-25*

Wait till the Lord comes. He will bring to light what is hidden in darkness and will expose the motives of men's hearts. At that time each will receive his praise from God. *1 Corinthians 4:5*

---

There are overshot waterwheels and undershot. In the one case the motive power falls from above; in the other the water turns the wheel from below. The first is more powerful. Men, like wheels, are turned by forces from various sources, and too many move by the undercurrent—mercenary desires and selfish aims drive them. But the good man's driving force falls from above; let him endeavor to prove to all men that this is the most mighty force in existence.

# Single-Minded Purpose

I eagerly expect and hope that I will in no way be ashamed, but will have sufficient courage so that now as always Christ will be exalted in my body, whether by life or by death. For to me, to live is Christ and to die is gain. If I am to go on living in the body, this will mean fruitful labor for me. Yet what shall I choose? I do not know! I am torn between the two: I desire to depart and be with Christ, which is better by far; but it is more necessary for you that I remain in the body. *Philippians 1:20-24*

---

It is said of Thomas Pett, the miser, that his pulse rose and fell with the funds. He never lay down or rose that he did not bless the inventor of compound interest. His one gloomy apartment was never brightened with coal, candle, or the countenance of a visitor, and he never ate a morsel at his own expense. Of course he made money, for he gave himself wholly to it, and we ought not to forget the same single-mindedness and self-denial would make Christians rich toward God. What is wanted in the service of Christ is the same unity of purpose that has ruled all men who have won the object for which they lived. He who makes God's glory the one and only aim before which all other things bow themselves, is the man to bring honor to his Lord.

# Preaching the Word

# Wisdom through the Spirit

My message and my preaching were not with wise and persuasive words, but with a demonstration of the Spirit's power, so that your faith might not rest on men's wisdom, but on God's power. We do, however, speak a message of wisdom among the mature, but not the wisdom of this age or of the rulers of this age, who are coming to nothing. No, we speak of God's secret wisdom, a wisdom that has been hidden and that God destined for our glory before time began. . . . but God has revealed it to us by his Spirit. The Spirit searches all things, even the deep things of God. For who among men knows the thoughts of a man except the man's spirit within him? In the same way no one knows the thoughts of God except the Spirit of God. We have not received the spirit of the world but the Spirit who is from God, that we may understand what God has freely given us. This is what we speak, not in words taught us by human wisdom but in words taught by the Spirit, expressing spiritual truths in spiritual words. *1 Corinthians 2:4-7, 10-13*

---

However learned, godly, and eloquent a minister may be, he is nothing without the Holy Spirit. The bell in the steeple may be well hung, fairly fashioned, and of soundest metal, but it is dumb until the ringer makes it speak. And in like manner the preacher has no voice of quickening for the dead in sin, or of comfort for living saints until the divine spirit gives him a gracious pull, and bids him speak with power. Hence the need of prayer from both preacher and hearers.

# Resting on God's Power

But God chose the foolish things of the world to shame the wise; God chose the weak things of the world to shame the strong. He chose the lowly things of this world and the despised things—and the things that are not—to nullify the things that are, so that no one may boast before him. It is because of him that you are in Christ Jesus, who has become for us wisdom from God—that is, our righteousness, holiness, and redemption. Therefore, as it is written: "Let him who boasts boast in the Lord." When I came to you, brothers, I did not come with eloquence or superior wisdom as I proclaimed to you the testimony about God. For I resolved to know nothing while I was with you except Jesus Christ and him crucified. I came to you in weakness and fear, and with much trembling. My message and my preaching were not with wise and persuasive words, but with a demonstration of the spirit's power, so that your faith might not rest on men's wisdom, but on God's power. *1 Corinthians 1:27—2:5*

---

*Swift of foot was Hiawatha,*
*He could shoot an arrow from him,*
*And run forward with such fleetness,*
*That the arrow fell behind him!*

The fable is even less than truth with the fervent preacher: he darts arrows of fire in flaming speech, but his eagerness to win souls far outruns his words. He projects himself far beyond his language. His heart outstrips his utterance. He embraces souls in his love, while his words as yet are but on the wing. Often and often he will weep when his sermon is over, because his words "fell behind him." Yet he has cause for joy, that he should have received so divine a spirit from his Master's hand: his very dissatisfaction proves his zeal.

# With the Holy Spirit and with Fire

John answered them all, "I baptize you with water. But one more powerful than I will come, the thongs of whose sandals I am not worthy to untie. He will baptize you with the Holy Spirit and with fire." *Luke 3:16*

---

In his travels, Humboldt observed, "It seems remarkable that in the hottest as well as the coldest climates, people display the same predilection for heat. On the introduction of Christianity into Iceland, the inhabitants would be baptized only in the hot springs of Hecla. And in the torrid zone, in the plains as well as on the Cordilleras, the natives flock from all parts to the thermal waters." The fact is not less noteworthy that men love spiritual warmth. Cold truth, even cold gospel truth, is never attractive. Ministers must be fervent, their spirits earnest, and their style energetic, or many will not come to them. Religion is a dish to be served hot; once it becomes lukewarm it is sickening. Our baptism must be with the Holy Ghost and with fire if we would win the masses to hear the gospel.

# Pearls before Swine

"Do not give dogs what is sacred; do not throw your pearls to pigs. If you do, they may trample them under their feet, and then turn and tear you to pieces." *Matthew 7:6*

---

Luther was told of a nobleman who, above all things, occupied himself with amassing money and was so buried in darkness that he gave no heed to the word of God, and even said to someone who witnessed to him, "But the gospel pays no interest."

"Have you no grains?" interposed Luther. And then he told this fable. "A lion was making a great feast, and invited all the beasts, among them some swine. When all types of dainty foods were set before the guests, the swine asked, 'Have you no grains?' It is the same way with carnal men today," Luther continued. "We preachers set before them the most dainty and costly dishes, such as everlasting salvation, the remission of sins, and God's grace. But they, like swine, turn up their snouts, and ask for money. Offer a cow a nutmeg, and she will reject it for old hay."

# The Wisdom of Winning Souls

The fruit of the righteous is a tree of life, and he who wins souls is wise. *Proverbs 11:30*

I have become all things to all men so that by all possible means I might save some. *1 Corinthians 9:22*

---

Sir Astley Cooper, on visiting Paris, was asked by the chief surgeon how many times he had performed a certain wonderful feat of surgery. He replied that he had performed the operation thirteen times.

"Ah, but, monsieur, I have done it one hundred and sixty times. How many times did you save the life?" continued the curious Frenchman, after he had looked into the blank amazement of Sir Astley's face.

"I," said the Englishman, "saved eleven out of the thirteen. How many did you save out of one hundred and sixty?"

"Ah, monsieur, I lost them all, but the operation was very brilliant!"

Of how many popular ministries might the same verdict be given! Souls are not saved, but the preaching is very brilliant. Thousands are attracted and operated on by the rhetorician's art, but what if he should have to say of his admirers, "I lost them all, but the sermons were very brilliant!"

# "Throwing Dirt" at the Gospel

You may command certain men not to teach false doctrines any longer nor to devote themselves to myths and endless genealogies. These promote controversies rather than God's work—which is by faith. The goal of this command is love, which comes from a pure heart and a good conscience and a sincere faith. Some have wandered away from these and turned to meaningless talk. They want to be teachers of the law, but they do not know what they are talking about or what they so confidently affirm. We know that the law is good if a man uses it properly. *1 Timothy 1:3-8*

---

The old fable tells us of a boy who mounted a scavenger's cart with the base intent to throw dirt at the moon. Another boy, with better intentions, but scarcely less foolishness, came running with a bucket of water to wash the moon, and make its face clean again. Certain skeptics are forever inventing new infidelities with which they endeavor to defile the fair face of the gospel, and many ministers forsake the preaching of Christ, and him crucified, to answer their endless quibbles: to both of these the ancient fable may be instructive.

# Bread that Nourishes

Jesus declared, "I am the bread of life. He who comes to me will never go hungry, and he who believes in me will never be thirsty. . . . Here is the bread that comes down from heaven, which a man may eat and not die. I am the living bread that came down from heaven. If a man eats of this bread, he will live forever. This bread is my flesh, which I will give for the life of this world. . . . I tell you the truth, unless you eat the flesh of the Son of Man and drink his blood, you have no life in you. Whoever eats my flesh and drinks my blood has eternal life, and I will raise him up at the last day. For my flesh is real food and my blood is real drink. Whoever eats my flesh and drinks my blood remains in me, and I in him. Just as the living Father sent me and I live because of the Father, so the one who feeds on me will live because of me." *John 6:35, 50-51, 53-57*

---

From the deck of an Austrian gunboat we threw into the Lago Garda a succession of little pieces of bread, and presently small fishes came in shoals till there seemed to be, as the old proverb puts it, more fish than water. They came to feed and needed no music. Let the preacher give his people food, and they will flock around him, even if the sounding brass of rhetoric and the tinkling cymbals of oratory are silent.

# They Come to Be Fed

"Come, all you who are thirsty, come to the waters; and you who have no money, come, buy and eat! Come, buy wine and milk without money and without cost. Why spend money on what is not bread, and your labor on what does not satisfy? Listen, listen to me, and eat what is good, and your soul will delight in the richest of fare. Give ear and come to me, hear me, that your soul may live." *Isaiah 55:1-3*

Taste and see that the LORD is good; blessed is the man who takes refuge in him. *Psalm 34:8*

Like newborn babies, crave pure spiritual milk, so that by it you may grow up in your salvation, now that you have tasted that the Lord is good. *1 Peter 2:2-3*

---

Everybody knows that large flocks of pigeons assemble at the stroke of the great clock in the square of St. Mark. Believe me, it is not the music of the bell that attracts them—they can hear that every hour. They come for the food, and no mere sound will long collect them. This is a hint for filling the preacher's meeting house: it must be done not merely by that fine, bell-like voice of yours, but by all the neighborhood's being assured that spiritual food is to be had when you open your mouth. Barley for pigeons, and the gospel for men and women. Try it in earnest and you cannot fail. You will soon be saying, "Who are these that fly as a cloud, and as doves to their windows?"

# Make the Message Available to Everyone

Though I am free and belong to no man, I make myself a slave to everyone, to win as many as possible. To the Jews I became like a Jew, to win the Jews. To those under the law I became like one under the law (though I myself am not under the law), so as to win those under the law. To those not having the law I became like one not having the law (though I am not free from God's law but am under Christ's law), so as to win those not having the law. To the weak I became weak, to win the weak. I have become all things to all men so that by all possible means I might save some. *1 Corinthians 9:19-22*

---

In the town of Goslar, in the Hartz mountains, there is in the principal square a medieval fountain, but the peculiarity of its construction is that no one can reach the water so as to fill a bucket or even get a drink to quench his thirst. Both the jets and the basin into which they fall are above the reach of any person of ordinary stature, yet the fountain was intended to supply the public with water, and it fulfills its design by a method that we never saw before. Every person brings a spout or trough with him long enough to reach the top of the fountain and bring the water down into his pitcher. We are afraid that all our reverence for antiquity did not prevent us from laughing—the slightest bit of mason's work with a chisel would have made the crystal stream available to all. But no, everyone had to bring a trough or go away unsupplied.

When preachers of the gospel talk in so lofty a style that each hearer needs to bring a dictionary, they remind us of the absurd fountain of Goslar. The use of six-syllabled jaw-breaking words is simply a most ludicrous vanity. A little labor on the part of such scholars would save a world of profitless toil to their hearers and enable those uneducated persons who have no means of reaching the preacher's altitude to derive some measure of instruction from his ministry.

# Teaching and Exhortation

Preach the Word; be prepared in season and out of season; correct, rebuke and encourage—with great patience and careful instruction. *2 Timothy 4:2*

For you know that we dealt with each of you as a father deals with his own children, encouraging, comforting and urging you to live lives worthy of God, who calls you into his kingdom and glory. And we also thank God continually because, when you received the word of God, which you heard from us, you accepted it not as the word of men, but as it actually is, the word of God, which is at work in you who believe. *1 Thessalonians 2:11-13*

---

"Those that are strong in exhortation but weak in doctrine are like those that snuff the lamp but don't pour in the oil. Again, those that are strong in doctrine and nothing in exhortation drown the wick in oil and then don't light it, making it fit for use if it had fire put to it, but as it is, having only a potential for good rather than actually being profitable for the present. Doctrine without exhortation makes men all brain, no heart; exhortation without doctrine makes the heart full, leaves the brain empty. Both together make a person. One makes a wise person, the other good. One serves that we may know our duty, the other that we may perform it. I will labor in both, but I do not know to which I ought to give most attention. People cannot practice unless they know, and they know in vain if they don't practice their faith."—*Bishop Hall*

# Making the Mystery Understandable

This grace was given me: to preach to the Gentiles the unsearchable riches of Christ, and to make plain to everyone the administration of this mystery, which for ages past was kept hidden in God, who created all things. His intent was that now, through the church, the manifold wisdom of God should be made known to the rulers and authorities in the heavenly realms, according to his eternal purpose which he accomplished in Christ Jesus our Lord. In him and through faith in him we may approach God with freedom and confidence. *Ephesians 3:8-12*

---

An inspector of schools mentions in his report for 1863 that he has nowhere heard such good reading as in a girls' school in Berkshire. The clergyman, who is also the acting manager, is rather deaf, and the girls are obliged to read with unusual clearness and distinctness of tone and articulation in order that he might not miss a word. The inspector considers the pleasure with which he listened to the girls' reading to be in great measure attributable to the fact that they ordinarily had to make what they read intelligible to someone who could not hear so well as many people do.

The best of teachers are those who have labored to be understood by the dullest capacities. Preachers who all along have aimed to suit the educated never become so simple or efficient as those who have made a point of explaining even the elements of faith to the ignorant.

# The Gospel, Plain and Simple

He is the image of the invisible God, the firstborn over all creation. . . . For God was pleased to have all his fullness dwell in him,
and through him to reconcile to himself all things, whether things
on earth or things in heaven, by making peace through his blood,
shed on the cross. Once you were alienated from God and were
enemies in your minds because of your evil behavior. But now he
has reconciled you by Christ's physical body through death to
present you holy in his sight, without blemish and free from
accusation—if you continue in your faith, established and firm, not
moved from the hope held out in the gospel. This is the gospel that
you heard and that has been proclaimed to every creature under
heaven. *Colossians 1:15, 19-23*

---

The great bell of Moscow is too large to be hung. The question
arises, then what was the purpose of making it? Some preachers
are so learned that they cannot make themselves understood, or
else cannot bring their minds to preach plain gospel sermons. The
same question might be asked—then why preach them at all?

# Preaching and Teaching for the Glory of God

If anyone speaks, he should do it as one speaking the very words of God. If anyone serves, he should do it with the strength God provides, so that in all things God may be praised through Jesus Christ. To him be the glory and the power for ever and ever. *1 Peter 4:11*

---

We ascended the Sacro Monte at Orta, expecting to find that its holy hill was like that at Varallo, consecrated to representations of the life of Christ. To our disappointment we found that everything was to the honor and glory of St. Francis of Assissi, who nevertheless was represented as saying, "God forbid that I should glory, save in the cross of our Lord Jesus Christ." Too often when the preacher should think only of his Master, and labor only to set forth the Redeemer's glories, he is occupied with his own style and oratory, and so honors himself at the expense of his Lord.

# Sharing the Good News with Natural Enthusiasm

See to it, brothers, that none of you has a sinful, unbelieving heart that turns away from the living God. But encourage one another daily, as long as it is called Today, so that none of you may be hardened by sin's deceitfulness. We have come to share in Christ if we hold firmly till the end the confidence we had at first. As has just been said: "Today, if you hear his voice, do not harden your hearts." *Hebrews 3:12-15*

---

The celebrated actor Garrick, having been requested by Dr. Stonehouse to favor him with his opinion as to the manner in which a sermon ought to be delivered, sent him the following judicious answer:

"My dear pupil, you know how you would feel and speak in a parlor concerning a friend who was in imminent danger of his life, and with what energetic pathos of diction and countenance you would enforce the observance of that which you really thought would be for his preservation. You could not think of playing the orator, or studying your emphases, cadences, and gestures. You would be yourself, and the interesting nature of your subject, impressing your heart, would furnish you with the most natural tone of voice, the most proper language, the most engaging features, and the most suitable and graceful gestures. What you would be in the parlor, be in the pulpit, and you will not fail to please, to affect, and to profit."

# Speaking Up Boldly for Christ

"Now, Lord, consider their threats and enable your servants to speak your word with great boldness. Stretch out your hand to heal and perform miraculous signs and wonders through the name of your holy servant Jesus." After they prayed, the place where they were meeting was shaken. And they were all filled with the Holy Spirit and spoke the word of God boldly. *Acts 4:29-31*

---

I had tried to drive certain long brass-headed nails into a wall but had never succeeded except in turning up their points, and rendering them useless. When a tradesman came who understood his work, I noticed that he filed off all the points of the nails, the very points on whose sharpness I had relied, and when he had quite blunted them, he drove them in as far as he pleased. With some consciences our fine points in preaching are worse than useless. Our keen distinctions and nice discriminations are thrown away on many; they need to be encountered with sheer force and blunt honesty. The truth must be hammered into them by main strength, and we know from whom to seek the needed power.

# Preaching with Purpose

"You diligently study the Scriptures because you think that by them you possess eternal life. These are the Scriptures that testify about me, yet you refuse to come to me to have life." *John 5:39-40*

"You have let go of the commands of God and are holding on to the traditions of men. . . . You have a fine way of setting aside the commands of God in order to observe your own traditions!" *Mark 7:8-9*

---

Two Chinese jugglers have been making a public exhibition of their skill. One of them is set up as a target, and the other shows his dexterity by hurling knives that stick into the board at his comrade's back, close to the man's body. These deadly weapons fix themselves between his arms and legs, and between each of his fingers, they fly past his ears, and over his head, and on each side of his neck. The art is *not* to hit him. There seem to be quite a number of preachers who are remarkably proficient in the same art in the mental and spiritual departments.

# Preaching the Gospel to Rich and Poor, Wise and Foolish

"Children, how hard it is to enter the kingdom of God! It is easier for a camel to go through the eye of a needle than for a rich man to enter the kingdom of God." *Mark 10:24-25*

I am obligated both to Greeks and non-Greeks, both to the wise and the foolish. . . . I am not ashamed of the gospel, because it is the power of God for the salvation of everyone who believes. *Romans 1:14, 16*

---

John Wesley always preferred the middle and lower classes to the wealthy. He said, "If I might choose, I would still, as I have done up till now, preach the gospel to the poor." Preaching in a Monktown church, a large old, ruinous building, he said, "I suppose it has rarely had such a congregation during this century. Many of them were gay, genteel people. So I spoke on the first elements of the gospel, but I was still out of their depth. Oh, how hard it is to be *shallow* enough for a polite audience!"

# Passing Fancies or the Solid Food of Truth?

You are slow to learn. In fact, though by this time you ought to be teachers, you need someone to teach you the elementary truths of God's word all over again. You need milk, not solid food! Anyone who lives on milk, being still an infant, is not acquainted with the teaching about righteousness. But solid food is for the mature, who by constant use have trained themselves to distinguish good from evil. *Hebrews 5:11-14*

---

People gathered in crowds around the statue and looked at it again and again. It was not the finest work of art in the city, nor the most intrinsically attractive. Why, then, did the citizens of Verona stand in such clusters around the effigy of Dante on that summer's evening? Do you guess the reason? Was it a fête in honor of the poet? No, it was an ordinary evening, and there was nothing peculiar in the date of the events of the day. The reason was very simple: *the statue was new.* It had, in fact, only been unveiled the day before. Everyone passes Dante now, having other things to think of; the citizens are well used to his solemn visage and scarcely care that he stands among them. Is not this the way people are?

I am sure it is so with us ministers. New brooms sweep clean. What crowds follow a newly popular minister! How they step on one another to hear him, not necessarily because he is very wise or eloquent, much less because he is eminently holy, but because he is new and curiosity must gratify itself! In a few short months, the idol of the hour is stale, flat, and unprofitable; he is a mediocrity, there are scores as good as he. Indeed, another new man, at the other end of town, is far better. And off go the wonder-hunters! Folly brought them; folly removes them. Babies must have new toys.

# Not Just Entertainment

Do not let any unwholesome talk come out of your mouths, but only what is helpful for building others up according to their needs, that it may benefit those who listen. *Ephesians 4:29*

Do not be quick with your mouth, do not be hasty in your heart to utter anything before God. God is in heaven and you are on earth, so let your words be few. As a dream comes when there are many cares, so the speech of a fool when there are many words. *Ecclesiastes 5:2-3*

---

When Handel's *Messiah* oratorio had won the admiration of many of the great, Lord Kinnoul took occasion to pay him some compliments on the noble entertainment that he had lately given the town.

"My lord," said Handel, "I should be sorry if I only entertained them. I wish to make them better."

It is to be feared that many speech-makers at public meetings could not say as much, and yet how dare any of us waste the time of our fellow immortals in mere amusing talk! If we have nothing to speak to edification, how much better to hold our tongues!

# The Church, God's Glory

His intent was that now, through the church, the manifold wisdom of God should be made known to the rulers and authorities in the heavenly realms, according to his eternal purpose which he accomplished in Christ Jesus our Lord. . . . Now to him who is able to do immeasurably more than all we ask or imagine, according to his power that is at work within us, to him be glory in the church and in Christ Jesus throughout all generations, for ever and ever!
*Ephesians 3:10-11, 20-21*

---

The palace of Versailles with its countless representations of battles, sieges, stormings, surprises, and all other forms of wholesale and retail murder, is dedicated, according to an inscription on its front, "To all the glories of France." One might as well consecrate a slaughterhouse to all the glories of a butcher.

But what a glorious spiritual palace is the church, and how truly is it dedicated to all the glories of the Lord Jesus! Within its walls hang memorials of battles far more worthy of the historian's quill than those of Austerlitz or Wagram; victories are there commemorated which put to the blush all the achievements of Charlemagnes or Napoleon. For the contests are with evil principles, and the conquests are triumphs over iniquity and rebellion. There are no garments rolled in blood; fire and vapor smoke are not there, but rather the efficacy of atonement, the energy of grace, the Omnipotence of the Holy Ghost, the power of eternal love, all these are there, and happy are the eyes that see them. May the life of each one of us contribute a new work of celestial art to those which already represent to angels and heavenly intelligences, "the glories of Christ."

# Trumpet Call

We believe that Jesus died and rose again and so we believe that God will bring with Jesus those who have fallen asleep in him. According to the Lord's own word, we tell you that we who are still alive, who are left till the coming of the Lord, will certainly not precede those who have fallen asleep. For the Lord himself will come down from heaven, with a loud command, with the voice of the archangel and with the trumpet call of God, and the dead in Christ will rise first. After that, we who are still alive and are left will be caught up together with them in the clouds to meet the Lord in the air. And so we will be with the Lord forever. *1 Thessalonians 4:14-17*

---

At Harzburg in the Hartz mountains, we were awakened early in the morning, according to an ancient custom, by the sound of a trumpet, which made us pray that when the last trumpet sounds it may awaken us to an endless Sabbath. It would be wonderful if all hearts and minds heard at the dawn of the Lord's day "the sound of a trumpet," so that every faculty might be aroused to the highest activity of holy service. Sleepy hearing, praying, and singing are terrible. Sleepy preaching and teaching are worse, yet how common they are, and how many need the trumpet at the ear!

# Evening Wolves

But there were also false prophets among the people, just as there will be false teachers among you. They will secretly introduce destructive heresies, even denying the sovereign Lord who bought them—bringing swift destruction on themselves. Many will follow their shameful ways and bring the way of truth into disrepute. *2 Peter 2:1-2*

If anyone teaches false doctrines and does not agree to the sound instruction of our Lord Jesus Christ and to godly teaching, he is conceited and understands nothing. He has an unhealthy interest in controversies and arguments that result in envy, quarreling, malicious talk, evil suspicions, and constant friction between men of corrupt mind, who have been robbed of the truth and who think that godliness is a means to financial gain. *1 Timothy 6:3-5*

---

There are no greater foes to sheep than wild dogs. In some regions, sheep were no longer to be found because these fierce creatures utterly devoured the flocks. The church has never had worse enemies than false teachers. Infidels and persecutors do but mild injury to her, but her heretical preachers have been as evening wolves.

# Melted Hearts

Live such good lives among the pagans that, though they accuse you of doing wrong, they may see your good deeds and glorify God on the day he visits us. *1 Peter 2:12*

---

The hand must be quick if it is to make an impression in melted wax. Once the wax is cool, you will press the seal in vain. It becomes cold and hard in just a few moments, therefore let the work be quickly done. When men's hearts are melted under the preaching of the Word, or by sickness, or the loss of friends, believers should be very eager to stamp the truth on the prepared mind. Such opportunities are to be seized with holy eagerness. If you love the Lord Jesus, hasten with the seal before the wax is cool.

# Holy Boldness

The righteous are as bold as a lion. *Proverbs 28:1*

Therefore, since we have such a hope, we are very bold. *2 Corinthians 3:12*

---

Holy boldness honors the gospel. In the olden times, when Oriental despots had things pretty much their own way, they expected all ambassadors from the West to lay their mouths in the dust if permitted to appear before his Celestial Brightness, the Brother of the Sun and the Cousin of the Moon. Money-loving traders agreed to all this and ate dust as readily as reptiles, but when England sent her ambassadors abroad, the daring islanders stood bolt upright. They were told that they could not be indulged with a vision of the Brother of the Sun and the Cousin of the Moon without going down on their hands and knees. "Very well," said the Englishmen, "we will dispense with the luxury. But tell his Celestial Splendor that it is very likely that his Serenity will hear our cannon at his palace gates before long, and that their booming is not quite so harmless as the cooing of his Sublimity's doves." The ambassadors of the British Crown were no cringing petitioners; the British empire rose in the respect of the Oriental nations.

Our cowardice has subjected the gospel to contempt. Jesus was humble, and his servants must not be proud, but Jesus was never mean or cowardly, nor must his servants be. There was no braver man than Christ. He could stoop to save a soul, but he would stoop to nothing by which his character might be compromised, or truth and righteousness insulted. To preach the gospel boldly is to deliver it as such a message ought to be delivered. Blush to preach of a dying Savior? Apologize for talking about the Son of God condescending to be made man, that he might redeem us from all iniquity? *Never!* Oh, by the grace of God let us purpose with Paul "to be yet more bold," that the gospel may be yet more fully preached throughout all ranks of mankind.

# Life or Death?

"Today, if you hear his voice, do not harden your hearts." *Hebrews 4:7*

Come near to me and listen to this . . . This is what the LORD says—your Redeemer, the Holy One of Israel: "I am the LORD your God, who teaches you what is best for you, who directs you in the way you should go. If only you had paid attention to my commands, your peace would have been like a river, your righteousness like the waves of the sea" . . . They did not thirst when he led them through the deserts; he made water flow for them from the rock; he split the rock and water gushed out. "There is no peace," says the LORD, "for the wicked." *Isaiah 48:16, 17-18, 21-22*

---

We crossed and recrossed a river several times by the ferry-boat with no purpose in the world but mere amusement and curiosity, to watch the simple machinery by which the same current is made to drift the boat in opposite directions from side to side. To other passengers it was a business, to us a sport.

Our hearers use our ministry in much the same manner when they come to it out of the idlest curiosity and listen to us as a means of spending a pleasant hour. That which should ferry them across to a better state of soul, they use as a mere pleasure-boat to sail up and down in, making no progress after years of hearing. It may be sport to them, but it is death to us, because we know it will before long be death to them.

# A Loving, Gentle Shepherd

Keep watch over yourselves and all the flock of which the Holy Spirit has made you overseers. Be shepherds of the church of God, which he bought with his own blood. *Acts 20:28*

Since an overseer is entrusted with God's work, he must be blameless—not overbearing, not quick-tempered, not given to drunkenness, not violent, not pursuing dishonest gain. Rather he must be hospitable, one who loves what is good, who is self-controlled, upright, holy and disciplined. He must hold firmly to the trustworthy message as it has been taught, so that he can encourage others by sound doctrine and refute those who oppose it. *Titus 1:7-9*

---

In a church in Verona stands, or rather sits, a wooden image of St. Zeno, an ancient bishop, with knees so ludicrously short that there is no lap on which a baby could be held. He was not the first nor the last ecclesiastic who has been utterly incapable of being a nursing father to the church. It would be good if all ministers had a heavenly instinct for the nourishing and bringing up of the Lord's little ones, but this quality is sadly lacking.

# A Burden for Evangelism

# Working for Christ until the End

"No one knows about that day or hour, not even the angels in heaven, nor the Son, but only the Father. . . . Therefore keep watch, because you do not know on what day your Lord will come. But understand this: If the owner of the house had known at what time of night the thief was coming, he would have kept watch and would not have let his house be broken into. So you also must be ready, because the Son of Man will come at an hour when you do not expect him. Who then is the faithful and wise servant, whom the master has put in charge of the servants in his household to give them their food at the proper time? It will be good for that servant whose master finds him doing so when he returns. *Matthew 24:36, 42-46*

---

The minister of Christ should feel like the old keeper of Eddystone lighthouse. Life was failing fast, but summoning all his strength, he crept round once more to trim the lights before he died. May the Holy Ghost enable his servants to keep the beacon fire blazing, to warn sinners of the rocks, shoals, and quicksands that surround them.

# Sharing the Good News with Fervency

Build yourselves up in your most holy faith and pray in the Holy Spirit. Keep yourselves in God's love as you wait for the mercy of our Lord Jesus Christ to bring you to eternal life. Be merciful to those who doubt; snatch others from the fire and save them; to others show mercy, mixed with fear—hating even the clothing stained by corrupted flesh. *Jude 20-23*

---

"A traveler was journeying in the darkness of night along a road that led to a deep and rapid river, which, swollen by sudden rains, was chafing and roaring within its precipitous banks. The bridge that crossed the stream had been swept away by the torrent, but he didn't know it. A man met him and said to him in an indifferent way, 'Are you aware that the bridge is gone? I heard such a report this afternoon, and though I am not certain about it, perhaps you had better not proceed.'

"Deceived by the hesitating and undecided manner in which the information was given, the traveler pushed on in the way of death. Soon another came along and cried out in consternation, 'Sir, sir, the bridge is gone!'

" 'Oh, yes,' " replied the traveler. " 'Someone told me that story a little while ago, but I'm sure it is an idle tale.' "

" 'Oh, it is true!' exclaimed the other. 'I barely escaped being carried away with it myself. You must not go on.' In the excitement of his feelings, he grasped the traveler by the hands, by the arms, by the clothes. Convinced by the earnest voice, the earnest eyes, the earnest gestures, the traveler turned back and was saved.

"So it is only through a burning zeal for the salvation of the lost—a zeal glowing in the heart and flashing out in look and action and utterance—that the confidence of unbelief can be overcome and the heedless travelers of the broad way won to the path of life and happiness. Love is the most potent logic: interest and sympathy are the most subduing eloquence."—*Christian Work*

# Rescue the Perishing

In the presence of God and of Christ Jesus, who will judge the living and the dead, and in view of his appearing and his kingdom, I give you this charge: Preach the Word. *2 Timothy 4:1-2*

---

Thomas Fuller gives the following interesting account of Gervase Scroop, Knight: "He engaged with his majesty in Edgehill fight, where he received twenty-six wounds and was left on the ground among the dead. Next day his son Adrian obtained leave from the king to find and fetch his father's corpse, and his hopes pretended no higher than to a decent interment thereof.

Hearty seeking makes happy finding. Indeed, some more commended the affection than the judgment of the young gentleman, concerning such a search in vain among many naked bodies, where pale death had confounded all complexions together.

However, he having some general hint of the place where his father fell, did light upon his body, which had some heat left therein. This heat was, with rubbing, within a few minutes, improved into motion; within some hours, into sense; that sense, within a day, into speech; that speech, within certain weeks, into a perfect recovery, living more than ten years after, a monument of God's mercy and his son's affection."

True love of souls will seek them out with all the eagerness of this heroic son, and finding them, will be as persevering in attempts to save. Not all at once shall we see all we could wish in the objects of our holy care, but no difficulties must daunt us. We must continue by God's grace to agonize for their souls until we see them safe in Christ. The little awakened interest that cheers us must be nursed into anxiety, and through the Holy Spirit we must labor to see anxiety turned into hope, and hope to faith and salvation. None are too far gone for zeal and prayer. Love is ever hopeful, and God is ever gracious. Let us renew our search, and the Lord send us good speed today.

# Courageous and Creative Witnesses

"But you will receive power when the Holy Spirit comes upon you; and you will be my witnesses in Jerusalem, and in Judea and Samaria, and to the ends of the earth." *Acts 1:8*

---

In Switzerland, where land is very precious because rock abounds and the rugged soil is chary in its yieldings, you see the husbandman looking after a little tuft of grass growing on one of the edges of a lofty cliff. From the valley he had caught a sight of it and thought of clambering up to where it grew, but the rock was all too steep. From a ledge nearer the top of the precipitous wall he looked down but could see no pathway to the coveted morsel of green. That armful of grass would feed his goat, or help to fill the cottage loft with winter fodder for the cow. Every armful is an item, and he cannot forego that tempting clump. He looks and looks, and looks again, but looks in vain. By and by, he fetches his bold boy who can follow wherever a chamois can climb, but the boy after a hard scramble comes back with the tidings, "Father, it cannot be done." The father's answer is, "Boy, it must be done." It is only an armful, and would not be worth a farthing to us, but to the poor mountaineer even a farthing or a farthing's worth is precious. The grass waves its flowers in the breeze and scorns the daring climbers from below. But where there is a will there is a way. And what cannot be reached from below may be gained from above. With a rope slung around him or firmly grasped in his accustomed hand, with a stout stake or tree to hold it up above, the man is let down till he gets to the jutting crag, there he stands with his sickle, reaps the grass, ties it into a bundle, puts it under his arm, and climbing back again, joyfully returns with his little harvest. Poor pay, you think, for such dangerous toil, but, fellow worker for Jesus, I wish we were as venturesome for souls and as careful of them, as these poor peasants are concerning miserable bundles of grass. I wish that we sometimes looked up or down on apparently inaccessible spots and resolved to reach immortal souls who are to be found there, and pined to bring them to Christ.

---

# Filled with God's Love

Since, then, you have been raised with Christ, set your hearts on things above, where Christ is seated at the right hand of God. Set your minds on things above, not on earthly things. For you died, and your life is now hidden with Christ in God. *Colossians 3:1-3*

---

When Audubon, the celebrated American ornithologist, was in Paris he grew quite weary of it, and his diary does not contain a cheerful word about that city until he writes, "The stock pigeon roosts in the trees of the garden of the Tuileries in great numbers; blackbirds also do the same, and are extremely noisy before dark; some rooks and magpies are seen there also. In the Jardin, or walks of the Palais Royal, common sparrows are prodigiously plentiful. The mountain finch passes in scattered numbers over Paris at this season, going northerly." So also when in London the great naturalist was quite out of his element and only seemed pleased when a flight of wildfowl passed over the city. Here was the secret of his success—his complete absorption in his one study—birds alone had charm for him. We who would attain to eminence in the service of Christ must let the love of souls, in an equal way, master and engross us. When writing a paper for the Natural History Society upon the habits of the wild pigeon, Audubon says, "So absorbed was my whole soul and spirit in the work, that I felt as if I were in the woods of America, among the pigeons, and my ears were filled with the sound of their rustling wings." We should all write, speak, and preach for our Lord Jesus far more powerfully if our love to the Lord were a passion so dominant as to make the great realities of eternity vividly real and supremely commanding in our minds.

# Waiting for an Invitation

"Everyone who calls on the name of the Lord will be saved." How, then, can they call on the one they have not believed in? And how can they believe in the one of whom they have not heard? And how can they hear without someone preaching to them? And how can they preach unless they are sent? As it is written, "How beautiful are the feet of those who bring good news!" *Romans 10:13-15*

---

"A Sunday school teacher once visited a poor family in one of the top apartments of a tenement in a small but clean room. From conversation with the father and mother, she soon discovered that since the beginning of a long illness of the father, the family had fallen from comparative comfort to poverty. He was now, however, better, and had been able for some time to work a little, so as to keep his family from destitution, but by no means to enable them to live in comfort. Having learned so much of their worldly concerns, their visitor next began to speak of their souls' interests. She asked them if they went to any church. 'No,' said the father. 'We used to go long ago, before I took ill, but we went no more after that.'

" 'But you have been better for a good while,' said the teacher.

" 'But nobody ever asked us to come!'

" 'Well,' said the visitor, 'I'll ask you now,' and she directed him to a church where he would hear the glad tidings from a faithful minister. The next Sunday several of the children were at her Sunday school and told her that their family had been at church. Since that day they have been hearers of the Word. How many souls are perishing 'because, though all things are now ready, nobody ever asked them to come!' Will not the blood of their souls be required at the hand of those who profess to have tasted a Savior's love, and yet make not one effort to pluck brands out of the fire?"—*Scottish Sunday School Teacher's Magazine*

---

# That All Would Be Saved

I urge, then, first of all, that requests, prayers, intercession and thanksgiving be made for everyone—for kings and all those in authority, that we may live peaceful and quiet lives in all godliness and holiness. This is good, and pleases God our Savior, who wants all men to be saved and to come to a knowledge of the truth. For there is one God and one mediator between God and men, the man Christ Jesus, who gave himself as a ransom for all men—the testimony given in its proper time. . . . I want men everywhere to lift up holy hands in prayer. *1 Timothy 2:1-6, 8*

---

What if a man convicted of high treason and condemned to die was not only pardoned but taken into the favor of his sovereign? If he were riding in the royal carriage and on the road he saw some of his fellow traitors pinioned and manacled, led forth in the midst of officers to die for the offense in which he had as deep a hand as they, wouldn't he entreat the gracious monarch to extend his clemency to his fellow rebels? Wouldn't the tears stand in his eyes as he admires the difference that his sovereign's free mercy has made? Wouldn't he be moved with emotions impossible to describe, of mingled joy and grief, pity and gratitude, wonder and compassion?

The Christian's likeness is drawn here. Surely each Christian must feel ready to fall down on his knees, and cry, "Lord, why do you reveal your mercy to me and not to these others? Save them, also, Lord, for your name's sake."

# Sharing the Great Discovery

How can they believe in the one of whom they have not heard? And how can they hear without someone preaching to them? And how can they preach unless they are sent? As it is written, "How beautiful are the feet of those who bring good news!" *Romans 10:14-15*

For Christ's love compels us, because we are convinced that one died for all, and therefore all died. And he died for all, that those who live should no longer live for themselves but for him who died for them and was raised again. *2 Corinthians 5:14-15*

---

Huber, the great naturalist, tells us that if a single wasp discovers a deposit of honey or other food, he will return to his nest and depart the good news to his companions, who will sally forth in great numbers to partake of the fare which has been discovered for them.

Shall we who have found honey in the rock Christ Jesus be less considerate of our fellow men than wasps are of their fellow insects? Ought we not rather like the Samaritan woman to hasten to tell the good news? Common humanity should prevent one of us from concealing the great discovery which grace has enabled us to make.

# A Burden for Souls

"My food," said Jesus, "is to do the will of him who sent me and to finish his work. Do you not say, 'Four months more and then the harvest'? I tell you, open your eyes and look at the fields! They are ripe for harvest. Even now the reaper draws his wages, even now he harvests the crop for eternal life, so that the sower and the reaper may be glad together." *John 4:34-36*

"It is not the healthy who need a doctor, but the sick. But go and learn what this means: 'I desire mercy, not sacrifice.' For I have not come to call the righteous, but sinners." *Matthew 9:12-13*

---

Living in the midst of the church of God is like sailing down the Nile in a boat. One is charmed with the luxuriance of either bank, and with much that is beautiful immediately around; but alas! at a little distance on either side lies a vast uncultivated, almost hopeless, desert. Some are at rest because they never look beyond the borders of the church, but those whose sympathies reach to all humanity will have to carry a lifelong "burden of the Lord."

# Tender-Hearted Sharing

"This is the one I esteem: he who is humble and contrite in spirit, and trembles at my word." *Isaiah 66:2*

In the presence of God and of Christ Jesus, who will judge the living and the dead, and in view of his appearing and his kingdom, I give you this charge: Preach the Word; be prepared in season and out of season; correct, rebuke, and encourage—with great patience and careful instruction. *2 Timothy 4:1-2*

---

"I was never fit to say a word to a sinner, except when I had a broken heart myself, when I was subdued and melted into penitency, and felt as though I had just received pardon to my own soul, and when my heart was full of tenderness and pity. No anger, no anger."
—*Payson*

# Growing in Godliness

# The Warmth of the Spirit

*Since we live by the Spirit, let us keep in step with the Spirit.*
*Galatians 5:25*

*Do not put out the Spirit's fire. 1 Thessalonians 5:19*

---

"On a winter's day I noticed a row of cottages with a deep load of snow on their roofs. As the day wore on, large fragments began to tumble from the eaves of this one and that other till, by and by, there was a simultaneous avalanche, and the whole heap slid over in powdery ruin on the pavement. Before the sun went down you could see each roof as clear and dry as on a summer evening. But here and there was a roof with its snow-mantle unbroken, and a ruff of stiff icicles around it. What made the difference? The difference was to be found within. Some of these cottages were empty, or the lonely inhabitant cowered over a scanty fire. In the peopled homes, the high-blazing kindling created such an inward warmth that grim winter melted and relaxed his grip, and the loosened mass folded off and tumbled over on the trampled street. It is possible by some outside process to push the main volume of snow from the frosty roof, or chip off the icicles one by one. But they will form again, and it needs an inward heat to create a total thaw. And so, by sundry processes, you may clear from a man's conduct the dead weight of conspicuous sins, but it needs a hidden heat, a vital warmth within, to produce such a separation between the soul and its besetting iniquities, that the whole wintry incubus, the entire body of sin, will come spontaneously away. That vital warmth is the love of God abundantly shed abroad—the kindly glow which the Comforter diffuses in the soul which he makes his home. His genial inhabitation thaws that soul and its favorite sins asunder, and makes the indolence and self-indulgence and indevotion fall off from their old resting-place on that dissolving heart. The easiest form of self-mortification is a fervent spirit."—*James Hamilton, D.D.*

# Pointing the Finger

"Why do you look at the speck of sawdust in your brother's eye and pay no attention to the plank in your own eye? How can you say to your brother, 'Let me take the speck out of your eye,' when all the time there is a plank in your own eye? You hypocrite, first take the plank out of your own eye, and then you will see clearly to remove the speck from your brother's eye." *Matthew 7:3-5*

---

Pedley, who was a well-known natural simpleton, often said, "God help the fool." None are more ready to pity the folly of others than those who have a small share of it themselves.

"There is no love among Christians," cries the man who is destitute of true charity.

"Zeal has vanished," exclaims the idle talker.

"Oh for more consistency," groans out the hypocrite.

"We want more vital godliness," protests the false pretender. As in the old legend, the wolf preached against sheep-stealing, so very many hunt down those sins in others which they gladly shelter in themselves.

# Fruit in Its Season

Blessed is the man who does not walk in the counsel of the wicked or stand in the way of sinners or sit in the seat of mockers. But his delight is in the law of the LORD, and on his law he meditates day and night. He is like a tree planted by streams of water, which yields its fruit in season and whose leaf does not wither. *Psalm 1:1-3*

Bear with each other and forgive whatever grievances you may have against one another. Forgive as the Lord forgave you. And over all these virtues put on love, which binds them all together in perfect unity. *Colossians 3:13-14*

---

It is said in praise of the tree firmly planted by the rivers of water that it brings forth its fruit *in its season.* Good men should aim to have seasonable virtues. For instance, a forgiving spirit is golden if it displays itself in the moment when an injury is received. It is but silver if it shows itself on speedy reflection. And it is merely lead if it be manifested only after a long time of cooling.

# Slow Growing

Make every effort to add to your faith goodness; and to goodness, knowledge; and to knowledge, self-control; and to self-control, perseverance; and to perseverance, godliness; and to godliness, brotherly kindness; and to brotherly kindness, love. For if you possess these qualities in increasing measure, they will keep you from being ineffective and unproductive in your knowledge of our Lord Jesus Christ. *2 Peter 1:5-8*

We will in all things grow up into him who is the Head, that is, Christ. From him the whole body, joined and held together by every supporting ligament, grows and builds itself up in love, as each part does its work. *Ephesians 4:15-16*

---

Lettuces, radishes, and such garden crops are soon out of the ground and ready for the table—a month almost suffices to perfect them. But an oak requires long centuries to come to the fullness of its growth.

Those graces which are most precious and durable will cost us longest to produce. Those good things which spring up hastily may have some transient worth about them, but we cannot look for permanence and value in them. There is no need to deplore the slowness of our spiritual growth, if that which comes of it is of a solid character.

# Know Them by Their Fruits

"You are the light of the world. A city on a hill cannot be hidden. Neither do people light a lamp and put it under a bowl. Instead they put it on its stand, and it gives light to everyone in the house. In the same way, let your light shine before men, that they may see your good deeds and praise your Father in heaven." *Matthew 5:14-16*

"By their fruit you will recognize them. Do people pick grapes from thornbushes, or figs from thistles? Likewise every good tree bears good fruit, but a bad tree bears bad fruit. . . . Thus, by their fruit you will recognize them." *Matthew 7:16-17, 20*

---

Longfellow in his Hiawatha sings of

*The pleasant watercourses,*
*You could trace them through the valley,*
*By the rushing in the Springtime,*
*By the alders in the Summer,*
*By the white fog in the Autumn,*
*By the black line in the Winter.*

So traceable are the lives of really gracious men and women. They are not solicitous to be observed, but the gracious "signs following" are sure to reveal them. Like their Master they cannot be hid.

# The King's Daughter

"The LORD does not look at the things man looks at. Man looks at the outward appearance, but the LORD looks at the heart." *1 Samuel 16:7*

---

"A poor but pious woman called upon two elegant young ladies who, regardless of her poverty, invited her to sit down with them in the drawing room and entered into conversation with her on religious subjects. While thus occupied, their brother, a dashing youth, by chance entered and appeared astonished to see his sisters so comfortable with the woman. One of them instantly exclaimed, 'Brother, don't be surprised! This is a king's daughter, though she has not yet put on her fine clothes.' "—*Pioneer*

# Speaking Words that Edify

The tongue of the righteous is choice silver. . . . The lips of the righteous nourish many. *Proverbs 10:20-21*

The tongue of the wise brings healing. *Proverbs 12:18*

The tongue of the wise commends knowledge. . . . The tongue that brings healing is a tree of life. *Proverbs 15:2, 4*

The lips of the wise spread knowledge. *Proverbs 15:7*

---

The Spaniards in Chili believed that no water was so wholesome or of so delicate a flavor as that which flowed through veins of gold. Certainly no conversation is so edifying to the hearers as that which pours forth from a heart stored with sacred knowledge, sanctified experience, devout contemplations, and such like precious treasures.

# Stony Places to Soft Soil

Have mercy on me, O God, according to your unfailing love; according to your great compassion blot out my transgressions. Wash away all my iniquity and cleanse me from my sin. . . . Create in me a pure heart, O God, and renew a steadfast spirit within me. Do not cast me from your presence or take your Holy Spirit from me. Restore to me the joy of your salvation and grant me a willing spirit, to sustain me. *Psalm 51:1-2, 10-12*

---

In preparing places for planting new trees, the diggers found it necessary in certain spots to lay aside the spade and use the pick-axe. In those positions there had been a well-graveled carriage road, and hence the ground was hard to deal with.

How often, when we are under sanctifying influences, do we find certain hard points of our character which are not touched by ordinary influences. These are most probably sins in which we have become hardened, tracks worn by habitual transgression. We must not wonder if the severest processes of affliction should be tried upon us, if the pick-axe is used instead of the spade, that our stony places may yet yield soil for the plants of grace and holiness.

# Ready and Active

Be strong in the Lord and in his mighty power. Put on the full armor of God so that you can take your stand against the devil's schemes. For our struggle is not against flesh and blood, but against the rulers, against the authorities, against the powers of this dark world and against the spiritual forces of evil in the heavenly realms. Therefore, put on the full armor of God, so that when the day of evil comes, you may be able to stand your ground, and after you have done everything, to stand. Stand firm then, with the belt of truth buckled around your waist, with the breastplate of righteousness in place, and with your feet fitted with the readiness that comes from the gospel of peace. In addition to all this, take up the shield of faith with which you can extinguish all the flaming arrows of the evil one. Take the helmet of salvation and the sword of the Spirit, which is the word of God. *Ephesians 6:10-17*

---

James the First once said of armor that "it was an excellent invention, for it not only saved the life of the wearer, but it hindered him from doing harm to anybody else." Equally destructive to all usefulness is that excessive prudence upon which some professing Christians pride themselves. Not only do they escape all persecution, but they are never able to strike a blow, much less fight a battle for the Lord Jesus.

# Guarding Your "Inner Springs"

*"Nothing outside a man can make him 'unclean' by going into him. Rather, it is what comes out of a man that makes him 'unclean.' "*
*Mark 7:15*

All a man's ways seem innocent to him, but motives are weighed by the LORD. *Proverbs 16:2*

---

Standing near the remarkable spring at Ewell, in Surrey, England, and watching the uprising of the waters, one sees at the bottom of the pool innumerable circles with smaller circles within them, from which extremely fine sand is continually being heaved up by the force of the rising water. Tiny geysers toss up their little founts, and a myriad of openings bubble up with the clear crystal. The perpetual motion of the water, and the leaping of the sand are most interesting. It is not like the spring-head in a field, where the cooling liquid pours forth perpetually from a spout, all unseen, till it plunges into its channel; nor like the river-head where the stream weeps from a mass of mossy rock. But here are the fountains of earth's hidden deeps all unveiled and laid bare, the very veins of nature opened to the public gaze. How it would amaze us if we could in this fashion peer into the springs of human character and see whence words and actions flow! What man would wish to have his designs and aims exposed to every onlooker? But why this aversion to being known and read of all men? The Christian's motives and springs of action should be so honest and pure that he might safely defy inspection. He who has nothing to be ashamed of has nothing to conceal. Sincerity can afford, like our first parents in Paradise, to be naked and not ashamed.

Stand by your inner springs and watch, and make faithful notes of what you see, lest you be deceived.

# Fleeing Temptation

Flee from sexual immorality. All other sins a man commits are outside his body, but he who sins sexually sins against his own body. Do you not know that your body is a temple of the Holy Spirit, who is in you, whom you have received from God? You are not your own; you were bought at a price. Therefore honor God with your body. *1 Corinthians 6:18-20*

You were taught, with regard to your former way of life, to put off your old self, which is being corrupted by its deceitful desires; to be made new in the attitude of your minds; and to put on the new self, created to be like God in true righteousness and holiness. *Ephesians 4:22-24*

---

One of the ancient fathers, we are told, had lived with a woman before his conversion, and a short time after she accosted him as usual. Knowing how likely he was to fall into sin, he ran away with all his might, and she ran after him, crying, "Why do you run away? It's only me."

He answered, "I run away because I am not myself. I am a new man."

# Happy in Your Youth

Be happy, young man, while you are young, and let your heart give you joy in the days of your youth. Follow the ways of your heart and whatever your eyes see, but know that for all these things God will bring you to judgment. . . . Remember your Creator in the days of your youth, before the days of trouble come. . . . Remember him—before the silver cord is severed, or the golden bowl is broken; before the pitcher is shattered at the spring, or the wheel broken at the well, and the dust returns to the ground it came from, and the spirit returns to God who gave it. *Ecclesiastes 11:9, 12:1, 6-7*

---

In an election the first votes recorded count all the day long, and they encourage the party all through the anxious hours of polling. When men give in their names for Jesus and his cause in the morning of their lives, their whole existence influences their time, and their encouragement to the good cause is lifelong.

# Devotion and Holiness

Guard the good deposit that was entrusted to you —guard it with the help of the Holy Spirit who lives in us. *2 Timothy 1·14*

---

While the Austrian general was staying at the Hotel de Ville, upon the Grand Canal at Venice, I lodged at the same house, and as often as I passed his rooms, whether during the day or at night, I encountered two sentries on guard at the door. My heart said to itself, whenever the King of kings deigns to make a chamber of my spirit, let me set holiness and devotion to be sentries at the entrance. When our Beloved visits us he must not be disturbed. Ill thoughts must be repulsed, and carnal desires kept at a distance. With drawn swords let watchfulness preserve the sanctity of Immanuel's rest. "I charge you, O ye daughters of Jerusalem, by the roes and by the hinds of the field, that ye stir not up nor awake my love, till he please."

# Practicing Godliness

Train yourself to be godly. For physical training is of some value, but godliness has value for all things, holding promise for both the present life and the life to come. *1 Timothy 4:7-8*

Do you not know that in a race all the runners run, but only one gets the prize? Run in such a way as to get the prize. Everyone who competes in the games goes into strict training. They do it to get a crown that will not last; but we do it to get a crown that will last forever. *1 Corinthians 9:24-25*

---

A neighbor near my study persists in practicing on the flute. He bores my ears as with an auger and renders it almost an impossibility to think. Up and down his scale he runs remorselessly, until even the calamity of temporary deafness would almost be welcome to me. Yet he teaches me that I must practice if I would be perfect, must exercise myself unto godliness if I would be skillful, must, in fact, make myself familiar with the word of God, with holy living, and saintly dying. Such practice, moreover, will be as charming as my neighbor's flute is intolerable.

# Christ, the Standard of Holiness

Therefore, prepare your minds for action; be self-controlled; set your hope fully on the grace to be given you when Jesus Christ is revealed. As obedient children, do not conform to the evil desires you had when you lived in ignorance. But just as he who called you is holy, so be holy in all you do; for it is written: "Be holy, because I am holy." Since you call on a Father who judges each man's work impartially, live your lives as strangers here in reverent fear. For you know that it was not with perishable things such as silver or gold that you were redeemed from the empty way of life handed down to you from your forefathers, but with the precious blood of Christ, a lamb without blemish or defect. He was chosen before the creation of the world, but was revealed in these last times for your sake. Through him you believe in God, who raised him from the dead and glorified him, and so your faith and hope are in God. *1 Peter 1:13-21*

---

The bloom of the hawthorn or White May looks like snow out in the country, but near the vast city or along the roadside its virgin whiteness is sadly stained. Too often contact with the world has just such an effect on our piety. We must make our way to the far-off garden of Paradise to see holiness in its unsullied purity, and meanwhile we must be much alone with God if we would maintain a gracious life below.

# Beautiful Obedience, Every Hour of the Day

Since the day we heard about you, we have not stopped praying for you and asking God to fill you with the knowledge of his will through all spiritual wisdom and understanding. And we pray this in order that you may live a life worthy of the Lord and may please him in every way: bearing fruit in every good work, growing in the knowledge of God, being strengthened with all power according to his glorious might so that you may have great endurance and patience, and joyfully giving thanks to the Father. *Colossians 1:9-12*

---

Linneaus, the great Swedish botanist, observing the beautiful order that reigns among flowers, proposed the use of a floral clock, to be composed of plants that open and close their blossoms at particular hours, as for instance the dandelion which opens its petals at six in the morning, the hawkweed at seven, the succory at eight, the celandine at nine, and so on; the closing of the flowers being marked with equal regularity so as to indicate the progress of the afternoon and evening.

> *Thus has each hour its own rich hue,*
> *And its graceful cup or bell,*
> *In whose colored vase may sleep the dew,*
> *Like a pearl in an ocean shell.*

Wouldn't it be lovely if in the same way, with flowers of grace and blossoms of virtue, we decorated every passing hour, fulfilling all the duties of each season and honoring him who makes the coming and going of morning and the evening to rejoice! Thus with undeviating regularity to obey the influence of the Sun of Righteousness, and give each following moment its due, were to begin the life of heaven beneath the stars.

---

# Joyful Obedience

For I delight in your commandments because I love them. I reach out my hands for your commandments, which I love, and I meditate on your decrees. . . . I have kept my feet from every evil path so that I might obey your word. I have not departed from your laws for you yourself have taught me. How sweet are your promises to my taste, sweeter than honey to my mouth! I gain understanding from your precepts; therefore I hate every wrong path. . . . Your commands are my delight. Your statutes are forever right; give me understanding that I may live. *Psalm 119:47-48, 101-104, 143-144*

---

" 'I wish I could mind God the way my little dog minds me,' said a little boy, looking thoughtfully on his shaggy friend. 'He always looks so *pleased* to mind, and I don't.' What a painful truth this child spoke! Shall the poor little dog thus readily obey his master, and we rebel against God, who is our Creator, our Preserver, our Father, our Savior, and the bountiful Giver of everything we love?"—*Christian Treasury*

# Life in Two Worlds

Therefore, I urge you, brothers, in view of God's mercy, to offer your bodies as living sacrifices, holy and pleasing to God—this is your spiritual worship. Do not conform any longer to the pattern of this world, but be transformed by the renewing of your mind. Then you will be able to test and approve what God's will is—his good, pleasing and perfect will. *Romans 12:1-2*

For he [the Father] has rescued us from the dominion of darkness and brought us into the kingdom of the Son he loves, in whom we have redemption, the forgiveness of sins. *Colossians 1:13-14*

---

"A Christian lives in two worlds at one and the same time—the world of the flesh and the world of the spirit. It is possible to do both. There are certain dangerous gases, which from their weight fall to the lower part of the place where they are, making it destructive for a dog to enter, but safe for a man who holds his head erect. A Christian, as living in the world of flesh, is constantly passing through these. Let him keep his head erect in the spiritual world, and he is safe. He does this so long as the Son of God is the fountain where he draws his inspiration, his motives, encouragement, and strength."—*George Philip*

# Short on Spirituality

Anyone who lives on milk, being still an infant, is not acquainted with the teaching about righteousness. But solid food is for the mature, who by constant use have trained themselves to distinguish good from evil. Therefore let us leave the elementary teachings about Christ and go on to maturity. *Hebrews 5:13-6:1*

---

There was once in London a club of small men, whose qualification for membership lay in their not exceeding five feet in height. These dwarves held, or pretended to hold, the opinion that they were nearer the perfection of manhood than others, for they argued that primeval man had been far more gigantic than the present race, and consequently that the way of progress was to grow less and less, and that the human race as it perfected itself would become as diminutive as themselves. Such a club of Christians might be established in most cities, and without any difficulty might attain an enormously numerous membership. For the notion is common that our dwarfish Christianity is, after all, the standard, and many even imagine that nobler Christians are enthusiasts, fanatical and hot-blooded, while they themselves are cool because they are wise, and indifferent because they are intelligent.

# Never Stop Learning

"Get wisdom, get understanding . . . Do not forsake wisdom, and she will protect you; love her, and she will watch over you. Wisdom is supreme; therefore get wisdom. Though it cost all you have, get understanding." *Proverbs 4:5-7*

The heart of the discerning acquires knowledge; the ears of the wise seek it out. *Proverbs 18:15*

---

Wise men know their own ignorance and are always ready to learn. Humility is the child of knowledge. Michelangelo was found by the Cardinal Farnese walking in solitude amid the ruins of the Coliseum, and when he expressed his surprise, the great artist answered, "I go yet to school that I may continue to learn."

We need to learn from everything around us. Every person we encounter is able to teach us something, and we would be very foolish not to be able to learn from him.

# Cheerful Humility

Clothe yourselves with humility toward one another, because "God opposes the proud but gives grace to the humble." Humble yourselves, therefore, under God's mighty hand, that he may lift you up in due time. *1 Peter 5:5-6*

The cheerful heart has a continual feast. *Proverbs 15:15*

---

"Observe the peculiar characteristics of the grass which adapt it especially for the service of man: *humility* and *cheerfulness*. Its humility, in that it seems created only for lowest service, appointed to be trodden on and fed upon. Its cheerfulness, in that it seems to exult under all kinds of violence and suffering. You roll it, and it is the stronger the next day. You mow it, and it multiplies its shoots, as if it were grateful. You tread upon it, and it only sends up richer perfume. Spring comes, and it rejoices with all the earth, glowing with variegated flame of flowers, waving in soft depth of fruitful strength. Winter comes, and though it will not mock its fellow plants by growing then, it will not pine and mourn and turn colorless or leafless as they. It is always green, and is only the brighter and more cheerful for the hoarfrost."

So Ruskin poetically writes of grass; should it not be so with believers? Their flesh is like grass in its perishing; it would be well if their spirits were like grass in its humility and cheerfulness in service.

# Meditation, a Spiritual Exercise

I will remember the deeds of the LORD; yes, I will remember your miracles of long ago. I will meditate on all your works and consider all your mighty deeds. *Psalm 77:11-12*

Praise be to you, O LORD; teach me your decrees. With my lips I recount all the laws that come from your mouth. I rejoice in following your statutes as one rejoices in great riches. I meditate on your precepts and consider your ways. I delight in your decrees; I will not neglect your word. *Psalm 119:12-16*

---

Those who would be in health do not sit still in their houses to breathe such air as may come to them, but they walk abroad and seek out rural and elevated spots that they may inhale the invigorating breezes. Thus those godly souls who would be in a vigorous spiritual state do not merely think on whatever holy doctrines might come into their minds in the ordinary course of thought, but they give time to meditation, they walk abroad in the fields of truth, and endeavor to climb the heights of gospel promises. It is said that Enoch walked with God. Here is not an idle but an active communion. The road to bodily health is said to be a footpath, and the way to spiritual health is to exercise one's self in holy contemplation.

# The Circle of Fellowship

# Strength in Fellowship

Two are better than one, because they have a good return for their work: If one falls down, his friend can help him up. But pity the man who falls and has no one to help him up! Also, if two lie down together, they will keep warm. But how can one keep warm alone? Though one may be overpowered, two can defend themselves. A cord of three strands is not quickly broken. *Ecclesiastes 4:9-12*

---

Communion is strength; solitude is weakness. Alone, the fine old beech yields to the blast and lies prone on the meadow. In the forest, supporting each other, the trees laugh at the hurricane. The sheep of Jesus flock together. The social element is the genius of Christianity.

# Members of One Body

Let the peace of Christ rule in your hearts, since as members of one body you were called to peace. And be thankful. Let the word of Christ dwell in you richly as you teach and admonish one another with all wisdom, and as you sing psalms, hymns and spiritual songs with gratitude in your hearts to God. And whatever you do, whether in word or deed, do it all in the name of the Lord Jesus, giving thanks to God the Father through him. *Colossians 3:15-17*

---

What the circulation of the blood is to the human body, that the Holy Spirit is to the body of Christ which is the church. Now, by virtue of the one life-blood, every limb of the body holds fellowship with every other, and as long as life lasts that fellowship is inevitable. If the hand be unwashed the eye cannot refuse communion with it on that account. If the finger be diseased, the hand cannot, by binding a cord around it, prevent the life-current from flowing. Nothing but death can break up the fellowship. You must tear away the member, or it must of necessity commune with the rest of the body. It is even thus in the body of Christ. No laws can prevent one living member of Christ from fellowship with every other. The pulse of living fellowship sends a wave through the whole mystical frame. Where there is but one life, fellowship is an inevitable consequence. Yet some talk of restricted communion and imagine that they can practice it. If they be alive unto God they may in mistaken conscientiousness deny their fellow Christians the outward sign of communion, but communion itself falls not under any rule or regulation of theirs. Tie a red tape round your thumb and let it decree that the whole body is out of fellowship with it. The thumb's decree is either ridiculously inoperative, or else it proves injurious to itself. God has made us one, one Spirit quickens us, and truly our fellowship is with the Father and with his Son Jesus. To deny any believer in Jesus is to refuse what you *must* of necessity give, and to deny in symbol what you *must* inevitably render in reality.

# The Spirit's Fire

*Do not put out the Spirit's fire. 1 Thessalonians 5:19*

---

There once was a blacksmith who had two pieces of iron which he wished to weld into one. He took them just as they were, all cold and hard, and put them on the anvil, and began to hammer with all this might, but they were still two pieces, and they would not unite. At last he remembered what he should never have forgotten. He thrust both of them into the fire, took them out red-hot, laid one on the other, and by one or two blows of the hammer they soon became one.

# The Poison of Slander

"Beware of your friends; do not trust your brothers. For every brother is a deceiver, and every friend a slanderer. Friend deceives friend, and no one speaks the truth. They have taught their tongues to lie; they weary themselves with sinning. You live in the midst of deception; in their deceit they refuse to acknowledge me . . . Their tongue is a deadly arrow; it speaks with deceit. With his mouth each speaks cordially to his neighbor, but in his heart he sets a trap for him. Should I not punish them for this?" declares the LORD. *Jeremiah 9:4-6, 8-9*

---

We saw in the Museum at Venice an instrument with which one of the old Italian tyrants was accustomed to shoot poisoned needles at the objects of his wanton malignity. We thought of gossips, backbiters, and secret slanderers, and wished that their mischievous devices might come to a speedy end. Their weapons of innuendo and whisper appear to be as insignificant as needles, but the venom which they instill is deadly to many a reputation.

# A Clever Reproof

Remind the people to be subject to rulers and authorities, to be obedient, to be ready to do whatever is good, to slander no one, to be peaceable and considerate, and to show true humility toward all men. *Titus 3:1-2*

---

The Rev. B. Jacobs of Cambridgeport could, when necessary, administer reproof quite forcibly, though the gentleness of his character was always seen in the manner in which it was done. Some young ladies at his house were one day talking about one of their female friends. As he entered the room, he heard the epithets "odd," "singular," etc. applied. He asked and was told the name of the young lady in question, and then said, very gravely, "Yes, she is an odd young lady—she is a very odd young lady. I consider her extremely singular." He then added very impressively, "She was never heard to speak ill of an absent friend." The rebuke was not forgotten by those who heard it.

# Keeping Warm

Blessed are those who have learned to acclaim you, who walk in the light of your presence, O LORD. They rejoice in your name all day long; they exult in your righteousness. *Psalm 89:15-16*

"Is not my word like fire," declares the LORD, "and like a hammer that breaks a rock in pieces?" *Jeremiah 23:29*

Fan into flame the gift of God, which is in you through the laying on of my hands. For God did not give us a spirit of timidity, but a spirit of power, of love and of self-discipline. *2 Timothy 1:6-7*

If two lie down together, they will keep warm. But how can one keep warm alone? *Ecclesiastes 4:11*

---

Philip Henry's advice to his daughter: "If you want to keep warm in this cold season (January, 1692), take these four directions: 1) Get into the sun; under his blessed beams there are warmth and comfort. 2) Go near the fire. 'Is not my word like a fire?' How many cheering passages there are! 3) Keep in motion and action—stirring up the grace and gift of God that is in you. 4) Seek Christian communion. 'How can one be warm alone?'"

# No Two Alike

Therefore judge nothing before the appointed time; wait till the Lord comes. He will bring to light what is hidden in darkness and will expose the motives of men's hearts. At that time each will receive his praise from God. . . . Then you will not take pride in one man over against another. For who makes you different from anyone else? What do you have that you did not receive? And if you did receive it, why do you boast as though you did not? *1 Corinthians 4:5, 6-7*

---

Ruskin, a most accurate observer, said, "Break off an elm bough three feet long, in full leaf, and lay it on the table before you, and try to draw it, leaf for leaf. It is ten to one if in the whole bough you find one leaf exactly like another. Perhaps you will not even have *one* complete. Every leaf will be oblique, or foreshortened, or curled, or crossed by another, or have something the matter with it. And though the whole bough will look graceful and symmetrical, you will scarcely be able to tell how or why it does, since there is not one line of it like another."

If such an infinite variety prevails in creation, we may reasonably expect to find the same in the experience of the saints. Uniformity is no rule of spiritual life. We must not judge others because their feelings have not been precisely similar to ours. All the saints are led in a right way, but no two of them precisely in the same way. Far be it from us to set up a standard and expect all to be conformed to it. If we reject all believers who labor under infirmities, or are marred with faults, our fellowship will be quite limited.

# Strength in Unity

If you have any encouragement from being united with Christ, if any comfort from his love, if any fellowship with the Spirit, if any tenderness and compassion, then make my joy complete by being like-minded, having the same love, being one in spirit and purpose. Do nothing out of selfish ambition or vain conceit, but in humility consider others better than yourselves. Each of you should look not only to your own interests, but also to the interests of others. *Philippians 2:1-4*

---

In his day, Melancthon mourned the divisions among Protestants and sought to bring them together through the parable of the war between the wolves and the dogs. The wolves were somewhat afraid, for the dogs were many and strong, and so they sent out a spy to observe them. On his return the scout said, "It is true the dogs are many, but there are not many mastiffs among them. There are dogs of so many sorts one can hardly count them. And as for the worst of them," he said, "they are little dogs, which bark loudly but cannot bite. However, this did not cheer me so much," said the wolf, "as this: that as they came marching on, I observed they were all snapping right and left at one another, and I could see clearly that though they all hate the wolf, yet each dog hates every other dog with all his heart." I fear it is true still, for there are many believers who snap right and left at their own brothers, when they should save their teeth for the wolves. If our enemies are to be put to confusion, it must be by the united efforts of all the people of God: unity is strength.

# From Small Spark to Raging Fire

The tongue is a small part of the body, but it makes great boasts. Consider what a great forest is set on fire by a small spark. The tongue also is a fire, a world of evil among the parts of the body. It corrupts the whole person, sets the whole course of his life on fire, and is itself set on fire by hell. *James 3:5-6*

---

"I saw a terrible fire some time ago, or rather I saw the reflection of it in the sky; the heavens were crimsoned with it. It burned a large factory to the ground, and the firemen had hard work to save the buildings that surrounded it. They poured streams of water on it from fifteen engines, but it licked it up, and would have its course until the walls gave way. That terrible fire was kindled by a penny candle! Some years ago, I saw the black ashes of what the night before had been a cheerful farm-yard, with its hay-ricks, corn stacks, stables, and cow sheds. Lying about on the ashes were the carcasses of a number of miserable horses and bulls that had perished in the flames. And all that was done by a friction match. American Indians could strike a spark from a flint and steel and set fire to the dry grass, and the flames spread and spread until they swept like a roaring torrent over vast prairies and men and cattle had to flee for their lives. 'Behold, how great a matter a little fire kindles!' And the tongue is a fire! A few rash words will set a family, a neighborhood, a nation, by the ears; they have often done it. Half the lawsuits, and half the wars have been brought about by the tongue."—*James Bolton*

# No Use for an Angry Man

Better a patient man than a warrior, a man who controls his temper than one who takes a city. *Proverbs 16:32*

An angry man stirs up dissension, and a hot-tempered one commits many sins. *Proverbs 29:22*

Everyone should be quick to listen, slow to speak and slow to become angry, for man's anger does not bring about the righteous life that God desires. *James 1:19-20*

---

The Adige at Verona appears to be a river quite broad and deep enough for navigation, but its current is so rapid as to make it quite unserviceable. Many men are so rash and impetuous, and at the same time so suddenly angry and excited, that their otherwise most valuable abilities are rendered useless for any good purpose.

# God's Delightful Provision

Share with God's people who are in need. *Romans 12:13*

He has caused his wonders to be remembered; the LORD is gracious and compassionate. He provides food for those who fear him; he remembers his covenant forever. He has shown his people the power of his works. *Psalm 111:4-6*

---

Occasionally a benevolent action done in faith brings with it an instantaneous recompense in kind. Therein Providence is seen as smiling upon the deed. While walking in Cheapside, the late John Andrew Jones, a poor Baptist minister, was appealed to by someone he knew for help. He had but a shilling in the world, and poised it in his mind, to give or not to give? The greater distress of his acquaintance prevailed, and he gave his all, walking away with a sweet remembrance of the promise, "He that has pity on the poor, lends to the Lord, and that which he has given, will he pay him again." He had not gone a hundred yards further before he met a gentleman who said, "Ah, Mr. Jones, I am glad to see you. I have had this sovereign in my waistcoat pocket this past week for some needy minister, and you may as well have it." Mr. Jones often added, when telling the story, "If I had not stopped to give relief I would have missed the gentleman and the sovereign too."

# Speaking the Truth in Love

An honest answer is like a kiss on the lips. *Proverbs 24:26*

Like an earring of gold or an ornament of fine gold is a wise man's rebuke to a listening ear. Like the coolness of snow at harvest time is a trustworthy messenger to those who send him; he refreshes the spirit of his masters. *Proverbs 25:12-13*

---

A lady who had lost a beloved child was so oppressed with grief that she even secluded herself from the society of her own family and kept herself locked in her chamber. But at length she was prevailed on by her husband to come downstairs and take a walk in the garden. While there, she stooped to pluck a flower, but her husband appeared as though he would hinder her. She plaintively said, "What! Deny me a flower?"

He replied, "You have denied God your flower, and surely you ought not to think it hard in me to deny you mine."

The lady suitably felt the gentle reproof, and had reason to say, "A word spoken in season, how good it is!"

# Good Intentions Gone Awry

Above all, love each other deeply, because love covers over a multitude of sins. *1 Peter 4:8*

---

We were riding along in the afternoon of a lovely but blazing day from Varallo to Riva, and to quench our thirst on the road we carried with us some bottles of an excellent lemonade. The empty bottles were of no use to us, and one of them was given to a friend on the box seat of the carriage to throw away. He happened to be the essence of gentleness and liberality, and seeing two very poor peasant women trudging along with huge empty baskets strapped on their backs, he thought it would delight them if he dropped the bottle into one of their receptacles—a bottle being far more precious there than in other places. But the motion of the carriage made him miss his aim, and the bottle fell on the head of the woman instead of into her basket. There was a shrill cry, and a good deal of blood, and speedy faintness. Of course, we were all in an instant binding up the wound with silver, and our friend we feel sure used golden ointment, so that the poor old creature would have cheerfully had her head broken ten times to receive such a sum. But still the incident saddened us all, and especially our dear tenderhearted friend from whose hand the missile dropped.

But how often are we in a similar situation! We meant to cheer a troubled conscience and instead we wounded it yet more. We intended nothing but love, but our words gave pain; we miscalculated and missed our aim. This has both astonished us and caused us deep regret. Yet such a blunder has made us more careful and has humbled us under a sense of our readiness to err. Moreover, it has led us to be still more liberal in the use of that precious treasure of the gospel, which easily recompenses for all our blundering. Be careful with your kindnesses, but be not too much depressed should they fail to comfort. The Lord knows your intentions.

# An Unselfish Spirit

Make my joy complete by being like-minded, having the same love, being one in spirit and purpose. Do nothing out of selfish ambition or vain conceit, but in humility consider others better than yourselves. Each of you should look not only to your own interests, but also to the interests of others. *Philippians 2:2-4*

---

An incident gives high proof to the natural generosity of the artist Turner. He was one of the hanging committee, as the phrase goes, of the Royal Academy. The walls were full when Turner's attention was attracted by a picture sent in by an unknown provincial artist by the name of Bird. "A good picture," he exclaimed. "It must be hung up and exhibited."

"Impossible!" responded the committee of academicians. "The arrangement cannot be disturbed. Quite impossible!"

"A good picture," reiterated Turner. "It must be hung up." And, finding his colleagues to be as obstinate as himself, he hitched down one of his own pictures and hung up Bird's in its place.

If only that same spirit ruled among the servants of the Lord Jesus. The desire to honor others and to give others a fair opportunity to rise should lead well-known leaders to give place to less eminent men. We are not to look every one of us on our own things, but every one of us also on the things of others.

# Glorify God with Who You Are

God has arranged the parts in the body, every one of them, just as he wanted them to be. If they were all one part, where would the body be? As it is, there are many parts, but one body. . . . Now you are the body of Christ, and each one of you has a part in it.
*1 Corinthians 12:18-20, 27*

---

Suppose the mole should cry out, "How I could have honored the Creator had I been allowed to fly!" It would be very foolish, for a mole flying would be a most ridiculous object; while a mole fashioning its tunnels and casting up its castles is viewed with admiring wonder by the naturalist, who perceives its remarkable suitability to its sphere. The fish of the sea might say, "How I could display the wisdom of God if I could sing, or mount a tree, like a bird," but a dolphin in a tree would be a very grotesque affair, and there would be no wisdom of God to admire in trouts singing in the groves. But when the fish cuts the wave with agile fin, all who have observed it say how wonderfully it is adapted to its habitat, how exactly its every bone is fitted for its mode of life. Brother, it is just so with you. If you begin to say, "I cannot glorify God where I am, and as I am," I answer, neither could you anywhere if not where you are. Providence, which arranged your surroundings, appointed them so that, all things being considered, you are in the position in which you can best display the wisdom and grace of God.

# Warm and Loving Reproofs

Speaking the truth in love, we will in all things grow up into him who is the Head, that is, Christ. From him the whole body, joined and held together by every supporting ligament, grows and builds itself up in love, as each part does its work. *Ephesians 4:15-16*

Correct, rebuke, and encourage—with great patience and careful instruction. *2 Timothy 4:2*

---

While preaching on John 13:14, the duty of disciples to wash one another's feet, Mr. Finlayson of Helmsdale observed, "One way in which disciples wash one another's feet is by reproving one another. But the reproof must not be couched in angry words, so as to destroy the effect; nor in tame, so as to fail of effect. Just as in washing a brother's feet, you must not use boiling water to scald, nor frozen water to freeze them."

# Blessings to Others Are Blessings to Ourselves

A man reaps what he sows. The one who sows to please his sinful nature, from that nature will reap destruction; the one who sows to please the Spirit, from the Spirit will reap eternal life. Let us not become weary in doing good, for at the proper time we will reap a harvest if we do not give up. Therefore, as we have opportunity, let us do good to all people, especially to those who belong to the family of believers. *Galatians 6:7-10*

---

If we view the microcosm of the human body, we find that the heart does not receive blood to store it up. While it pumps blood in at one valve, it sends it out at another. The blood is always circulating everywhere, and is never stagnant. The same is true of all the fluids in a healthy body; they are in a constant state of expenditure. If one cell stores for a few moments its particular secretion, it only retains it until it is perfectly fitted for its appointed use in the body. For if any cell in the body should begin to store up its secretion, its store would soon become the cause of inveterate disease. The organ would soon lose the power to secrete at all, if it did not give forth its products. The whole of the human system lives by giving. The eye cannot say to the foot, I have no need of thee and will not guide thee; for if it does not perform its watchful office, the whole man will be in the ditch, and the eye will be covered with mire. If the members refuse to contribute to the general stock, the whole body will become poverty-stricken and be given up to the bankruptcy of death. Let us learn, then, from the analogy of nature, the great lesson, that to get we must give; that to accumulate we must scatter, that to make ourselves happy, we must make others happy; and that to get good and become spiritually vigorous, we must do good and seek the spiritual good of others.

# Words that Build Up

A word aptly spoken is like apples of gold in settings of silver.
*Proverbs 25:11*

Let us therefore make every effort to do what leads to peace and to mutual edification. *Romans 14:19*

---

Jesus arrived at the gates of a certain city, and he sent his disciples forward to prepare supper while he himself walked through the streets into the marketplace. He saw, at the corner of the market, some people gathered together looking at some object, and he drew near to see what it might be.

It was a dead dog with a halter round his neck, by which he appeared to have been dragged through the dirt, and a viler, more abject, more unclean thing never met the eyes of man.

"Ugh!" said one, holding his nose, "It pollutes the air!"

"How long," said another, "will this foul beast offend our sight?"

"Look at his torn hide," said a third. "You couldn't even cut a shoe out of it."

"And his ears," said a fourth, "all bedraggled and bleeding."

Jesus looked down compassionately on the dead creature said, "Pearls are not equal to the whiteness of his teeth."

The people turned to him with amazement and said among themselves, "Who is this? This must be Jesus of Nazareth, for only he could find something to pity and approve even in a dead dog." Ashamed, they bowed their heads and went each on his way.

# The Blessing of Affliction

# How God Gets Our Attention

Therefore, since we are surrounded by such a great cloud of witnesses, let us throw off everything that hinders and the sin that so easily entangles, and let us run with perseverance the race marked out for us. Let us fix our eyes on Jesus, the author and perfecter of our faith. *Hebrews 12:1-2*

---

Payson beautifully writes: "I have been all my life like a child whose father wishes to fix his undivided attention. At first the child runs about the room, but his father ties up his feet. He then plays with his hands until they likewise are tied. Thus he continues to do, till he is completely tied up. Then, when he can do nothing else, he will attend to his father. Just so has God been dealing with me, to induce me to place my happiness in him alone. But I blindly continued to look for it here, and God has kept cutting off one source of enjoyment after another, till I find that I can do without them all and yet enjoy more happiness than ever in my life before."

# The Honor of God's Heavy Hand

Consider it pure joy, my brothers, whenever you face trials of many kinds, because you know that the testing of your faith develops perseverance. Perseverance must finish its work so that you may be mature and complete, not lacking anything. *James 1:2-4*

"I will refine them like silver and test them like gold. They will call on my name and I will answer them; I will say, 'They are my people,' and they will say, 'The LORD is our God.' " *Zechariah 13:9*

---

In the ancient times, a box on the ear given by a master to a slave meant liberty—little would the freedman care how hard he was struck, when the blow meant release. By a stroke from the sword the warrior was knighted by his monarch—it was a small matter to the new knight if the royal hand was heavy. When the Lord intends to lift his servants into a higher stage of spiritual life, he frequently sends them a severe trial; he makes his Jacobs to be prevailing princes, but he confers the honor after a night of wrestling, and accompanies it with a shrunken sinew in the thigh. So we should not wish to be deprived of trials if they are the necessary attendants of spiritual advancement.

# Precious Words of Promise

"When you pass through the waters, I will be with you; and when you pass through the rivers, they will not sweep over you. When you walk through the fire, you will not be burned; the flames will not set you ablaze." *Isaiah 43:2*

The LORD is a refuge for the oppressed, a stronghold in times of trouble. *Psalm 9:9*

---

We never prize the precious words of promise till we are placed in conditions in which their suitability and sweetness are manifested. We all of us value those golden words, "When thou walkest through the fire thou shalt not be burned, neither shall the flame kindle upon thee," but few if any of us have read them with the delight of the martyr Bilney, to whom this passage was a comfort and help while he was in prison awaiting his execution at the stake. His Bible, still preserved in the library of Corpus Christi College, Cambridge, has the passage marked with a pen in the margin. Perhaps, if all were known, every promise in the Bible has borne a special message to some one saint, and so the whole volume might be scored in the margin with mementos of Christian experience, every one appropriate to the very letter.

# The Blessing of a Storm

For his anger lasts only a moment, but his favor lasts a lifetime; weeping may remain for a night, but rejoicing comes in the morning. *Psalm 30:5*

Blessed is the man who perseveres under trial, because when he has stood the test, he will receive the crown of life that God has promised to those who love him. *James 1:12*

---

How different are summer storms from winter ones! In winter they rush over the earth with their violence; and if any poor remnants of foliage or flowers have lingered behind, these are swept along at one gust. Nothing is left but desolation; and long after the rain has ceased, pools of water and mud bear tokens of what has been. But when the clouds have poured out their torrents in summer, when the winds have spent their fury, and the sun breaks forth again in glory, all things seem to rise with renewed loveliness from their refreshing bath. The flowers, glistening with rainbows, smell sweeter than before; the grass seems to have gained another brighter shade of green; and the young plants which had hardly come into sight have taken their place among their fellows in the borders, so quickly have they sprung up from the showers. The air, too, which may previously have been oppressive, has become clear, and soft, and fresh.

Such, too, is the difference when the storms of affliction fall on hearts unrenewed by Christian faith, and on those who abide in Christ. In the former they bring out the dreariness and desolation which may before have been unapparent. The gloom is not relieved by the prospect of any cheering ray to follow it or of any flowers or fruits to show its beneficence. But for the true Christian soul, "though weeping may endure for a night, joy comes in the morning." A sweet smile of hope and love follows every tear; and tribulation itself is turned into the chief of blessings.

# Growing Up in God

So then, just as you received Christ Jesus as LORD, continue to live in him, rooted and built up in him, strengthened in the faith as you were taught, and overflowing with thankfulness. *Colossians 2:6-7*

Be joyful in hope, patient in affliction, faithful in prayer. *Romans 12:12*

---

Latimer described the way in which his father trained him as a yeoman's son: "I had my bows bought for me according to my age and strength. As I increased in them, so my bows were made bigger and bigger." Thus boys grew into crossbowmen, and by a similar increase in the force of their trials, Christians become veterans in the Lord's host. The affliction which is suitable for a babe in grace would little serve the young man, and even the well-developed man needs more severe trials as his strength increases. God, like a wise father, trains us wisely, and as we are able to bear it he makes our service and our suffering more arduous. As boys rejoice to be treated like men, so will we rejoice in our greater tribulations, for here is man's work for us, and by God's help we will not flinch from doing it.

# Lizards and Other Peculiar Mercies

I have learned to be content whatever the circumstances. I know what it is to be in need, and I know what it is to have plenty. I have learned the secret of being content in any and every situation, whether well fed or hungry, whether living in plenty or in want.
*Philippians 4:11-12*

---

Afflictions, when sanctified, make us grateful for mercies which before we treated with indifference. We sat for half an hour in a calf's shed the other day, quite grateful for the shelter from the driving rain, yet at no other time would we have entered such a hovel. Discontented people need a course of the bread of adversity and the water of affliction to cure them of the wretched habit of complaining. Even things which we loathed before, we shall learn to value when in troubling circumstances. We are not fond of lizards, and yet at Pont St. Martin, in the Aosta valley, where the mosquitoes, flies, and insects of all sorts drove us nearly to distraction, we prized the little green fellows, and felt quite an attachment to them as they darted out their tongues and devoured our worrying enemies. Sweet are the uses of adversity, and this among them—that it brings into proper estimation mercies which were before lightly esteemed.

# A Tree Firmly Planted

Blessed is the man who does not walk in the counsel of the wicked or stand in the way of sinners or sit in the seat of mockers. But his delight is in the law of the LORD, and on his law he meditates day and night. He is like a tree planted by streams of water, which yields its fruit in season and whose leaf does not wither. Whatever he does prospers. *Psalm 1:1-3*

---

The pine is nearly always placed in disordered and desolate places, and it brings all possible elements of order and precision. Lowland trees may lean to this side and that with only a meadow breeze to bend them or a bank of cowslips to make their trunks lean sideways. But let storm and avalanche do their worst, and let the pine find only a ledge of vertical precipice to cling to, the tree will nevertheless grow straight. Thrust a rod from its last shoot down the stem, it shall point to the center of the earth as long as the tree lives.

The most upright Christians are usually reared amid the sternest trials. The divine life within them so triumphs over every difficulty as to render the men, above all others, true and exact. What a noble spectacle is a man whom nothing can warp, a firm decided servant of God, defying hurricanes of temptation!

# Revealing the Hidden

We also rejoice in our sufferings, because we know that suffering produces perseverance; perseverance, character; and character, hope. And hope does not disappoint us, because God has poured out his love into our hearts by the Holy Spirit, whom he has given us. *Romans 5:3-5*

---

When the green leaves decorate the trees and the season is fair, one cannot readily find the birds' nests, but when the winter strips the trees, anyone with half an eye may see them. In the same way the Christian may scarcely be discerned amid the press of business and prosperity; his hidden life is concealed amid the thick and throng of the things of earth. But let affliction come, a general sickness, or severe losses in the family, and you shall see the Christian man plainly enough in the gracious patience by which he rises superior to trial. The sick bed reveals the man; the burning house, the sinking ship, the panic on the exchange—all these make manifest the hidden ones. In many a true believer, true piety is like a drum which nobody hears of unless it be beaten.

# Proof of the Father's Love

Endure hardship as discipline; God is treating you as sons. . . . God disciplines us for our good, that we may share in his holiness. No discipline seems pleasant at the time, but painful. Later on, however, it produces a harvest of righteousness and peace for those who have been trained by it. *Hebrews 12:7, 10-11*

---

When we wish to keep a lawn in the best condition, we mow it very frequently; the grass scarcely has a break from the mower's blade. Out in the meadows there is no such repeated cutting; sometimes they are mown, but only once or twice in a year. In the same way the nearer we are to God, and the more regard he has for us, the more frequent will be our adversities. To be very dear to God involves no small degree of chastisement.

# Moment by Moment

No temptation has seized you except what is common to man. And God is faithful; he will not let you be tempted beyond what you can bear. But when you are tempted, he will also provide a way out so that you can stand up under it. *1 Corinthians 10:13*

---

"A celebrated writer once said, 'Take care of the *minutes*, and the *hours* will take care of themselves.' This is an admirable remark and might be very seasonably recollected when we begin to be 'weary in well-doing' from the thought of having too much to do. The present moment is all we have to handle now. The past is irrecoverable; the future is uncertain. Nor is it fair to burden one moment with the weight of the next. Sufficient unto the *moment* is the trouble thereof. If we had to walk a hundred miles, we would still have to take but one step at a time, and this process continued would infallibly bring us to our journey's end. Fatigue generally begins, and is always increased, by calculating in a minute the exertion of hours. Thus, in looking forward to future life, remember that we have not to sustain all its toil, to endure all its sufferings, or encounter all its crosses at once. One moment comes laden with its own *little* burdens, then flies, and is succeeded by another no heavier than the last. If *one* could be borne, so can another, and another. Even in looking forward to a single day, the spirit may sometimes faint from an anticipation of duties, the labors, the trials to temper and patience, that may be expected. Now, this is unjustly laying the burden of many thousand moments upon one."—*Youth's Magazine for November, 1819*

# Satisfied in God's Will

But he said to me, "My grace is sufficient for you, for my power is made perfect in weakness." Therefore I will boast all the more gladly about my weaknesses, so that Christ's power may rest on me. That is why, for Christ's sake, I delight in weaknesses, in insults, in hardships, in persecutions, in difficulties. For when I am weak, then I am strong. *2 Corinthians 12:9-10*

---

When under great bodily affliction, Payson was asked if he could see any particular reason for this dispensation. "No," he replied, "but I am as well satisfied as if I could see ten thousand. God's will is the very perfection of all reason."

# An Obedient Servant

But if anyone obeys his word, God's love is truly made complete in him. This is how we know we are in him: Whoever claims to live in him must walk as Jesus did. *1 John 2:5-6*

---

Old Betty was converted late in her life, and though she was very poor she was very active. She visited the sick; out of her own poverty she gave to those who were still poorer; she collected a little money from others when she could give none of her own, and told many of the love of the Savior. At last she caught a cold and rheumatism and lay in bed month after month, pain-worn and helpless. A good minister went to see her and asked if after her active habits she did not find the change very hard to bear.

"No sir, not at all. When I was well, I used to hear the Lord say day by day, 'Betty, go here. Betty, go there. Betty, do this. Betty do that," and I used to do it as well as I could. And now I hear him say every day, 'Betty, lie still and cough.' "

# The Sympathy from Experience

Praise be to the God and Father of our Lord Jesus Christ, the Father of compassion and the God of all comfort, who comforts us in all our troubles, so that we can comfort those in any trouble with the comfort we ourselves have received from God. For just as the sufferings of Christ flow over into our lives, so also through Christ our comfort overflows. *2 Corinthians 1:3-5*

---

Hone recorded the following anecdote about Charles Pratt, Earl Camden, when he was Chief Justice of the Common Pleas. "Being on a visit to Lord Dacre, he walked out with a gentleman—a very absent-minded man—to a hill, on the top of which the stocks of the village stood. The Chief Justice sat down, and wanting to feel what the punishment was, he asked his companion to open them and put him in. This being done, his friend took a book from his pocket, sauntered on and completely forgot the judge. In the meantime, the Chief Justice tried in vain to release himself. Seeing a countryman, he endeavored to convince him to let him out, but obtained nothing by his persuasion. 'No, no, old gentleman,' said the man, 'You were not set there for nothing,' and left him until he was released by a servant dispatched from the house.

"Later he presided at a trial in which a magistrate was charged for false imprisonment and for sitting in the stocks. The counsel for the magistrate made light of the whole charge and especially of sitting in the stocks, which he said everybody knew was no real punishment.

"The Chief Justice rose and, leaning over the bench, said in a half-whisper, 'Brother, have you ever been in the stocks?'

" 'Really, my lord, never!'

" 'Well, I have,' said the judge, 'and I assure you, it is no such trifle as you represent.' "

A little experience of the real trials of life would be of essential service to many professing believers, and especially to those religious teachers whose path in life has been smooth and prosperous. Nothing promotes true sympathy like a kindred experience.

# The Comfort of Sympathy

Rejoice with those who rejoice; mourn with those who mourn. *Romans 12:15*

Finally, all of you, live in harmony with one another; be sympathetic, love as brothers, be compassionate and humble. *1 Peter 3:8*

---

The story goes that Harry the Eighth, wandering one night in the streets of London in disguise, was met at the foot of a bridge by some of the night watchmen; and, not giving a good account of himself, he was carried off to the Poultry Compter and shut up for the night without fire or candle. On his liberation he made a grant of thirty chaldrons of coals and a quantity of bread for the solace of night prisoners in the Compter. Experience brings sympathy. Those who have felt sharp afflictions, terrible convictions, racking doubts, and violent temptations, will be zealous in consoling those in a similar condition. It would be good if the great Head of the church would put unsympathizing pastors into the Compter of trouble for a season until they could weep with those who weep.

# Loving Discipline

"My son, do not make light of the Lord's discipline, and do not lose heart when he rebukes you, because the Lord disciplines those he loves, and he punishes everyone he accepts as a son." Endure hardship as discipline; God is treating you as sons. For what son is not disciplined by his father? If you are not disciplined (and everyone undergoes discipline), then you are illegitimate children and not true sons. Moreover, we have all had human fathers who disciplined us and we respected them for it. How much more should we submit to the Father of our spirits and live! Our fathers disciplined us for a little while as they thought best; but God disciplines us for our good, that we may share in his holiness. No discipline seems pleasant at the time, but painful. Later on, however, it produces a harvest of righteousness and peace for those who have been trained by it. *Hebrews 12:5-11*

---

Augustine said that his God was "mercifully rigorous" to him, sprinkling with most bitter alloy all his unlawful pleasures, "that he might seek pleasures without alloy."

# Our Troubles and God's Power

He said to me, "My grace is sufficient for you, for my power is made perfect in weakness." Therefore I will boast all the more gladly about my weaknesses, so that Christ's power may rest on me. That is why, for Christ's sake, I delight in weaknesses, in insults, in hardships, in persecutions, in difficulties. For when I am weak, then I am strong. *2 Corinthians 12:9-10*

Rejoice that you participate in the sufferings of Christ, so that you may be overjoyed when his glory is revealed. *1 Peter 4:13*

---

Some of the arable land along the shore on the southeast coast of Sutherland is almost covered with shore stones, from the size of a turkey's egg to eight pounds weight. Several experiments have been made to collect these off the land, expecting a better crop. But in every case the land proved *less* productive after having removed the stones, and on some small spots of land it was found so evident, that they were spread on the land again, to ensure their usual crop of oats or peas.

We would like to be rid of all our infirmities which, to our superficial conceptions, appear to be great hindrances to our usefulness, and yet it is most questionable if we should bring forth any fruit unto God without them. Much rather, therefore, will I glory in infirmities that the power of Christ may rest upon me.

# Maybe I'm Dead?

"I have come that they may have life, and have it to the full." *John 10:10*

You have made known to me the path of life; you will fill me with joy in your presence, with eternal pleasures at your right hand. *Psalm 16:11*

---

In doubt and discouragement, a Christian once considered the darkness that overspread her soul as a proof that she was finally cast away. She stumbled over mole-hills when she should have been removing mountains. To an old minister who was trying to comfort her, she said with impassioned emphasis, "I'm *dead, dead,* twice *dead,* and plucked up by the roots!"

After a pause, the minister replied, "Well, while sitting in my study the other day, I heard a sudden scream—'John's in the well! John's fallen in the well!' Before I could reach the spot, I heard the sad and mournful cry, 'John's dead—poor little Johnny's dead!' Bending over the curb, I called out, 'John, are you dead?' 'Yes, grandfather,' replied John, 'I'm dead.' I was glad to hear it from his own mouth."

Many doubts are so absurd that the only way to combat them is by gentle ridicule.

# Persecuted—for God's Glory

Among God's churches we boast about your perseverance and faith in all the persecutions and trials you are enduring. All this is evidence that God's judgment is right, and as a result you will be counted worthy of the kingdom of God, for which you are suffering. God is just: He will pay back trouble to those who trouble you and give relief to you who are troubled, and to us as well. This will happen when the Lord Jesus is revealed from heaven in blazing fire with his powerful angels. He will punish those who do not know God and do not obey the gospel of our Lord Jesus. They will be punished with everlasting destruction and shut out from the presence of the Lord and from the majesty of his power on the day he comes to be glorified in his holy people and to be marveled at among all those who have believed. . . . With this in mind, we constantly pray for you, that our God may count you worthy of his calling, and that by his power he may fulfill every good purpose of yours and every act prompted by your faith. *2 Thessalonians 1:4-10, 11*

---

The cold water of persecution is often thrown on the church's face to bring her to herself when she is in a swoon of indolence or pride.

# Something Worth Living and Dying For

Now there is in store for me the crown of righteousness, which the Lord, the righteous Judge, will award to me on that day—and not only to me, but also to all who have longed for his appearing. *2 Timothy 4:8*

---

There is an old Greek story of a soldier under Antigonus who had an extremely painful disease that was likely to bring him soon to the grave. This soldier was always first in the charge, rushing into the hottest part of the fray, as the bravest of the brave. His pain prompted him to fight, that he might forget it; and he was not afraid of death, because he knew that in any case he had not long to live. Antigonus greatly admired the valor of his soldier, and discovered his malady and had him cured by one of the most eminent physicians of the day. But from that moment the warrior was absent from the front of the battle. Now he sought his ease; for, as he remarked to his companions, he had something worth living for—health, home, family, and other comforts, and he would not risk his life now as he had before.

So, when our troubles are many we are often by grace made courageous in serving our God. We feel that we have nothing to live for in this world, and we are driven, by hope of the world to come, to exhibit zeal, self-denial, and industry. But how often is it otherwise in better times! For then the joys and pleasures of this world make it hard for us to remember the world to come, and we sink into inglorious ease.

# A Need for Night

Weeping may remain for a night, but rejoicing comes in the morning. *Psalm 30:5*

---

Speaking of a Norwegian summer, the Rev. H. Macmillan says, "The long daylight is very favorable to the growth of vegetation, plants growing in the night as well as in the day in the short but ardent summer. But the stimulus of perpetual solar light is peculiarly trying to the nervous systems of those who are not accustomed to it. It prevents proper repose and banishes sleep. I never felt before how needful darkness is for the welfare of our bodies and minds. I longed for night, but the farther north we went, the farther we were fleeing from it, until at last, when we reached the most northern point of our tour, the sun set for one hour and a half. Consequently, the heat of the day never cooled down, and accumulated until it became almost unendurable at last. Truly for a most wise and beneficent purpose did God make light and create darkness. "Light is sweet, and it is a pleasant thing to the eyes to behold the sun." But darkness is also sweet. It is the nurse of nature's kind restorer, balmy sleep, and without the tender drawing around us of its curtains the weary eyelid will not close, and the jaded nerves will not be soothed to refreshing rest. Not till the everlasting day breaks, and the shadows flee away, and the Lord himself shall be our light, and our God our glory, can we do without the cloud in the sunshine, the shade of sorrow in the bright light of joy, and the curtain of night for the deepening of the sleep which God gives his beloved."

# Trials Lead to Greater Growth

Consider it pure joy, my brothers, whenever you face trials of many kinds, because you know that the testing of your faith develops perseverance. Perseverance must finish its work so that you may be mature and complete, not lacking anything. *James 1:2-4*

---

In his *Sacred Philosophy of the Seasons*, Duncan tells us there is an insect *(musca pumilionis)* that deposits its eggs in the very core of the *plumula*, or primary shoot of wheat, so that this shoot is completely destroyed by the larvae. If the plant possessed no means within itself, no means of repairing this injury, the whole previous labor of the gardener would have been in vain. But since this destruction occurs in the spring of the year, when the vegetable power of the plant is in its greatest vigor, an effect is produced that is somewhat analogous to that of heading down a fruit tree. Shoots immediately spring up from the knots, the plant becomes more firmly rooted, and produces probably a dozen stems and ears, when but for the temporary mischief it might have sent forth only one. Thus may it often occur that those early trials which appear almost to destroy the faith of young believers are their best friends, since they never would have been so useful had they been left to flourish as their hearts desired.

# A Blinded Spirit

The god of this age has blinded the minds of unbelievers, so that they cannot see the light of the gospel of the glory of Christ. *2 Corinthians 4:4*

---

Too long a period of fair weather in the Italian valleys creates such a superabundance of dust that the traveler sighs for a shower. He is smothered, his clothes are white, his eyes smart, the grit even grates between his teeth and finds its way down his throat. The rain clouds are welcome, as they promise to abate the nuisance. Prosperity long continued breeds a plague of dust even more injurious, for it almost blinds the spirit and insinuates itself into the soul. A shower or two of grief proves a mighty blessing, for it deprives the things of earth of some of their smothering power. A Christian making money fast is just a man in a cloud of dust—it will fill his eyes if he is not careful. A Christian full of worldly care is in the same condition, and should look to it lest he be choked with earth. Afflictions might almost be prayed for if we never had them, even as in long stretches of fair weather men beg for rain to lay the dust.

# The Buried Seed

"I tell you the truth, unless a kernel of wheat falls to the ground and dies, it remains only a single seed. But if it dies, it produces many seeds. The man who loves his life will lose it, while the man who hates his life in this world will keep it for eternal life. Whoever serves me must follow me; and where I am, my servant also will be. My Father will honor the one who serves me." *John 12:24-26*

---

Two seeds lie before us—the one is warmed in the sun, the other falls from the sower's hand into the cold dark earth, and there it lies buried beneath the soil. That seed which suns itself in the noontime beam may rejoice in the light in which it basks, but it is liable to be devoured by the bird. And certainly nothing can come of it, however long it might linger above ground. But the other seed, hidden beneath the clods in a damp, dark sepulcher, soon swells, germinates, bursts its sheath, throws off the mold, springs up a green blade, buds, blossoms, becomes a flower, exhales perfume, and loads the wings of every wind. Better far for the seed to pass into the earth and die than to lie in the sunshine and produce no fruit. And even so for you the future in its sorrow shall be as a sowing in a fertile land. Tears shall moisten you, grace shall increase within you, and you shall grow up in the likeness of your Lord unto perfection of holiness, to be such a flower of God's own planting as even angels shall delight to gaze upon in the day of your transplanting to celestial soil.

# Warm Seasons of the Spirit

Repent, then, and turn to God, so that your sins may be wiped out, that times of refreshing may come from the Lord, and that he may send the Christ, who has been appointed for you—even Jesus. *Acts 3:19-20*

---

The decline of revival is a great testing season. It discovers the true believers by chilling the false. A frosty night or two suffices to nip all the exotic plants of a garden, but the hardy shrubs, the true natives of the soil, live on even in the severest cold. Converts raised in the hot-bed of excitement soon droop and die if the spiritual temperature of the church falls below summer heat. What are these worth compared with the hardy children of divine grace, whose inward life will continue in enduring vigor when all around is dead! Yet we do not desire to see the revival spirit droop among us, for even the evergreens of our garden delight in a warmer season, for then they send forth their shoots and clothe themselves with new leaves. And thus it will be seen that the best of the saints are all the better for the holy glow of the "times of refreshing."

# Braving the Storms

The God of all grace, who called you to his eternal glory in Christ, after you have suffered a little while, will himself restore you and make you strong, firm and steadfast. *1 Peter 5:10*

"Let us acknowledge the LORD; let us press on to acknowledge him. As surely as the sun rises, he will appear; he will come to us like the winter rains, like the spring rains that water the earth." *Hosea 6:3*

---

Sir Francis Drake, caught in a dangerous storm in the Thames, was heard to say, "Must I who have escaped the rage of the ocean be drowned in a ditch?!" Will you, experienced saints, who have passed through a world of tribulation, lie down and die of despair, or give up your profession of faith because you are passing through some light affliction? Let your past preservation inspire you with courage and constrain you to brave all storms for Jesus' sake.

# The Glory of the Rainbow

"I will remember my covenant between me and you and all living creatures of every kind. Never again will the waters become a flood to destroy all life. Whenever the rainbow appears in the clouds, I will see it and remember the everlasting covenant between God and all living creatures of every kind on the earth." *Genesis 9:15-16*

---

Looking from the little wooden bridge which passes over the brow of the beautiful waterfall of Handeck, on a bright day one will see a circular rainbow surrounding the fall like a coronet of gems. Every hue is there from the red to where the violet fades into the sky.

This fair vision reminded me of the mystic rainbow which the seer of Patmos beheld around the throne. It was seen by John as a *complete circle;* we see but half on earth. The upper arch of manifest glory we rejoice to gaze upon, but the lower and foundational arch of the eternal purpose, upon which the visible display of grace is founded, is reserved for our contemplation in another world.

I compared the little stream to the church of God, which in peaceful times flows on like a village brook, quiet and obscure, blessed and blessing others, but yet little known or considered by the sons of men. But when the church advances over the steeps of opposition and is dashed down the crags of persecution, then her glory is revealed. Then it is that the eternal God glorifies her with the rainbow of his everlasting grace, makes the beauty of her holiness to shine forth, and reveals a heavenly radiance, which all behold with astonishment.

The majestic rainbow of the divine presence encircles the chosen people when tribulation, affliction, and distress break them, as the stream is broken by the precipitous rocks on which it boldly casts itself, that its current may advance in its predestined channel. When forebodings foretell the coming of evil times for the church, remember that before the Spirit revealed to the beloved disciple the terrible beasts, the thundering trumpets, the falling stars, and the dreadful vials, he bade him mark with attention that the covenant rainbow was round about the throne. All is well, for God is true.

---

# Strength of Character

# Sight and Sincerity

We have not stopped praying for you and asking God to fill you with the knowledge of his will through all spiritual wisdom and understanding. And we pray this in order that you may live a life worthy of the Lord and may please him in every way: bearing fruit in every good work, growing in the knowledge of God. *Colossians 1:9-10*

---

In reference to painters, Ruskin declares that "a person false at heart may, when it suits his purposes, seize a stray truth here or there, but the relations of truth, its perfectness, that which makes it wholesome truth, he can never perceive. As wholeness and wholesomeness go together, so also sight with sincerity. It is only the constant desire of, and submissiveness to truth, which can measure its strange angles, and mark its infinite aspects, and fit them and knit them into the strength of sacred invention."

The like remark, with keener edge, applies to those who would be disciples in Christ's school, or aspire to be teachers in his church.

# Pillars of the Church

Set an example for the believers in speech, in life, in love, in faith and in purity. *1 Timothy 4:12*

Since an overseer is entrusted with God's work . . . he must be hospitable, one who loves what is good, who is self-controlled, upright, holy and disciplined. He must hold firmly to the trustworthy message as it has been taught. *Titus 1:8-9*

Be on your guard; stand firm in the faith; be men of courage; be strong. Do everything in love. *1 Corinthians 16:13-14*

---

In the Cathedral of St. Mark in Venice—a marvelous building, lustrous with an Oriental splendor far beyond description—there are pillars said to have been brought from Solomon's Temple. These are of alabaster, a substance firm and durable as granite, and yet transparent, so that the light glows through them.

They are an emblem of what all true pillars of the church should be—firm in their faith and transparent in their character; people of simple mold, ignorant of tortuous and deceptive ways, and yet people of strong will, not readily led aside or bent from uprightness. We know a few such alabaster people; may the great Master-builder place more of them in his temple!

# Keep Trying!

I can do everything through him who gives me strength. *Philippians 4:13*

---

No person who moodily indulges a despondent view of his own capacities is likely to accomplish much. By God's help the weakest of us may be strong, and it is the way to become so, to resolve never to give up a good work until we have tried our best to achieve it. To think nothing impossible is the privilege of faith. We deprecate the indolent cowardice of the person who always felt assured that every new enterprise would be too much for him, and therefore declined it, but we admire the pluck of the plowman who was asked on his cross-examination if he could read Greek, and replied that he did not know because he had never tried. Those Suffolk horses that pull at a post until they drop are worth a thousand times as much as jibbing animals that run back as soon as ever the collar begins to press them.

# Never Give Up!

"Suppose one of you has a friend, and he goes to him at midnight and says, 'Friend, lend me three loaves of bread, because a friend of mine on a journey has come to me, and I have nothing to set before him.'

"Then the one inside answers, 'Don't bother me. The door is already locked, and my children are with me in bed. I can't get up and give you anything.' I tell you, though he will not get up and give him the bread because he is his friend, yet because of the man's persistence he will get up and give him as much as he needs.

"So I say to you: Ask and it will be given to you; seek and you will find; knock and the door will be opened to you. For everyone who asks receives; he who seeks finds; and to him who knocks the door will be opened." *Luke 11:5-10*

---

"An old man in Watton, whom Mr. Thornton had in vain urged to come to church, was taken ill and confined to his bed. Mr. Thornton went to the cottage and asked to see him. The old man, hearing his voice below, answered in a very discourteous tone, 'I don't want you here, you may go away.'

"The following day the curate was again at the foot of the stairs. 'Well, my friend, may I come up today and sit beside you?'

"Again he received the same reply, 'I don't want you here.'

"Twenty-one days successively Mr. Thornton paid his visit to the cottage, and on the twenty-second his perseverance was rewarded. He was permitted to enter the room of the aged sufferer, to read the Bible, and to pray by his bedside. The elderly man recovered and became one of the most regular attendants at the house of God."—*Memoirs of Rev. Spencer Thornton*

# Faithful to the Tasks Before Us

Therefore, my dear brothers, stand firm. Let nothing move you. Always give yourselves fully to the work of the Lord, because you know that your labor in the Lord is not in vain. *1 Corinthians 15:58*

It is required that those who have been given a trust must prove faithful. *1 Corinthians 4:2*

---

A poor woman had a supply of coal laid at her door by a charitable neighbor. A very little girl came out with a small fire-shovel and began to take up a shovelful at a time and carry it to a sort of bin in the cellar.

I said to the child, "Do you expect to get all that coal in with that little shovel?"

She was quite confused by my question, but her answer was very striking, "Yes sir, if I work long enough."

Make up for your lack of ability by abundant continuance in well-doing, and your life-work will not be trivial. The repetition of small efforts will accomplish more than the occasional use of great talents.

# Unquestioning Obedience

Give me understanding, and I will keep your law and obey it with all my heart. *Psalm 119:34*

We know that we have come to know him if we obey his commands. The man who says, "I know him," but does not do what he commands is a liar, and the truth is not in him. But if anyone obeys his word, God's love is truly made complete in him. This is how we know we are in him: Whoever claims to live in him must walk as Jesus did. *1 John 2:3-6*

---

"Sirs," said the Duke of Wellington to an office of engineers who complained of the impossibility of executing the directions he had received, "I did not ask your opinion. I gave you my orders, and I expect them to be obeyed." Such should be the obedience of every follower of Jesus. The words which he has spoken are our law, not our judgments or fancies. Even if death appears in the way, it is

*Not ours to reason why—*
*Ours, but to dare and die,*

and, at our Master's bidding, advance through flood or flame.

# Undaunted Devotion to Duty

I eagerly expect and hope that I will in no way be ashamed, but will have sufficient courage so that now as always Christ will be exalted in my body, whether by life or by death. For to me, to live is Christ and to die is gain. *Philippians 1:20-21*

---

After the disgraceful defeat of the Romans at the battle of Allia, Rome was sacked, and it seemed as if the Gauls might take the Capitol at any moment. Among the garrison was a young man of the Fabian family, and on a certain day the anniversary of a sacrifice returned, when his family had always offered sacrifice upon the Quirinal Hill. This hill was in the possession of the Gauls, but when the morning dawned, the young man took the sacred utensils of his god, went down from the Capitol, passed through the Gallic sentries, through the main body, up the hill, offered sacrifice, and came back unharmed. It was always told as a wonder among Roman legends.

This is just how the Christian should act when a decision for Christ is called for. Though he be a solitary man in the midst of a thousand opponents, let him, at the precise moment when duty calls, fearless of all danger, go straight to the appointed spot, do his duty, and remember that consequences belong to God and not to us. I pray God that after this style we may witness for Christ.

# Courage in Action

Be on your guard; stand firm in the faith; be men of courage; be strong. Do everything in love. *1 Corinthians 16:13-14*

"Be strong and courageous. Do not be terrified; do not be discouraged, for the LORD your God will be with you wherever you go." *Joshua 1:9*

---

Courage maintains itself by ardent action, as some birds rest on the wing. There is an energy about agility that will often give a man strength which he might not have possessed otherwise. We can picture a gallant regiment into the valley of death at a dashing gallop, but we could scarcely imagine soldiers marching slowly up to the guns, coolly calculating all the deadly odds of the adventure. We should obey as our Lord did: "straightway." When the Lord gives his servants grace to follow out their convictions as they feel them, then they act courageously. First thoughts are best in the service of God; they are like Gideon's men that lapped water. Second thoughts come up timorously and limpingly, and incite us to make provision for our weaknesses; they are like those men whom Gideon discarded because they went down on their knees to drink, they took things too leisurely to be fit for the Lord's battles.

# Onward, Christian Soldiers

Train a child in the way he should go, and when he is old he will not turn from it. *Proverbs 22:6*

Don't let anyone look down on you because you are young, but set an example for the believers in speech, in life, in love, in faith and in purity. *1 Timothy 4:12*

---

"In the early French revolution, the schoolboys of Bourges from twelve to seventeen years of age formed themselves into a Band of Hope. They wore a uniform and were taught drill. On their holidays, their flag was unfurled, displaying in shining letters the sentence, 'Tremblez, Tyrans, nous grandirons!' *(Tremble, Tyrants, we shall grow up!).*

"Without any charge of spurious enthusiasm, we may in imagination hear the shouts of confidence and courage uttered by the young Christians of the future, as they say, 'Tremble, Oh enemy, *we are growing up for God!'* "—*Mr. S.R. Pattison's Address at the Meeting of the Baptist Union, 1869*

# Acting Out of Courage and Sincerity

Obey your earthly masters in everything; and do it, not only when their eye is on you and to win their favor, but with sincerity of heart and reverence for the Lord. Whatever you do, work at it with all your heart, as working for the Lord, not for men, since you know that you will receive an inheritance from the Lord as a reward. It is the Lord Christ you are serving. *Colossians 3:22-24*

---

A brigade of artillery passed at full gallop over a piece of uneven ground intersected by a ditch full of water. One of the guns, from the horses not making a sufficient spring, got stuck in the ditch. The first gunner, a man of great strength, jumped down into the water and, setting his shoulders to one of the wheels, lifted it out of the mud. He resumed his seat, and the gun crossed the ditch.

Prince Augustus of Prussia, who came up at the moment, cried, "Bravo, my lad," and tearing off a strip from his sash, gave it to the artilleryman, telling him to fasten it to his sword-belt in remembrance. In the evening, the soldier, when in his barracks, was surprised by receiving a gratuity of 150 golden crowns.

A short time after, another artilleryman, having heard this anecdote, wished in his turn to display his strength. Prince Augustus, when one day at the arsenal of Berlin, ordered a 24-pounder to be mounted on its carriage. The man in question immediately raised the piece from the ground and, unassisted, put it on its carriage. The prince, however, said, "This man is a fool. He has risked his limbs, and wasted his strength without any necessity. Let him be under arrest for three days."

The tale furnishes us with a warning against being mere copyists. An action may from the time and circumstances be noble and praiseworthy in one man, but another would render himself ridiculous who, forgetting the surrounding circumstances, should merely repeat the action itself. True grace, like a truly soldierly spirit, guides its possessor as emergencies arise, but that mimicry of religion that only follows precedents is to be despised.

# A Child's Grateful Heart

So then, just as you received Christ Jesus as Lord, continue to live in him, rooted and built up in him, strengthened in the faith as you were taught, and overflowing with thankfulness. *Colossians 2:6-7*

I have learned to be content whatever the circumstances. I know what it is to be in need, and I know what it is to have plenty. I have learned the secret of being content in any and every situation, whether well fed or hungry, whether living in plenty or in want. I can do everything through him who gives me strength. *Philippians 4:11-13*

---

I once heard a touching story about a poor woman with two children who had no bed for them to sleep in and scarcely any clothes to cover them. In the depth of winter they were nearly frozen, and the mother took the door of a cellar off the hinges, and set it up before the corner where they crouched to sleep, that some of the draft and cold might be kept from them. One of the children whispered to her, when she complained, "Mother, what do those dear little children do who have no cellar door to put up in front of them?" Even there, you see, the little heart found cause for thankfulness.

# Complain, Complain

Do everything without complaining or arguing, so that you may become blameless and pure, children of God without fault in a crooked and depraved generation, in which you shine like stars in the universe as you hold out the word of life. *Philippians 2:14-16*

And whatever you do, whether in word or deed, do it all in the name of the Lord Jesus, giving thanks to God the Father through him. *Colossians 3:17*

---

A heavy wagon was being dragged along a country lane by a team of oxen. The axles groaned and creaked terribly, when the oxen turning around thus addressed the wheels, "Hey there, why do you make so much noise? We bear all the labor, and we—not you—ought to cry out!" Those complain first in our churches who have the least to do. The gift of grumbling is largely dispensed among those who have no other talents, or who keep what they have wrapped up in a napkin.

# Sweet Song of Excellence

Make it your ambition to lead a quiet life, to mind your own business and to work with your hands, just as we told you, so that your daily life may win the respect of outsiders and so that you will not be dependent on anybody. *1 Thessalonians 4:11-12*

Live such good lives among the pagans that, though they accuse you of doing wrong, they may see your good deeds and glorify God on the day he visits us. *1 Peter 2:12*

---

I was once in a spot on the Lago Lugano where the song of the nightingale swelled sweetly from the thickets on the shore in a matchless rush of music, so that the oars lay motionless and I was hushed into silent entrancement. Yet I did not see a single bird; the orchestra was as hidden as the notes were clear.

Such is a virtuous life, and such the influence of modest holiness. The voice of excellence is heard when the excellent themselves are not seen.

# Who Do You Imitate?

Be imitators of God, therefore, as dearly loved children and live a life of love, just as Christ loved us and gave himself up for us as a fragrant offering and sacrifice to God. *Ephesians 5:1*

Dear friend, do not imitate what is evil but what is good. Anyone who does what is good is from God. Anyone who does what is evil has not seen God. *3 John 11*

---

Plutarch says that among the Persians those persons were considered most beautiful who were hawk-nosed, for no other reason than that Cyrus had such a nose. In Richard the Third's court hunchbacks were the height of fashion. According as the various potentates who have condescended to rule mankind have lisped, or stuttered, or limped, or squinted, or spoken through their noses, these infirmities have been elevated into graces and commanded the admiration of silly mortals.

But is there not more than a possibility that what we ridicule in the kingdoms of earth may have its counterpart in the church? Is there not a tendency among Christians to imitate the spiritual infirmities of their religious leaders, or more often still of departed saints? We may follow holy people so far as they follow Christ. The mischief is that we do not readily stop where we should, but rather where we should not. By all means imitate the great heroes of the faith, but not indiscriminately, not slavishly, or you will do so ridiculously. One is your Master, to copy him in every jot and tittle will be safe enough.

# Living Examples

Dear friends, I urge you, as aliens and strangers in the world, to abstain from sinful desires, which war against your soul. Live such good lives among the pagans that, though they accuse you of doing wrong, they may see your good deeds and glorify God on the day he visits us. . . . It is God's will that by doing good you should silence the ignorant talk of foolish men. Live as free men, but do not use your freedom as a cover-up for evil; live as servants of God. *1 Peter 2:11-12, 15-16*

"I have been crucified with Christ and I no longer live, but Christ lives in me. The life I live in the body, I live by faith in the Son of God, who loved me and gave himself for me." *Galatians 2:20*

---

Lord Peterborough spoke of the celebrated Fénélon in this way: "He is a delicious creature. I was forced to get away from him as fast as I possibly could, else he would have made me pious."

I wish that all of us had such an influence over godless men!

# Never Satisfied

Do you not know that in a race all the runners run, but only one gets the prize? Run in such a way as to get the prize. Everyone who competes in the games goes into strict training. They do it to get a crown that will not last; but we do it to get a crown that will last forever. Therefore I do not run like a man running aimlessly; I do not fight like a man beating the air. No, I beat my body and make it my slave so that after I have preached to others, I myself will not be disqualified for the prize.... If you think you are standing firm, be careful that you don't fall! *1 Corinthians 9:24-27; 10:12*

---

"During the nine years that I was his wife," says the wife of the great artist Opie, "I never saw him satisfied with one of his productions, and often, very often, have I seen him enter my sitting room and, throwing himself in an agony of despondence on the sofa, exclaim, 'I never, never shall be a painter as long as I live!'" It was a noble despair, such as is never felt by the self-complacent daubers of signboards, and it bore the panting aspirant up to one of the highest niches in the artistic annals of his country. The same dissatisfaction with present attainments is a potent force to bear the Christian onward to the most eminent degree of spirituality and holiness.

# Remembered for Righteousness

Blessed is the man who fears the LORD, who finds great delight in his commands. His children will be mighty in the land; each generation of the upright will be blessed. Wealth and riches are in his house, and his righteousness endures forever.... Surely he will never be shaken; a righteous man will be remembered forever.
*Psalm 112:1-3, 6*

---

Sir Bernard Burke thus touchingly writes in his *Vicissitudes of Families*, "In 1850 a pedigree research caused me to pay a visit to the village of Finderne, about five miles southwest of Derby. I sought for the ancient hall. Not a stone remained to tell where it had stood! I entered the church. Not a single record of a Finderne was there! I accosted a villager, hoping to glean some stray traditions of the Findernes. 'Findernes!' said he, 'We have no Findernes here, but we have something that once belonged to them. We have Findernes' flowers.'

" 'Show them to me,' I replied, and the old man led me into a field that still retained faint traces of terraces and foundations. 'There,' said he, pointing to a bank of garden flowers grown wild, 'there are the Findernes' flowers, brought by Sir Geoffrey from the Holy Land, and do what we will, they will never die!' "

So be it with each of us. Should our names perish, may the truths we taught, the virtues we cultivated, the good works we initiated, live on and blossom with undying energy.

# A Wisdom Full of Grace and Fear

Who is wise and understanding among you? Let him show it by his good life, by deeds done in the humility that comes from wisdom. *James 3:13*

Clothe yourselves with humility toward one another, because, "God opposes the proud but gives grace to the humble." Humble yourselves, therefore, under God's mighty hand, that he may lift you up in due time. *1 Peter 5:5-6*

---

Quinctilian said of some in his time that they might have become excellent scholars had they not been so persuaded of their scholarship already. Grant, most precious God, that I may never hold so high an opinion of my own spiritual health as to prevent my being in my deeds full of your grace and fear!

# Dangerous Prejudices

When they saw the courage of Peter and John and realized that they were unschooled, ordinary men, they were astonished and they took note that these men had been with Jesus. *Acts 4:13*

---

When people refuse to hear the gospel from the lips of a gracious but uneducated preacher, they remind us of the Spaniard in South America who suffered severely from the gout but refused to be cured by an Indian. "I know," said he, "that he is a famous man and would certainly cure me, but he is an Indian and would expect to be treated with attentions which I cannot pay to a man of color, and therefore I prefer to remain as I am."

# All the Glory Must Be to the Lord

"All men are like grass, and all their glory is like the flowers of the field. The grass withers and the flowers fall, because the breath of the LORD blows on them. Surely the people are grass. The grass withers and the flowers fall, but the word of our God stands forever." *Isaiah 40:6-8*

May the glory of the LORD endure forever; may the LORD rejoice in his works. *Psalm 104:31*

---

A certain king had a minstrel whom he commanded to play before him. It was a day of high feasting. The cups were flowing and many great guests were assembled. The minstrel laid his fingers among the strings of his harp, and woke them all to the sweetest melody, but the hymn was to the glory of himself. It was a celebration of the exploits of song which the bard had himself performed. In high-sounding strains he sang himself and all his glories. When the feast was over, the harper said to the monarch, "Oh king, give me my pay; let the minstrel's fee be paid."

Then the monarch replied, "You have sung to yourself, pay yourself. Your own praises were your theme; be your own pay-master."

The harpist cried, "Didn't I sing sweetly? Oh king, give me my gold!"

But the king answered, "So much the worse for your pride, that you should lavish such sweetness on yourself. Go away, you shall not serve in my train."

If a man should grow grey-headed in the performance of good works, yet when the last it is known that he has done them all for himself, that he may be honored by his works, his Lord will say, "You have done well enough in the eyes of men, but so much the worse, because you did it only to yourself, that your own praises might be sung, and that your own name might be extolled."

# Stand Firm!

So, if you think you are standing firm, be careful that you don't fall!
No temptation has seized you except what is common to man. And
God is faithful; he will not let you be tempted beyond what you
can bear. But when you are tempted, he will also provide a way out
so that you can stand up under it. *1 Corinthians 10:12-13*

---

"The Hindu Brahmins say that Benares is not a part of this sinful
earth, but that it is on the outside of the world. A recent earthquake,
however, has rather nonplused them, as it proves that what shakes
the earth shakes Benares, too." It is easy enough for those who have
been long at ease to imagine themselves protected from the common lot of humankind, but a shaking trial in their estates or persons
soon convinces them that they are as others are. Spiritual presumption leads many believers to imagine that they are beyond the
power of temptation and are no longer such frail beings as their
fellow Christians. Let but the Lord conceal his face, or Satan assail
them, and in their sore trouble they will discover that they are
people of like passions with the rest.

# The Danger of Hypocrisy

# Living a Lie

The LORD says, "These people come near to me with their mouth and honor me with their lips, but their hearts are far from me. Their worship of me is made up only of rules taught by men. Therefore once more I will astound these people with wonder upon wonder; the wisdom of the wise will perish, the intelligence of the intelligent will vanish." *Isaiah 29:13-14*

---

Louis XI made a donation to the Virgin Mary of the whole country of Boulogne, retaining, however, for his own use, the revenues thereof! A solemn deed was drawn up, signed, sealed, and delivered, and it bears the date 1478. What a ridiculous farce! The instrument gives away just nothing at all. But are there no such farces among us? When people of mean and miserly dispositions sing certain of our hymns, are they not guilty of just such a pretense of generosity? With abundance of goods in their power, they fumble for a nickel in their pockets, singing, meanwhile,

> *"Were the whole realm of nature mine,*
> *That were a present far too small;*
> *Love so amazing, so divine*
> *Demands my soul, my life, my all."*

# Life with the Power of the Spirit

I pray that out of his glorious riches he may strengthen you with power through his Spirit in your inner being, so that Christ may dwell in your hearts through faith. And I pray that you, being rooted and established in love, may have power, together with the saints, to grasp how wide and long and high and deep is the love of Christ, and to know this love that surpasses knowledge—that you may be filled to the measure of all the fullness of God. *Ephesians 3:16-19*

---

Don't forget that the pretense of religion without the power of it is one of the most comfortless things in the world. It is like a man who should call his servant and say to him, "Is the larder well stocked?"

"There is nothing, sir, not even a moldy bread crust."

"Set the table," he says. All is laid out, the tablecloth and all the dishes. "And now," he says, "I will sit down to my meal, and you shall wait on me."

The empty dishes are brought in proper course. From invisible joints he cuts imperceptible slices, and from the empty plates he lifts on his fork mouthfuls of nothingness and dainty morsels of vacuum. There, the cloth can be removed, the feaster has finished the atmospheric banquet, and rises from the table free from any charge of immoderate eating. Now, this may be a very pleasant operation for once, although its charms require a very poetic and imaginative mind to appreciate them, but if continued several days, this unsubstantial festival would, I conceive, become somewhat undesirable and cheerless, and in the end the guest might perish amid his empty platters. Yet such must be the life of the man who professes to feed on the bread of heaven and knows not its sustaining virtues, who boasts of drinking the water of life and has never sipped that heavenly stream.

# True Soldiers for the Kingdom

Finally, be strong in the Lord and in his mighty power. Put on the full armor of God so that you can take your stand against the devil's schemes. For our struggle is not against flesh and blood, but against the rulers, against the authorities, against the powers of this dark world and against the spiritual forces of evil in the heavenly realms. Therefore put on the full armor of God, so that when the day of evil comes, you may be able to stand your ground, and after you have done everything, to stand. *Ephesians 6:10-13*

Be on your guard; stand firm in the faith; be men of courage; be strong. *1 Corinthians 16:13*

---

There was an age of chivalry when no coward courted knighthood, for it involved the hard blows, the dangerous wounds, the rough unhorsings, and the ungentle perils of the tournament. And these were but child's play! There were the distant eastern fields, where warriors must be slain by valiant hands, and blood must flow in rivers from the Red-cross knights. Then men who lacked valor preferred hawks and jesters, and left heroes to court death and glory on the battlefield. This genial time of peace breeds carpet knights, who flourish their untried weapons, and bear the insignia of valor, without incurring its inconvenient toils. Many are crowding to the seats of the heroes, since prowess and patience are no more required. The war is over, and every man is willing to enlist.

It is not otherwise today. Into the triumphs of martyrs and confessors few are unwilling to enter; in a national respect to religion, which is the result of their holiness, even ungodly men are willing to share. They have gone before us with true hearts valiant for truth, and false traitors are willing to divide their spoils.

# A True Test of Godliness

"I the LORD search the heart and examine the mind, to reward a man according to his conduct, according to what his deeds deserve." *Jeremiah 17:10*

The lamp of the LORD searches the spirit of a man; it searches out his inmost being. *Proverbs 20:27*

"Acknowledge the God of your father, and serve him with whole-hearted devotion and with a willing mind, for the LORD searches every heart and understands every motive behind the thoughts. If you seek him, he will be found by you; but if you forsake him, he will reject you forever." *1 Chronicles 28:9*

---

In the olden times even the best rooms were usually made of bare brick or stone, damp and moldy. But in great houses where the family was resident, arras or hangings of rich materials were hung over these. People could conceal themselves behind these so that literally the walls had ears. I'm afraid that many brave shows of godliness are like an arras to conceal rank hypocrisy. This accounts for some people's religion being only occasional, since it is folded up or exposed to view as need may demand. Is there no room for conscience to pry between professed godliness and real ungodliness? If conscience won't do it, certainly "the watcher and the Holy One" will make a thorough search in you.

# A Form of Godliness

". . . having a form of godliness but denying its power." *2 Timothy 3:5*

Not long ago I stood for a while in a cheese shop. Being in a fidgety mood, and having a stick in my hand, I was not content with seeing but felt a need to touch as well. My stick came gently upon a fine cheese in the window. To my surprise a most metallic sound emanated from it. The sound was rather hollow, and there was a sort of crockery jingle in the sound, like the ring of a huge bread or milk pan. I came to the very correct conclusion that I had found a very well disguised hypocrite in the shop window. And ever since that time, when I pass by, I mentally whisper, "Pottery." Even if the fakes have been exchanged for real cheeses, it will take a long time to convince me. In my mind the stock has become potsherds, and the fine show in the window only suggests the potter's vessel. This illustration is simply introduced because we find people of this sort in our churches, looking extremely like what they should be, yet having no substance in them, so that if, accidentally, one happens to tap them somewhere or other with sudden temptation or stern duty, the baked earth gives forth its own ring, and the pretender is esteemed no longer.

# The Danger of Hypocrisy

"Others, like seed sown on rocky places, hear the word and at once receive it with joy. But since they have no root, they last only a short time. When trouble or persecution comes because of the word, they quickly fall away. Still others, like seed sown among thorns, hear the word; but the worries of this life, the deceitfulness of wealth and the desires for other things come in and choke the word, making it unfruitful." *Mark 4:16-19*

So, if you think you are standing firm, be careful that you don't fall! *1 Corinthians 10:12*

---

"The meteor, once it falls, cannot be rekindled." When those who once flashed before the eyes of the religious public with the blaze of a vain profession fall into open and scandalous sin, it is impossible to renew their glory. Once the egg of hypocrisy is broken, who can repair the damage?

# No Secret Sins

"Am I only a God nearby," declares the LORD, "and not a God far away? Can anyone hide in secret places so that I cannot see him?" declares the LORD. "Do not I fill heaven and earth?" declares the LORD. *Jeremiah 23:23-24*

He who conceals his sins does not prosper, but whoever confesses and renounces them finds mercy. *Proverbs 28:13*

"You may be sure that your sin will find you out." *Numbers 32:23*

"There is nothing concealed that will not be disclosed, or hidden that will not be made known." *Matthew 10:26*

---

Coals of fire cannot be concealed beneath the most sumptuous apparel, they will betray themselves with smoke and flame. Neither can pet sins be long hidden beneath the most ostentatious profession of faith; they will sooner or later discover themselves, and burn sad holes in a person's reputation. Sin needs quenching in the Savior's blood, not concealing under the garb of religion.

# Remember the Last Great Day

Nothing in all creation is hidden from God's sight. Everything is uncovered and laid bare before the eyes of him to whom we must give account. *Hebrews 4:13*

" 'As surely as I live,' says the Lord, 'Every knee will bow before me; every tongue will confess to God.' " So then, each of us will give an account of himself to God. *Romans 14:11-12*

---

How many are like that famous painting of olden times, in which the artist depicted what seemed at a distance a holy friar with a book before him, and his hands crossed in devotion, looking like a saint indeed, but when you came close to the venerable impostor, you found that his hands, though clasped, enclosed a lemon, and instead of a book there was a punch-bowl into which he was squeezing juice. *To seem to be* answers men's purposes so well that it is little marvel if pretenders swarm like the flies in Egypt's plague. Yet if they would remember the last great day, men would abhor hypocrisy.

# Rainless Clouds, Fruitless Trees, Foaming Waves, Wandering Stars

For certain men whose condemnation was written about long ago have secretly slipped in among you. They are godless men, who change the grace of our God into a license for immorality and deny Jesus Christ our only Sovereign and Lord. . . . These men are blemishes at your love feasts, eating with you without the slightest qualm—shepherds who feed only themselves. They are clouds without rain, blown along by the wind; autumn trees, without fruit and uprooted—twice dead. They are wild waves of the sea, foaming up their shame; wandering stars, for whom blackest darkness has been reserved forever. *Jude 4, 12-13*

---

After a refreshing shower that has made all the flowers to smile till the teardrops of joy stand in their eyes, you will see your garden paths spotted over with slugs and snails. These creatures lay concealed till the genial rain called them forth to make their slimy way toward whatever they might devour.

In the same way, revivals, of necessity, sometimes develop hypocrites. Yet who would deplore the shower because of the snails, and who would complain about "times of refreshing" because mere pretenders are excited to make a base profession of a grace to which they are strangers?

# Lying Lips

Like a coating of glaze over earthenware are fervent lips with an evil heart. A malicious man disguises himself with his lips, but in his heart he harbors deceit. Though his speech is charming, do not believe him, for seven abominations fill his heart. His malice may be concealed by deception, but his wickedness will be exposed in the assembly. *Proverbs 26:23-26*

The LORD says: "These people come near to me with their mouth and honor me with their lips, but their hearts are far from me. Their worship of me is made up only of rules taught by men. Therefore once more I will astound these people with wonder upon wonder; the wisdom of the wise will perish, the intelligence of the intelligent will vanish." *Isaiah 29:13-14*

---

"God is in the hypocrite's mouth, but the world is in his heart, which he expects to gain through his good reputation. I have read of one that offered his prince a great sum of money to have permission once or twice a day to come into his presence, and only say, 'God save your Majesty!' The prince, wondering at this large offer for so small a favor, asked him, 'What advantage would this afford him?'

" 'Oh sire,' he said, 'this, though I have nothing else at your hands, will get me a name in the country for one who is a great favorite at court and such an opinion will help me more than it costs me for the purchase.'

"Thus some, by the name they get for great saints, advance their worldly interests, which lie at the bottom of all their profession of faith."—*Gurnall*

# Though the Wicked Seem to Prosper . . .

But as for me, my feet had almost slipped; I had nearly lost my foothold. For I envied the arrogant when I saw the prosperity of the wicked. They have no struggles; their bodies are healthy and strong. They are free from the burdens common to man; they are not plagued by human ills. . . . This is what the wicked are like—always carefree, they increase in wealth. . . . Surely you place them on slippery ground; you cast them down to ruin. How suddenly are they destroyed, completely swept away by terrors! . . . Those who are far from you will perish; you destroy all who are unfaithful to you. But as for me, it is good to be near God. I have made the Sovereign LORD my refuge. *Psalm 73:2-5, 12, 18-19, 27-28*

---

See how the eagle mounts! Does it care for the ethereal blue, or aspire to commune with the stars of heaven? Not a whit; such airy considerations have no weight with the ravenous bird, and yet you will not wonder that it soars aloft when you remember that it thus obtains a broader range of vision and so becomes more able to provide for its nest. The bird mounts toward heaven, but it keeps its eye evermore on the outlook for its prey. No celestial impulse is needed, its love of blood suffices to bear it aloft. It soars only that it may flash downward with fell swoop on the object of its desires. Wonder not that people with the hearts of devils yet mount like angels: there is a reason that explains it all.

# No Tricks in Prayer

"Two men went up to the temple to pray, one a Pharisee and one a tax collector. The Pharisee stood up and prayed about himself; 'God, I thank you that I am not like all other men—robbers, evildoers, adulterers—or even like this tax collector. I fast twice a week and give a tenth of all I get.' But the tax collector stood at a distance. He would not even look up to heaven, but beat his breast and said, 'God, have mercy on me, a sinner.' I tell you that this man, rather than the other, went home justified before God. For everyone who exalts himself will be humbled, and he who humbles himself will be exalted." *Luke 18:10-14*

---

"You have no doubt heard of beggars who tie up a leg when they go begging and then make hideous lamentation of their lameness. Why, it is the same thing when you go to church praying, which is begging, and tie your righteous heart up and then make woeful outcry for mercy on us miserable sinners. These tricks may pass awhile unnoticed, but Jesus Christ will apprehend such cheats at last and give them what they deserve."—*John Berridge*

# Yoking Two Lions

"No servant can serve two masters. Either he will hate the one and love the other, or he will be devoted to the one and despise the other. You cannot serve both God and Money . . . God knows your hearts. What is highly valued among men is detestable in God's sight." *Luke 16:13, 15*

God is light; in him there is no darkness at all. If we claim to have fellowship with him yet walk in the darkness, we lie and do not live by the truth. But if we walk in the light, as he is in the light, we have fellowship with one another, and the blood of Jesus, his Son, purifies us from every sin. *1 John 1:5-7*

---

Mark Antony once yoked two lions together and drove them through the streets of Rome, but no human skill can ever yoke together the Lion of the Tribe of Judah and the Lion of the Pit. I did see a man once trying to walk on both sides of the street at one time, but he was undoubtedly drunk. And when we see a person laboring day by day to walk on both sides of the street morally—in the shady side of sin and the sunny side of holiness, or reeling in the evening, at one time toward the bright lights of virtue, and then staggering back to sin in dark places, where no lamp is shining—we say of him, "He is morally intoxicated," and wisdom adds, "He is mad, and if the Great Physician heal him not, his madness will bring him to destruction."

# True Repentance Required

Godly sorrow brings repentance that leads to salvation and leaves no regret, but worldly sorrow brings death. See what this godly sorrow has produced in you: what earnestness, what eagerness to clear yourselves, what indignation, what alarm, what longing, what concern, what readiness to see justice done. *2 Corinthians 7:10-11*

---

The gondoliers at Venice, when we were sojourning in that queen of the Adriatic, frequently quarreled with each other, and used such high words and ferocious gestures that we were afraid murder would come of it. Yet they never came to blows, it was only their rough way of disputing. Often and often have we heard men upbraiding themselves for their sins, and crying out against the evil which their follies have wrought them. Yet these very people have continued in their transgressions, and have even gone from bad to worse. They barked too much at sin to fall to and destroy it. Their enmity to evil was mere feigning—like the sword-play of the stage, which looks like an earnest fight, but no wounds are given or received. Let those who play at repentance remember that they who repent in mimicry shall go to hell in reality.

# Holiness That Holds Up Under Scrutiny

LORD, who may dwell in your sanctuary? Who may live on your holy hill? He whose walk is blameless and who does what is righteous, who speaks the truth from his heart and has no slander on his tongue, who does his neighbor no wrong and casts no slur on his fellow man, who despises a vile man but honors those who fear the LORD, who keeps his oath even when it hurts, who lends his money without usury and does not accept a bribe against the innocent. He who does these things will never be shaken. *Psalm 15:1-5*

---

"In the sweet valley between Chamouni and the Valais, at every turn of the pleasant pathway, where the scent of thyme lies richest upon its rocks, we shall see a little cross and shrine set under one of them, and go up to it, hoping to receive some happy thought of the Redeemer, by whom all these lovely things were made, and still consist. But when we come near, behold, beneath the cross a rude picture of souls tormented in red tongues of hell fire, and pierced by demons."—*Ruskin*

Too often the house of him who professes to be a Christian turns out to be the same. The beauty at a distance changes into hideous deformity when near. Oh, to be found, when closest watched, better than observers would at first sight have conceived us to be!

# A Facade of Godliness

See to it, brothers, that none of you has a sinful, unbelieving heart that turns away from the living God. But encourage one another daily, as long as it is called Today, so that none of you may be hardened by sin's deceitfulness. We have come to share in Christ if we hold firmly till the end the confidence we had at first. *Hebrews 3:12-14*

The crucible for silver and the furnace for gold, but the LORD tests the heart. *Proverbs 17:3*

But your hearts must be fully committed to the LORD our God, to live by his decrees and obey his commands. *1 Kings 8:61*

---

How like a Christian a person may be and yet possess no vital godliness! Walk through a museum and you will see all the orders of animals standing in their various places and exhibiting themselves with the utmost possible propriety. The rhinoceros demurely retains the position in which he was set at first, the eagle does not soar through the window, the wolf does not howl at night. Every creature, whether bird, beast, or fish, remains in the particular glass case allotted to it. But we know that these are not the creatures, but only the outward semblances of them. Yet in what do they differ? Certainly in nothing which you could readily see, for the well-stuffed animal is precisely like what the living animal would have been. That eye of glass even appears to have more brightness in it than the natural eye of the creature itself. But there is a secret inward something lacking, which, when it has once departed, you cannot restore. So in the churches of Christ, many professing believers are not living believers, but stuffed Christians. They possess all the externals of religion, and every outward morality that you could desire. They behave with great propriety, they keep their places, and there is no outward difference between them and the true believer, except upon the vital point, the life which no power on earth can possibly confer. There is this essential distinction, spiritual life is absent.

---

# Stewardship of Self and Possessions

# Stewardship and Freedom

From everyone who has been given much, much will be demanded; and from the one who has been entrusted with much, much more will be asked. *Luke 12:48*

For we will all stand before God's judgment seat. It is written: " 'As surely as I live,' says the Lord, 'Every knee will bow before me; every tongue will confess to God.' " So then each of us will give an account of himself to God. *Romans 14:10-12*

---

When Bishop Latimer resigned, Foxe tells us that as he put off his rochet from his shoulders he gave a skip on the floor for joy, "feeling his shoulders so light at being discharged of such a burden." To be relieved of wealth or high position is to be unloaded of weighty responsibilities, and should not be a cause for worry, but rather for rejoicing as those who are lightened of a great load. If we step down from office in the church, or from public honors, or from power of any sort, we may be consoled by the thought that there is just so much the less for us to answer for at the great audit, when we must give an account of our stewardship.

# Stewardship of the Soul

"For whoever wants to save his life will lose it, but whoever loses his life for me will find it. What good will it be for a man if he gains the whole world, yet forfeits his soul? Or what can a man give in exchange for his soul? For the Son of Man is going to come in his Father's glory with his angels, and then he will reward each person according to what he has done." *Matthew 16:25-27*

---

" 'Two things a master commits to his servants' care,' someone said, 'the child and the child's clothes.' It would be a poor excuse for the servant to say, at his master's return, 'Sir, here are all the child's clothes, neat and clean, but the child is lost!'

"It is the same way with the account that many will give to God of their souls and bodies at the great day. 'Lord, here is my body. I was very grateful for it. I neglected nothing that belonged to its content and welfare. But as for my soul, that is lost and cast away forever. I took little care and thought about it!' "—*Flavel*

# Traveling Light

"Do not worry about your life, what you will eat; or about your body, what you will wear. Life is more than food, and the body more than clothes. Consider the ravens: They do not sow or reap, they have no storeroom or barn; yet God feeds them. And how much more valuable you are than birds! Who of you by worrying can add a single hour to his life? Since you cannot do this very little thing, why do you worry about the rest? . . . Do not be afraid, little flock, for your Father has been pleased to give you the kingdom."
*Luke 12:22-26, 32*

---

"A person says, 'I cannot understand how I am to get along when I leave my father's house.' Why should he understand it until that time comes? What if a person going on a journey of five years should undertake to carry provisions, clothes, and money enough to last him during the whole time, lugging them as he traveled, like a veritable Englishman, with all creation at his back! If he is wise he will supply himself at the different points where he stops. When he gets to London, let him buy what he needs there. When he gets to Rome, let him buy what he needs there. And when he gets to Vienna, Dresden, Munich, St. Petersburg, and Canton, let him buy what he needs at these places! He will find at each of them, and all the other cities he visits, whatever thing he requires. Why, then, should he undertake to carry them around the globe with him? It would be the greatest folly imaginable."—*Henry Ward Beecher*

# Humble Beginnings

Brothers, think of what you were when you were called. Not many of you were wise by human standards; not many were influential; not many were of noble birth. But God chose the foolish things of the world to shame the wise; God chose the weak things of the world to shame the strong. He chose the lowly things of this world and the despised things—and the things that are not—to nullify the things that are, so that no one may boast before him. It is because of him that you are in Christ Jesus, who has become for us wisdom from God—that is, our righteousness, holiness and redemption. *1 Corinthians 1:26-30*

---

When the hot-air balloon was first discovered, a matter-of-fact gentleman contemptuously asked Dr. Franklin what the use of it was. The doctor answered this question by asking another: "What is the use of a new-born infant? It may become a man!" This anticipation of great things springing from small beginnings should induce us to put into practice those holy promptings which at certain seasons move our souls. What if we ourselves and our work should be little in Zion? Can't the Lord cause the grandest issues to proceed from insignificant beginnings? Don't despise the small things.

# Too Much Is Too Much

Command those who are rich in this present world not to be arrogant nor to put their hope in wealth, which is so uncertain, but to put their hope in God, who richly provides us with everything for our enjoyment. Command them to do good, to be rich in good deeds, and to be generous and willing to share. In this way they will lay up treasure for themselves as a firm foundation for the coming age, so that they may take hold of the life that is truly life. *1 Timothy 6:17-19*

---

Beware of growing covetousness, for of all sins this is one of the most insidious. It is like the silting up of a river. As the stream comes down from the land, it brings with it sand and earth and deposits all these at its mouth, so that by degrees, unless the conservators watch it carefully, it will block itself up and leave no channel for ships of great burden. By daily deposit it imperceptibly creates a bar which is dangerous to navigation. Many a man when he begins to accumulate wealth commences at the same moment to ruin his soul, and the more he acquires, the more closely he blocks up his liberality, which is, so to speak, the very mouth of spiritual life. Instead of doing more for God he does less. The more he saves the more he wants, and the more he wants of this world the less he cares for the world to come.

# Caught by Covetousness

"Watch out! Be on your guard against all kinds of greed; a man's life does not consist in the abundance of his possessions." *Luke 12:15*

"Do not store up for yourselves treasures on earth, where moth and rust destroy, and where thieves break in and steal. But store up for yourselves treasures in heaven, where moth and rust do not destroy, and where thieves do not break in and steal. For where your treasure is, there your heart will be also." *Matthew 6:19-21*

---

Covetous men must be the sport of Satan, for their grasping avarice neither lets them enjoy life nor escape from the second death. They are held by their own greed as surely as beasts with cords, or fish with nets, or men with chains. They may be likened to those foolish apes which in some countries are caught by narrow-necked vessels. Into these corn is placed, the creatures thrust in their hands, and when they have filled them they cannot draw out their fists unless they let go the grain. Sooner than let go they submit to be captured. Are covetous men then so like to animals? Let them ponder and be ashamed.

# Getting Ahead—At the Expense of Others

Do nothing out of selfish ambition or vain conceit, but in humility consider others better than yourselves. Each of you should look not only to your own interests, but also to the interests of others. *Philippians 2:3-4*

---

Ambition, a good enough thing within reasonable bounds, is an Apollyon among men, when it gets the mastery over them. Have you ever seen boys climbing a greasy pole to reach a hat or handkerchief? If so, you will have noticed that the aspiring youths for the most part adopt plans and tricks quite as slimy as the pole. One covers his hands with sand, another twists a knotted cord, and still another one climbs fairly (and he is the one boy whose chance is smallest!). The hasty desire to rise is the cause of many a fall. Those who see the glittering heaps of gold before them are frequently in so much haste to thrust their arms in up to the elbow among the treasures that they take shortcuts, leave the beaten road of honest labor, break through hedges, and find themselves before long in a ditch. It is hard to keep great riches without sin, and we have heard that it is harder still to get them. Walk warily, successful friend! Growing wealth will prove no blessing to you unless you acquire growing grace. Prosperity destroys a fool and endangers a wise man. Be on your guard, for whichever you are, your testing hour has come.

# The Dangerous Lure of Riches

For we brought nothing into the world, and we can take nothing out of it. But if we have food and clothing, we will be content with that. People who want to get rich fall into temptation and a trap and into many foolish and harmful desires that plunge men into ruin and destruction. For the love of money is a root of all kinds of evil. Some people, eager for money, have wandered from the faith and pierced themselves with many griefs. *1 Timothy 6:7-10*

---

"I was walking through an orchard when I saw a low tree laden more heavily with fruit than the rest. On a nearer examination, it appeared that the tree had been dragged to the very earth, and broken by the weight of its treasures. 'Oh!' said I, gazing on the tree, 'here lies one who has been ruined by his riches.'

"Then I met a man hobbling along on two wooden legs, leaning on two sticks. 'Tell me,' said I, 'my poor fellow, how you came to lose your legs.'

" 'Why, sir,' said he, 'in my younger days I was a soldier. With a few comrades I attacked a party of the enemy. We overcame them and began to load ourselves with spoil. My comrades were satisfied with little, but I burdened myself with as much as I could carry. We were pursued. My companions escaped, but I was overtaken and so cruelly wounded that I only saved my life afterward by losing my legs. It was a bad affair. But it is too late to repent now.'

" 'Ah, friend,' thought I, 'like the fruit tree, you may date your downfall to your possessions. It was your riches that ruined you.'

"Do not be over-anxious about riches. Get as much of true wisdom and goodness as you can, but be satisfied with a very moderate portion of this world's good. Riches may prove a curse as well as a blessing.

" 'Give me neither poverty nor riches; feed me with food convenient for me: lest I be full and deny thee, and say, Who is the Lord? or lest I be poor and steal, and take the name of my God in vain' (Proverbs 30:8-9)."—*Old Humphrey*

---

# Dangerous Wealth

"Store up for yourselves treasures in heaven, where moth and rust do not destroy, and where thieves do not break in and steal. For where your treasure is, there your heart will be also. *Matthew 6:20-21*

"How hard it is for the rich to enter the kingdom of God! Indeed, it is easier for a camel to go through the eye of a needle than for a rich man to enter the kingdom of God." *Luke 18:24-25*

---

Did the eye ever rest upon a more utter desolation than that which surrounds the gold mines near Goldau in the Hartz mountains? It is worse than a howling wilderness; it is a desert with its bowels torn out and scattered in horrid confusion. More or less is true of all gold mining regions. Humboldt, when writing of the Pearl Coast, says that it presents the same aspect of misery as the countries of gold and diamonds.

Is it so then? Are riches so closely akin to horror? Lord, let me set my affections on better things and seek for less dangerous wealth.

# Fueling the Voracious Fire

Whoever loves money never has money enough; whoever loves wealth is never satisfied with his income. This too is meaningless. *Ecclesiastes 5:10*

You open your hand and satisfy the desires of every living thing. The LORD is righteous in all his ways and loving toward all he has made. *Psalm 145:16-17*

---

Ambition is like the sea which swallows all the rivers and still is not more full; or like the insatiable grave which forever craves the bodies of men. In all probability, Napoleon never longed for a scepter till he had gained the baton, nor dreamed of being emperor of Europe till he had gained the crown of France. Caligula, with the world at his feet, was mad with a longing for the moon, and if he could have gained it the imperial lunatic would have coveted the sun. It is in vain to feed a fire which grows the more voracious the more it is supplied with fuel. He who lives to satisfy his ambition has before him the labor of Sisyphus, who rolled up hill an ever-rebounding stone, and the task of the daughters of Danaus, who are condemned forever to attempt to fill a bottomless vessel with buckets full of holes. If we knew the secret heartbreaks and weariness of ambitious men, we would flee from ambition as from the most accursed blood-sucking vampire which ever rose up from the caverns of hell.

# A Holy Day

Observe the Sabbath day by keeping it holy, as the LORD your God has commanded you. Six days you shall labor and do all your work, but the seventh day is a Sabbath to the LORD your God. *Deuteronomy 5:12-14*

---

When a gentleman was inspecting a house in Newcastle, with a view to renting it as a residence, the landlord took him to the upper window, expatiated on the extensive prospect, and added, "You can see Durham Cathedral from this window on a Sunday."

"Why on a Sunday and not any other day?" inquired our friend, with some degree of surprise.

The reply was conclusive enough. "Because on that day there is no smoke from those tall chimneys."

Blessed is the Sabbath to us when the earth-smoke of care and turmoil no longer clouds our view. Then our souls often behold the goodly land, and the city of the New Jerusalem.

# Stewardship of the Self

For the grace of God that brings salvation has appeared to all men. It teaches us to say "No" to ungodliness and worldly passions, and to live self-controlled, upright and godly lives in this present age, while we wait for the blessed hope—the glorious appearing of our great God and Savior, Jesus Christ, who gave himself for us to redeem us from all wickedness and to purify for himself a people that are his very own, eager to do what is good. *Titus 2:11-14*

---

An old writer, speaking of people as stewards of God, urges upon them as wise traders and servants to look to themselves carefully, and take care of four houses that are under their charge.

1. The warehouse—or heart and memory—where they should store up precious things, holy affections, grateful remembrances, celestial preparations, etc. Without a good stock in the warehouse there can be no good trade.

2. The workhouse—or actions—where they retail to others for God's glory the grace entrusted to them, teaching the ignorant, comforting the poor, visiting the sick, etc. We must be active, or we cannot be acceptable servants.

3. The clockhouse—meaning speech—which must always, like a well-timed bell, speak the truth accurately; also meaning observance of time, redeeming it by promptly doing the duties of every hour. We must use time well, or our spiritual gains will be small.

4. The counting-house—or the conscience—is to be scrupulously watched, and no false reckonings allowed, lest we deceive our own souls. The Master will call for our accounts; let us keep them honestly.

# Letting Everything Else Go

I consider everything a loss compared to the surpassing greatness of knowing Christ Jesus my Lord, for whose sake I have lost all things. I consider them rubbish, that I may gain Christ and be found in him, not having a righteousness of my own that comes from the law, but that which is through faith in Christ—the righteousness that comes from God and is by faith. I want to know Christ and the power of his resurrection and the fellowship of sharing in his sufferings, becoming like him in his death, and so, somehow, to attain to the resurrection from the dead. *Philippians 3:8-11*

---

Maturity in grace makes us willing to part with worldly goods. The green apple needs a sharp twist to separate it from the bough, but the ripe fruit parts readily from the wood. Maturity in grace makes it easier to part with life itself. The unripe pear is scarcely beaten down with much labor, while its mellow companion drops readily into the hand with the slightest shake. Rest assured that love for the things of this life and cleaving to this present state are sure indications of immaturity in the divine life.

# The Rich Need Heaven's Help

Do not wear yourself out to get rich; have the wisdom to show restraint. Cast but a glance at riches, and they are gone, for they will surely sprout wings and fly off to the sky like an eagle. *Proverbs 23:4-5*

---

It was as much as we could do to keep our feet on the splendid mosaic floor of the Palace Giovanelli at Venice: we found no such difficulty in the cottage of the poor glassblower in the rear. Is it one of the advantages of wealth to have one's abode polished till all comfort vanishes, and the very floor is as smooth and dangerous as a sheet of ice, or is there merely an accidental circumstance typical of the dangers of abundance? Observation shows us that there is a fascination in wealth that renders it extremely difficult for the possessors of it to maintain their equilibrium. And this is more especially the case where money is suddenly acquired, for then, unless grace prevent, pride, affectation, and other mean vices stupify the brain with their sickening fumes, and he who was respectable in poverty becomes despicable in prosperity. Pride may lurk under a threadbare cloak, but it prefers the comely broadcloth of the merchant's coat. Moth will eat any of our garments, but they seem to fly first to the costly furs. It is so much easier for men to fall when walking on wealth's sea of glass, because all men aid them to do so. Flatterers don't haunt cottages; the poor may hear an honest word from his neighbor, but etiquette forbids that the rich man should enjoy the same privilege. For is it not a maxim in Babylon, that rich men have no faults, or only such as their money, like charity, covers with a mantle? What man can help slipping when everybody is intent on greasing his ways, so that the smallest chance of standing may be denied him? The world's proverb is, "God help the poor, for the rich can help themselves," but to our mind, it is just the rich who have most need of heaven's help. Dives in scarlet is worse off than Lazarus in rags, unless divine love shall uphold him.

---

# The Day of Judgment

# "My Sin Is Always Before Me"

Have mercy on me, O God, according to your unfailing love; according to your great compassion blot out my transgressions. Wash away all my iniquity and cleanse me from my sin. For I know my transgressions, and my sin is always before me. *Psalm 51:1-3*

---

When that famous statesman Mirabeau died, all France bewailed his loss, and people for some hours could think or speak of little else. A waiter in one of the restaurants of the Palais Royal, after the manner of his race, saluted a customer with the usual remark, "Fine weather, Monsieur."

"Yes, my friend," replied the other, "very fine. But Mirabeau is dead."

If one absorbing thought can thus take precedence of every other in the affairs of life, is it so very amazing that people aroused to care for the life to come should be altogether swallowed up with grief at the dread discovery that they are by reason of sin condemned of God? Whether the weather may be fine or foul, if the soul is under the wrath of God its woeful condition will make it careless of surroundings. If his former security be dead, and the fear of coming judgment is alive in the man's heart, it is little wonder if eating and drinking can be forgotten, if sleep forsake his eyelids and even household joys become insipid. Let but the one emotion be great enough, and it will push out every other. The bitterness of spiritual grief will destroy both the honey of earthly bliss and the quassia of bodily pain.

# "I Never Thought of That!"

The LORD Almighty has a day in store for all the proud and lofty, for all that is exalted (and they will be humbled) . . . The arrogance of man will be brought low and the pride of men humbled; the LORD alone will be exalted in that day, and the idols will totally disappear. *Isaiah 2:12, 17*

Search me, O God, and know my heart; test me and know my anxious thoughts. See if there is any offensive way in me, and lead me in the way everlasting. *Psalm 139:23-24*

---

Is it not foolish to be living in this world without a thought of what you will do at the end of it? A man goes into an inn, and as soon as he sits down he begins to order his wine, his dinner, his bed; there is no delicacy in season that he forgets to order. He stays at the inn for some time. By and by, the bill comes due, and it takes him by surprise. "I never thought of that—I never thought of that!"

"Why," says the landlord, "here is a man who is either a born fool or else a knave. What! Never thought of reckoning—never thought of settling with me!"

After this fashion too many live. They eat, and drink, and sin, but they forget the inevitable hereafter, when for all the deeds done in the body, the Lord will bring us into judgment.

# Warnings of the Wrath of God

Since we have now been justified by his blood, how much more shall we be saved from God's wrath through him! For if, when we were God's enemies, we were reconciled to him through the death of his Son, how much more, having been reconciled, shall we be saved through his life! *Romans 5:9-10*

---

A very skillful bowman went to the mountains in search of game. All the beasts of the forest fled at his approach. The lion alone challenged him to combat. The bowman immediately let fly an arrow and said to the lion, "I send you my messenger, that from him you might learn what I myself will be when I assail you." The lion thus wounded rushed away in great fear, and when a fox exhorted him to be of good courage and not to run away at the first attack, he said, "You counsel me in vain, for if he sends so fearful a messenger, how shall I abide the attack of the man himself?"

If the warning admonitions of God's ministers fill the conscience with terror, what must it be to face the Lord himself? If one bolt of judgment brings a man into a cold sweat, what will it be to stand before an angry God in the last great day?

# The Deceptive Nature of Sin

Sow for yourselves righteousness, reap the fruit of unfailing love, and break up your unplowed ground; for it is time to seek the LORD, until he comes and showers righteousness on you. But you have planted wickedness, you have reaped evil, you have eaten the fruit of deception. *Hosea 10:12-13*

They are darkened in their understanding and separated from the life of God because of the ignorance that is in them due to the hardening of their hearts. Having lost all sensitivity, they have given themselves over to sensuality so as to indulge in every kind of impurity, with a continual lust for more. *Ephesians 4:18-19*

---

"Those who give themselves up to the service of sin enter the palace of pleasure by wide portals of marble, which conceal the low wicket behind which leads into the fields, where they are in a short time sent to feed swine."—*James D. Burns*

# Dangerous Pleasures

Do not love the world or anything in the world. If anyone loves the world, the love of the Father is not in him. For everything in the world—the cravings of sinful man, the lust of his eyes and the boasting of what he has and does—comes not from the Father but from the world. The world and its desires pass away, but the man who does the will of God lives forever. *1 John 2:15-17*

---

What a diabolical invention was the "Virgin's kiss" once used by the fathers of the Inquisition! The victim was pushed forward to kiss the image, then its arms enclosed him in a deadly embrace, piercing his body with a hundred hidden knives. The tempting pleasures of sin offer to the unwary just such a virgin's kiss. The sinful joys of the flesh lead, even in this world, to results most terrible, while in the world to come the daggers of remorse and despair will cut and wound beyond all remedy.

# The Consequences of Transgression

Therefore, just as sin entered the world through one man, and death through sin, and in this way death came to all men, because all sinned—for before the law was given, sin was in the world. *Romans 5:12-13*

---

Sages of old contended that no sin was ever committed whose consequences rested on the head of the sinner alone, that no man could do ill and others not suffer. They illustrated it in this way: "A vessel sailing from Joppa carried a passenger who, beneath his berth, cut a hole through the ship's side. When the men of the watch rebuked him, 'What are you doing, you miserable man?' the offender calmly replied, 'What does it matter to you? The hole I have made is under my own berth.' "

This ancient parable is worthy of the utmost consideration. No man perishes alone in his iniquity. No man can guess the full consequences of his transgression.

# A Surprise for the Self-Righteous

Now, brothers, about times and dates we do not need to write to you, for you know very well that the day of the Lord will come like a thief in the night. While people are saying, "Peace and safety," destruction will come on them suddenly, as labor pains on a pregnant woman, and they will not escape. But you, brothers, are not in darkness so that this day should surprise you like a thief.
*1 Thessalonians 5:1-4*

---

When the lofty spire of Old St. Paul's was destroyed by lightning, there were many superstitious people who were amazed beyond measure at the calamity, for in the cross there had long been deposited relics of certain saints which were considered sufficient to avert all danger of tempests. With what amazement will ignorant, self-righteous sinners see their own destruction come upon them, notwithstanding all the refuge of lies in which they trusted.

# The Way to Hell Is Easy

"Enter through the narrow gate. For wide is the gate and broad is the road that leads to destruction, and many enter through it. But small is the gate and narrow the road that leads to life, and only a few find it." *Matthew 7:13-14*

Jesus looked at him and loved him. "One thing you lack," he said. "Go, sell everything you have and give to the poor, and you will have treasure in heaven. Then come, follow me."

At this the man's face fell. He went away sad, because he had great wealth.

Jesus looked around and said to his disciples, "How hard it is for the rich to enter the kingdom of God!" *Mark 10:21-23*

---

A holy woman used to say of the rich, "They are hemmed around with no common misery; they go down to hell without thinking of it, because their staircase thither is of gold and porphyry."

# Sin Obscures the Imminent Danger

But the day of the Lord will come like a thief. The heavens will disappear with a roar; the elements will be destroyed by fire, and the earth and everything in it will be laid bare. Since everything will be destroyed in this way, what kind of people ought you to be? You ought to live holy and godly lives as you look forward to the day of God and speed its coming. *2 Peter 3:10-12*

---

A writer in the *Edinburgh Review* said, "A Swiss traveler describes a village situated on the slope of a great mountain. Huge crags, directly overhanging the village, and massive enough to sweep the whole of it into the torrent below, have become separated from the main body of the mountain in the course of ages by great fissures and now barely adhere to it. When they give way, the village must perish; it is only a question of time, and the catastrophe may happen any day. The villagers, for more than one generation, have been aware of their danger. They have been encouraged to move, yet they live on in their doomed dwellings, from year to year, fortified against the ultimate certainty and daily probability of destruction by the common sentiment, 'Things may last their time and longer.' "

Like the dwellers in this doomed village, the world's inhabitants have grown careless and secure in sin. The scoffers of the last days are around us, saying, "Where is the promise of his coming? For since the fathers fell asleep, all things continue as they were from the beginning of creation." But in saying this, they are too confident. Nothing is permanent that has sin about it, nothing secure that has wrath above it, and flames of fire beneath it. Sin has once deluged the world with water, it shall deluge it again with waves of fire. Sodom and Gomorrah are the types that foreshadow the doom of those that live ungodly in these latter times, and he who can walk this reeling world unmoved by all the tokens of its fiery doom, must either have a rock of refuge where his soul may rest secure, or else must have fallen into a strange carelessness, and a sad forgetfulness of God.

# Do Not Harden Your Hearts

See to it, brothers, that none of you has a sinful, unbelieving heart that turns away from the living God. But encourage one another daily, as long as it is called Today, so that none of you may be hardened by sin's deceitfulness. We have come to share in Christ if we hold firmly till the end the confidence we had at first. As has just been said: "Today, if you hear his voice, do not harden your hearts." *Hebrews 3:12-15*

---

Do any of you remember the loss of the vessel called the "Central America"? She was in a bad state, had sprung a leak, and was going down. She therefore hoisted a signal of distress. A ship came close to her, and its captain asked, through the trumpet, "What is wrong?"

"We are in bad repair and are going down. Wait till morning," was the answer.

But the captain on board the rescue ship said, "Let me take your passengers on board now."

"Wait until morning," was the message that came back.

Once again the captain cried, "You had better let me take your passengers on board now."

"Wait until morning," was the reply that sounded through the trumpet.

About an hour and a half later, the lights were gone, and though no sound was heard, she and all on board had gone down to the fathomless abyss. Unconverted friends, for God's sake, do not say, "Wait until morning." Today, hear God's voice.

# Don't Put It Off—Be Ready!

"Two men will be in the field; one will be taken and the other left. Two women will be grinding with a hand mill; one will be taken and the other left. Therefore keep watch, because you do not know on what day your Lord will come. But understand this: If the owner of the house had known at what time of night the thief was coming, he would have kept watch and would not have let his house be broken into. So you also must be ready, because the Son of Man will come at an hour when you do not expect him." *Matthew 24:40-44*

---

Be not like the foolish drunkard who, staggering home one night, saw his candle lit for him. "Two candles!" said he, for his drunkenness made him see double, "I will blow out one," and as he blew it out, in a moment he was in the dark. Many a person sees double through the drunkenness of sin. He has one life to sow his wild oats in, and then he half expects another in which to turn to God. So, like a fool, he blows out the only candle that he has, and in the dark he will have to lie down forever. Remember, you only have one sun, and after that sets, you will never reach your home. Make haste!

# A Deceptive Peace

Why does the way of the wicked prosper? Why do all the faithless live at ease? You have planted them, and they have taken root; they grow and bear fruit. You are always on their lips but far from their hearts. . . . This is what the LORD says: "As for all my wicked neighbors who seize the inheritance I gave my people Israel, I will uproot them from their lands and I will uproot the house of Judah from among them." *Jeremiah 12:1-2, 14*

---

The sinner's peace is that terribly prophetic calm that the traveler occasionally experiences on the higher Alps. Everything is still. The birds suspend their notes, fly low, and cower down with fear. The hum of bees among the flowers is hushed. A horrible stillness rules the hour, as if death had silenced all things by stretching his awful scepter over them. But the tempest is preparing—the lightning will soon cast abroad its flames of fire. Earth will rock with thunder-blasts; granite peaks will be dissolved. All nature will tremble beneath the fury of the storm. That calm is what the sinner is experiencing. He should not rejoice in it, because the hurricane of wrath is coming, the whirlwind and the tribulation that can sweep him away and utterly destroy him.

# Spiritual Death

If they have escaped the corruption of the world by knowing our Lord and Savior Jesus Christ and are again entangled in it and overcome, they are worse off at the end than they were at the beginning. It would have been better for them not to have known the way of righteousness, than to have known it and then to turn their backs on the sacred commandment that was passed on to them. *2 Peter 2:20-21*

---

Often, when traveling among the Alps, one sees a small black cross planted on a rock or on the brink of a stream or on the verge of the highway to mark the spot where men have met with sudden death by accident. These are solemn reminders of our mortality, but they lead our minds still further. For if the places where men seal themselves for the second death could be thus manifestly indicated, what a scene this world would present! Here the memorial of a soul undone by yielding to a foul temptation, there a conscience seared by the rejection of a final warning, and yonder a heart forever turned into stone by resisting the last tender appeal of love. Our places of worship would hardly hold the sorrowing monuments that might be erected over spots where spirits were forever lost—spirits that date their ruin from sinning against the gospel while under the sound of it.

# Weighed on the True Balance

"The LORD reigns." The world is firmly established, it cannot be moved; he will judge the peoples with equity. Let the heavens rejoice, let the earth be glad; let the sea resound, and all that is in it; let the fields be jubilant, and everything in them. Then all the trees of the forest will sing for joy; they will sing before the LORD, for he comes, he comes to judge the earth. He will judge the world in righteousness and the peoples in his truth. *Psalm 96:10-13*

---

Our judgment may be compared to the scales and weights of the merchant. It should be correct, but it seldom is quite accurate. Even ordinary wear and tear in this world will suffice to put it out of gear. We need to call in the Rectifier often and entreat him to search out our secret shortcomings, lest we deviate from equity and don't realize it. It would be good if the scales of conscience would turn even at the finest dust, but how rarely is this the case! False weights and balances are an abomination to the Lord, yet many use them, and they use balances far too favorable to themselves. They give the Lord a portion sadly too small, and to their own pleasures a dowry much too great. Tradesmen who have one set of weights to buy with and others to sell with, are evidently rogues. We may convict ourselves of injustice at once if we find ourselves severe to other men and lenient to ourselves. Fraudulent shopkeepers will use a movable piece of metal; by removing it they can lighten the weight of the scale. We too may have a convenient indignation which we may restrain or indulge according as the person whose fault we judge may be the object of our goodwill or our displeasure. Some of the pawnbrokers or door-to-door salespeople pretend to judge weight by feeling of their hand, and they are no worse than those who settle everything by prejudice and will not wait for reason. There is a great weighing time coming, for which it will be well to be prepared, for woe to him whom the infallible balances shall find wanting.

# Our Future Hope

# Resting on the Promise

"For I will forgive their wickedness and will remember their sins no more." *Jeremiah 31:34*

He saved us, not because of righteous things we had done, but because of his mercy. He saved us through the washing of rebirth and renewal by the Holy Spirit, whom he poured out on us generously through Jesus Christ our Savior, so that, having been justified by his grace, we might become heirs having the hope of eternal life. *Titus 3:5-7*

---

"Old Mr. Lyford being desired, a little before his death, to let his friends know in what condition his soul was and what his thoughts were about that eternity to which he seemed very near, he answered with a cheerfulness suitable to a believer and a minister, 'I will let you know how it is with me.' And then, stretching out a hand that was withered and consumed with age and sickness, 'Here is,' said he, 'the grave, the wrath of God, and devouring flames, the just punishment of sin, on the one side. And here am I, a poor sinful soul, on the other side. But this is my comfort, the covenant of grace which is established on so many sure promises has saved me from all. There is an act of oblivion passed in heaven. *I will forgive their iniquities, and their sins I will remember no more.* This is the blessed privilege of all within the covenant, among whom I am one.' "—*from T. Rogers, on "Trouble of Mind"*

# Approaching the Journey's End

Now there is in store for me the crown of righteousness, which the Lord, the righteous Judge, will award to me on that day—and not only to me, but also to all who have longed for his appearing. *2 Timothy 4:8*

---

"It is a blessed thing to know the Savior and to feel that your soul is safe. If you have been in a ship when it entered the harbor, you have noticed the different looks of the passengers as they turned their eyes ashore. There was one who, that he might not lose a moment's time, had got everything ready for landing long ago, and now he smiles and beckons to yonder party on the pier, who in their turn, are so eager to meet him that they almost press over the margin of the quay. But there is another who gazes with pensive eye on the nearer coast and seems to grudge that the trip was over. He is a stranger going among strangers, and though sometimes during the voyage he had a momentary hope that some friendly face might recognize him in regions where he was an alien and an adventurer, no such welcoming face is there, and with reluctant steps he leaves the vessel and commits himself to the unknown country. And now that everyone else has disembarked, who is this unhappy man whom they have brought on deck, and whom, groaning in his heavy chains, they are conducting to the dreaded shore? A felon and a runaway, whom they are bringing back to take his trial there, and no wonder he is loath to land.

"Now, dear brethren, our ship is sailing fast. We shall soon hear the rasping of the shallows and the commotion overhead, which bespeak the port in view. When it comes to that, how shall you feel? Are you a stranger, or a convict, or are you going home? Can you say, ' "I know whom I have believed" '? Have you a Friend within the veil? And however much you may enjoy the voyage, and however much you may like your fellow passengers, does your heart sometimes leap up at the prospect of seeing Jesus as he is, and so being ever with the Lord?"—*James Hamilton, D.D.*

# The Eye of Christ Jesus

"Be strong and courageous. Do not be afraid or terrified because of them, for the LORD your God goes with you; he will never leave you nor forsake you." *Deuteronomy 31:6*

---

"There is a touching fact related in a history of a Highland chief, of the noble house of McGregor, who fell wounded by two bullets at the battle of Prestonpans. Seeing their chief fall, the clan wavered and gave the enemy an advantage. The old chieftain, beholding the effect of his disaster, raised himself up on his elbow, while the blood gushed in streams from his wounds, and cried out loud, 'I am not dead, my children. I am watching to see you do your duty.' These words revived the sinking courage of his brave Highlanders. There was a charm in the fact that they still fought under the eye of their chief. It encouraged them to put forth their mightiest energies, and they did all that human strength could do to turn and stem the dreadful tide of battle.

"And isn't it impressive to believers that they contend in the battlefield of life under the eye of the Savior? Wherever they are, however they are oppressed by foes, however exhausted by the stern strife with evil, the eye of Christ is fixed most lovingly upon them. Nor is Jesus the only observer of their conduct. They are also 'a spectacle unto angels.' They are 'surrounded by a cloud of witnesses.' Human and angelic minds are the spectators of deeds. Thus is the theater of life made sublime. Believers contend for salvation under circumstances sufficiently grand, and with results before them sufficiently awful to arouse their most latent powers, and to stimulate them to strive bravely, vigorously, and perseveringly even unto victory."—D. *Wise*

# Ready for the Great Day

We will not all sleep, but we will all be changed—in a flash, in the twinkling of an eye, at the last trumpet. For the trumpet will sound, the dead will be raised imperishable, and we will be changed. For the perishable must clothe itself with the imperishable, and the mortal with immortality. When the perishable has been clothed with the imperishable, and the mortal with immortality, then the saying that is written will come true: "Death has been swallowed up in victory." *1 Corinthians 15:51-54*

---

When Bernard Gilpin was privately informed that his enemies had caused thirty-two articles to be drawn up against him in the strongest manner, and presented to Bonner, bishop of London, he said to his favorite servant, "At length they have prevailed against me. I am accused to the bishop of London, from whom there will be no escaping. God forgive their malice, and grant me strength to undergo the trial." He then ordered his servant to provide a long garment for him, in which he might go decently to the stake, and desired it might be got ready with all expedition. "For I know not," says he, "how soon I may have occasion for it." As soon as this garment was provided, it is said, he used to put it on every day until the bishop's messengers apprehended him. If we all thus realized to ourselves the hour of our departure, we ought by anticipation to sleep in our shrouds and go to bed in our sepulchers. To put on our burial clothes now is wisdom.

# After the Masquerade

For we will all stand before God's judgment seat. It is written: " 'As surely as I live,' says the Lord, 'Every knee will bow before me; every tongue will confess to God.' " So then, each of us will give an account of himself to God. *Romans 14:10-12*

---

Today the world is like a masquerade. High carnival is being held, and men wear their masks and dominoes and strut about, and we think that man a king, and this a mighty Oriental prince, and this a haughty Indian chief. But the time is over for the mask; daylight dawns; strip off your garnishings; every one of you put on your ordinary garments. Who goes out to the unrobing-room with greatest confidence? The man who feels that his next outfit will be a far more glorious vestment. Who shall go to that disrobing-room with the greatest tremor? Those who feel that the splendid character they once wore will give place to beggary and meanness; when for robes they shall have rags; for riches, poverty; for honor, shame; and for regal splendor, hissing and reproach. If any of our readers seem to be what they are not, let them be wise enough to think of the spade, the shroud, and the silent dust. Let everyone among us now put his soul into the crucible, and as we shall test ourselves in the silence of the dying hour, so let us judge ourselves now.

# All the Flowers of His Field

The Spirit of the Sovereign LORD is on me, because the LORD has anointed me to preach good news to the poor. He has sent me to bind up the brokenhearted . . . to bestow on them a crown of beauty instead of ashes, the oil of gladness instead of mourning, and a garment of praise instead of a spirit of despair. They will be called oaks of righteousness, a planting of the LORD for the display of his splendor. *Isaiah 61:1, 3*

---

You can buy complete sets of all the flowers of the Alpine district at the hotel near the foot of the Rosenlaui glacier, very neatly pressed and enclosed in cases. Some of the flowers are very common, but they must be included, or the flora would not be completely represented. The botanist is as careful to see that the common ones are there as he is to note that the rarer specimens are not excluded.

Our blessed Lord will be sure to make a perfect collection of the flowers of his field, and even the ordinary believer, the everyday worker, the common convert, will not be forgotten. To Jesus' eye, there is beauty in all his plants, and each one is needed to perfect the flora of Paradise. May I be found among his flowers, if only as one out of myriad daisies, who with sweet simplicity shall look up and wonder at his love forever.

# A Haven for Meditation or a Potato Field?

Therefore, since the promise of entering his rest still stands, let us be careful that none of you be found to have fallen short of it. For we also have had the gospel preached to us, just as they did; but the message they heard was of no value to them, because those who heard did not combine it with faith. *Hebrews 4:1-2*

---

The unfitness of unrenewed souls for heaven may be illustrated by the incapacity of certain uneducated and coarse-minded persons for elevated thoughts and intellectual pursuits. When a little child, I lived some years in my grandfather's house. In his garden there was a fine old hedge of yew of considerable length, which was clipped and trimmed until it made quite a wall of verdure. Behind it was a wide grass walk which looked on the fields and afforded a quiet outlook. The grass was kept mown, so as to make pleasant walking. Here, ever since the old Puritan chapel was built, godly ministers had walked, prayed, and meditated. My grandfather often used it as his study. He would walk up and down it when preparing his sermons, and always on Sundays when it was fair, he had half an hour there before preaching. To me it seemed to be a perfect paradise, and being forbidden to stay there when grandfather was meditating, I viewed it with no small degree of awe. I love to think of the green and quiet walk at this moment, and wish for just such a study. But I was once shocked and even horrified by hearing a farming man remark concerning this santum sanctorum, "It'd grow many 'taturs if it wor plowed up!" What did he care for holy memories? What were meditation and contemplation to him? Is it not the chief end of man to grow potatoes and eat them? Such, on a larger scale, would be an unconverted man's estimate of joys so elevated and refined as those of heaven, if he by any possibility were permitted to gaze on them.

# Hurrying Home

"Do not let your hearts be troubled. Trust in God; trust also in me. In my Father's house are many rooms; if it were not so, I would have told you. I am going there to prepare a place for you. And if I go and prepare a place for you, I will come back and take you to be with me that you also may be where I am." *John 14:1-3*

For here we do not have an enduring city, but we are looking for the city that is to come. Through Jesus, therefore, let us continually offer to God a sacrifice of praise—the fruit of lips that confess his name. *Hebrews 13:14-15*

---

My horse invariably comes home in less time than he makes on the journey away. He pulls the carriage with a hearty good will when his face is toward home. Should not I also both suffer and labor the more joyously because my way lies toward heaven, and I am on pilgrimage to my Father's house, my soul's dear home and resting place?

# Setting Your Sights on Eternal Things

Since, then, you have been raised with Christ, set your hearts on things above, where Christ is seated at the right hand of God. Set your minds on things above, not on earthly things. For you died, and your life is now hidden with Christ in God. When Christ, who is your life, appears, then you also will appear with him in glory. *Colossians 3:1-4*

---

"Suppose I were shut up within a round tower whose massive wall had in some time of trouble been pierced here and there with holes for guns. Suppose further, that by choice or necessity, I am whirled rapidly and incessantly around the inner circumference of the tower. Will I appreciate the beauties of the surrounding landscape or recognize the features of the men who labor in the field below? No! Why? Are there not openings in the wall which I pass at every circuit? Yes, but the eye, set for objects near, does not have time to adjust itself to objects at a distance until it has passed the openings. So the result is the same as if it were a windowless wall all around. This is something like the circle of human life. Throughout the whole circumference of the earth, a dead wall, very near and very thick, obstructs the view. Here and there, on a Sunday or another season of seriousness, a slit is left open in its side. Heaven might be seen through these slits, but the eye that is habitually set for earthly things cannot, during such momentary glimpses, adjust itself to higher things. Unless you pause and look steadfastly, you will see neither clouds nor sunshine through these openings, nor the distant sky. The soul has looked on the world so long, and the world's picture is so firmly fixed in its eye, that when the soul is turned for a moment toward heaven, it feels only a quiver of inarticulate light and retains no distinct impression of the things that are unseen and eternal."—W. Arnot

# Death Has Lost Its Sting

"Where, O death, is your victory? Where, O death, is your sting?"
The sting of death is sin, and the power of sin is the law. But thanks
be to God! He gives us the victory through our Lord Jesus Christ.
*1 Corinthians 15:55-57*

---

The doctrine of the resurrection is full of joy to the bereaved. It
clothes the grave with flowers and wreathes the tomb with unfad-
ing laurel. The sepulchre shines with a light brighter than the sun,
and death grows fair, as we say, in full assurance of faith, "I know
that my brother shall rise again." Torn from the degrading shell the
pearl is gone to deck the crown of the Prince of Peace; buried
beneath the sod the seed is preparing to bloom in the King's garden.
Altering a word or two of Beattie's verse we may even now find
ourselves singing,

> *'Tis night and the landscape is lovely no more;*
> *Yet ye beautiful woodlands I mourn not for you.*
> *For morn is approaching your charms to restore,*
> *Perfumed with fresh fragrance, and glittering with dew.*
> *Nor yet for the ravage of winter I mourn;*
> *Kind nature the embryo blossom will save.*
> *The spring shall yet visit the mouldering urn;*
> *The day shall yet dawn on the night of the grave.*

# Hope Doesn't Disappoint Us

Therefore, since we have been justified through faith, we have peace with God through our Lord Jesus Christ, through whom we have gained access by faith into this grace in which we now stand. And we rejoice in the hope of the glory of God. Not only so, but we also rejoice in our sufferings, because we know that suffering produces perseverance; perseverance, character; and character, hope. And hope does not disappoint us, because God has poured out his love into our hearts by the Holy Spirit, whom he has given us. *Romans 5:1-5*

---

Once upon a time, certain strong laborers were sent forth by the great King to level a primeval forest, to plow it, to sow it, and to bring to him the harvest. They were stout-hearted and strong, and willing enough for labor, and much they needed all their strength and more. One stalwart laborer was named Industry—consecrated work was his. His brother Patience, with muscles of steel, went with him, and tired not in the longest days under the heaviest labors. To help them they had Zeal, clothed with ardent and indomitable energy. Side by side there stood his kinsman Self-denial, and his friend Importunity. These went forth to their labor, and they took with them, to cheer their toils, their well-beloved sister Hope; and well it was they did, for they needed the music of her consolation before the work was done, for the forest trees were huge and demanded many sturdy blows of the axe before they would fall upon the ground. One by one the giant forest kings were overthrown, but the labor was immense and incessant. At night when they went to their rest, the day's work always seemed so light, for as they crossed the threshold, Patience, wiping the sweat from his brow, would be encouraged, and Self-denial would be strengthened by hearing the sweet voice of Hope within singing, "God will bless us; God, even our own God, will bless us." They felled the lofty trees to the music of that strain; they cleared the acres one by one, they tore from their sockets the huge roots, they delved the soil, they sowed the corn and waited for the harvest, often much discouraged, but they still held to their work as by silver chains and golden fetters by the sweet sound of the voice that chanted so constantly, "God, even our own God, will bless us." They never could refrain from service, for Hope could never refrain from song. They were ashamed to be discouraged, they were shocked to be despairing, for still the voice rang clearly out at noon and eventide, "God will bless us; God, even our own God, will bless us." You know the parable, you recognize the voice. May you hear it in your souls today!

# Holy Boldness

If Christ has not been raised, your faith is futile; you are still in your sins. Then those also who have fallen asleep in Christ are lost. If only for this life we have hope in Christ, we are to be pitied more than all men. But Christ has indeed been raised from the dead, the firstfruits of those who have fallen asleep. *1 Corinthians 15:17-20*

---

In Queen Mary's time a man named Palmer was condemned to die. Many tried to persuade him to recant. Among other things a friend said to him, "Take pity on your golden years and pleasant flowers of youth, before it is too late."

His reply was as beautiful as it was conclusive: "Friend, I long for those spring flowers which shall never fade away." When he was in the midst of the flames he exhorted his companions to constancy, saying, "We shall not end our lives in the fire, but make a change for a better life. Yes, for coals we shall receive pearls." From his testimony we clearly see that although "if in this life only we have hope in Christ, we are of all men most miserable," yet the prospect of a better and enduring substance enables us to meet all the trials and temptations of this present life with holy boldness and joy.

# Heavenly Joys

You have come to Mount Zion, to the heavenly Jerusalem, the city of the living God. You have come to thousands upon thousands of angels in joyful assembly, to the church of the firstborn, whose names are written in heaven. You have come to God, the judge of all men, to the spirits of righteous men made perfect, to Jesus the mediator of a new covenant. *Hebrews 12:22-24*

"Hallelujah! For our Lord God Almighty reigns. Let us rejoice and be glad and give him glory! For the wedding of the Lamb has come, and his bride has made herself ready." *Revelation 19:6-7*

---

Heavenly joys shall be like the tree of life in the New Jerusalem, which brings forth twelve types of fruits and yields her fruit every month. Robert Hall used to cry, "Oh for the everlasting rest!" but Wilberforce would sigh to dwell in unbroken love. Hall was a man who suffered—he longed for rest. Wilberforce was a man of amiable spirit, loving society and fellowship—he looked for love. Hall shall have his rest, and Wilberforce shall have his love. There are joys at God's right hand suitable for the spiritual tastes of all those who come there. The heavenly manna tastes to every man's peculiar liking.

# Looking toward an Eternal World of Joy

Now we know that if the earthly tent we live in is destroyed, we have a building from God, an eternal house in heaven, not built by human hands. . . . While we are in this tent, we groan and are burdened, because we do not wish to be unclothed but to be clothed with our heavenly dwelling, so that what is mortal may be swallowed up by life. Now it is God who has made us for this very purpose and has given us the Spirit as a deposit, guaranteeing what is to come. Therefore we are always confident and know that as long as we are at home in the body we are away from the Lord. We live by faith, not by sight. We are confident, I say, and would prefer to be away from the body and at home with the Lord. So we make it our goal to please him, whether we are at home in the body or away from it. For we must all appear before the judgment seat of Christ. *2 Corinthians 5:1, 4-10*

---

An old theologian once said, "Who chides a servant for taking away the first course of a feast when the second consists of far greater delicacies?" Who then can feel regret that this present world passes away when he sees that an eternal world of joy is coming? The first course is grace, but the second is glory, and that is as much better as the fruit is better than the blossom.

# Far Beyond Our Imagination

"No eye has seen, no ear has heard, no mind has conceived what God has prepared for those who love him." *1 Corinthians 2:9*

Then I saw a new heaven and a new earth, for the first heaven and the first earth had passed away, and there was no longer any sea. I saw the Holy City, the new Jerusalem, coming down out of heaven from God, prepared as a bride beautifully dressed for her husband.... He carried me away in the Spirit to a mountain great and high, and showed me the Holy City, Jerusalem, coming down out of heaven from God. It shone with the glory of God, and its brilliance was like that of a very precious jewel ... I did not see a temple in the city, because the Lord God Almighty and the Lamb are its temple. The city does not need the sun or the moon to shine on it, for the glory of God gives it light, and the Lamb is its lamp. *Revelation 21:1-2, 10-11, 22-23*

---

"Oh, when we meet in heaven, we shall see how little we knew about it on earth."—*Payson*

# Scripture Index

# Topical Index

Printed in the United States
by Baker & Taylor Publisher Services